Indonesian Pluralities

CONTENDING MODERNITIES

Series editors: Ebrahim Moosa, Atalia Omer, and Scott Appleby

As a collaboration between the Contending Modernities initiative and the University of Notre Dame Press, the Contending Modernities series seeks, through publications engaging multiple disciplines, to generate new knowledge and greater understanding of the ways in which religious traditions and secular actors encounter and engage each other in the modern world. Books in this series may include monographs, co-authored volumes, and tightly themed edited collections.

The series will include works that frame such encounters through the lens of "modernity." The range of themes treated in the series might include war, peace, human rights, nationalism, refugees and migrants, development practice, pluralism, religious literacy, political theology, ethics, multi- and intercultural dynamics, sexual politics, gender justice, and postcolonial and decolonial studies.

Indonesian Pluralities

Islam, Citizenship, and Democracy

Edited by

ROBERT W. HEFNER

and

ZAINAL ABIDIN BAGIR

UNIVERSITY OF NOTRE DAME PRESS

NOTRE DAME, INDIANA

University of Notre Dame Press
Notre Dame, Indiana 46556
undpress.nd.edu

Copyright © 2021 by the University of Notre Dame

Published in the United States of America

Library of Congress Control Number: 2020947032

ISBN: 978-0-268-10861-8 (Hardback)
ISBN: 978-0-268-10862-5 (Paperback)
ISBN: 978-0-268-10864-9 (WebPDF)
ISBN: 978-0-268-10863-2 (Epub)

CONTENTS

ACKNOWLEDGMENTS

The present book has a long but happy history. Its core aspiration originated in discussions that began a decade ago under the leadership of R. Scott Appleby, in the course of preparations for his multidimensional project "Contending Modernities: Catholics, Muslims, and Secularists in the Late Modern World." In those years the project was organized out of the Kroc Institute for International Peace Studies at the University of Notre Dame. One of the editors of the present book, Bob Hefner, participated in some of the project's founding meetings and along the way met some of the scholars who went on to play leadership roles in the larger CM program: Ebrahim Moosa, Atalia Omer, and Mun'im Sirry among them.

Although Hefner had earlier been involved in one of the CM projects, "Catholics, Muslims, and the New Plurality in Western Europe and North America," in 2014-15, Scott, Ebrahim, and Mun'im resolved to open another front in the CM's multiple projects, this one focused on aspects of religion and plurality in Indonesia and Africa. Scott subsequently invited the editors of the present book, Zainal Abidin Bagir and Bob Hefner, to submit a proposal for a project, which we did in 2015. The project was entitled "Scaling-Up Pluralism: Local-National Collaborations for Civic Coexistence in Contemporary Indonesia." The book is the product of the collaborative research project carried out from late 2015 to late 2017.

Both of the editors for this book have benefited enormously from the generosity, collegiality, and intellectual counsel of Scott, Ebrahim, Mun'im, and Atalia. We cannot thank them sufficiently for their kindness and support, or for the intellectual vision they have shown in the Contending Modernities project as a whole. We also thank Dr. Toby A. Volkman, director of the Religion and World Affairs program at the Henry Luce Foundation, for her and the Foundation's generous support of our research and the filmmaking sequel to the original field research. Six films based in part on some of the field sites described in this book are currently being produced and will be available for university and general distribution in late 2020.

Zainal Abidin Bagir and Bob Hefner visited all of the field sites several times over the course of the research and were the recipients of great kindness on the part of many local hosts. Although there are far too many individuals to mention in person, we want at the least to give special thanks to Margaretha Hendriks, Jacky Manuputty, Yance Rumahru, Hasbollah Toisuta, and Abidin Wakono. We also thank our American and Indonesian research partners in the project and the present book. All our colleagues in the research team took time away from their families and careers in Indonesia and the United States to cooperate in this multidisciplinary endeavor. We also thank our friends and colleagues at our respective institutes: Pak Zainal at the Center for Religious and Cross-Cultural Studies at the Graduate School of Gadjah Mada University and Bob Hefner at the Pardee School of Global Affairs at Boston University.

Last but not least, we dedicate the volume to the memory of the great Indonesian public intellectual Nurcholish Madjid (1939–2005), who in the 1990s was Bob's teacher and friend in things Indonesian. Cak Nur, as he was known, remains an intellectual and ethical exemplar for all who care about religion and pluralist recognition in the unfinished but great project that is the nation of Indonesia.

Bob Hefner and Zainal Abidin Bagir

ONE

The Politics and Ethics of
Social Recognition and Citizenship
in a Muslim-Majority Democracy

ROBERT W. HEFNER

The question of how to live together in a religiously plural society is much in the air these days, and for good reason. In Western democracies, the confluence of mass immigration, ISIS/Daesh terrorism, and alt-right populisms has shaken public confidence in once widely held assumptions as to civility and citizenship in a context of deep social difference (Mouffe 2005). Calls heard in the 1990s for some variety of multicultural citizenship have long since given way to demands for the exclusion of new immigrants and the coercive assimilation of those long arrived, not least if they happen to be Muslim (Joppke 2017; Modood 2007).

What is arguably a crisis of confidence in pluralist recognition and citizenship in the West is paralleled by an even greater sense of alarm in the Muslim-majority world, and nowhere more anxiously than in the Arab Middle East. By early 2013, the hopeful dreams of the 2011 "Arab Spring" had given way to the somber realization that in all but one of the Arab Muslim nations, Tunisia (Zeghal 2016), progress toward pluralist democracy had not merely stalled but ended. Political observers spoke with good reason of a "crisis of citizenship" in the Arab-Muslim world (Challand 2017; Meijer and Butenschøn 2017). As if this inventory were not distressing enough, even in Southeast Asia's once hopeful democracies, one hears today that, to borrow a phrase from the political scientist William Case (2011, 360), "After a long run of global good fortune, democracy has fallen on hard times."

It is against this backdrop of democratic hope and challenge that Indonesia today takes on its public and policy importance. With its population of 266 million people, 87.2 percent of whom are Muslim, Indonesia is the largest Muslim-majority country in the world. It is also the third-largest democracy, having undertaken a return to electoral democracy in 1998–99 in the aftermath of thirty-two years of authoritarian rule. Some analysts, including the distinguished scholar of democratic transitions Alfred Stepan, have argued that Indonesia offers clear proof of the compatibility of Islam and pluralist democracy (Stepan 2014). But skeptics are not so sure. They argue that, however impressive Indonesia's electoral achievements, the larger transition from the authoritarianism of the New Order regime (1966–98) to the democratic politics of the *Reformasi* era (1998–today) has been so marred by antiminority violence as to discredit any claim to democratic exemplarity (Harsono 2012).

Although the issues at its heart remain vexing, this disagreement has had a salutary effect on ongoing studies of politics and civic coexistence in contemporary Indonesia. The debate has underscored that, in assessing the quality of democracy, plurality, and citizenship in Indonesia today, it is important to examine not just elections and state-centered politics but the less formal but more pervasive processes of social *recognition* (Taylor 1994; Honneth 2001) at work in this deeply plural society. *Social recognition* refers to the social-psychological, ethical, and political practices through which actors evaluate, acknowledge, and otherwise engage their fellows in society. If the related and no less important concept of "citizenship" refers to an individual's relationship with a political community that conveys certain reciprocal rights and obligations between that individual and political community and/or that individual and the state (Berenschot and van Klinken 2019b; Isin and Nyers 2014), *social recognition* refers to the more general and less state-focused processes through which actors perceive, categorize, and evaluate their social fellows within a particular sociopolitical community and then draw on those processes of recognition to understand and enact their own identities, rights, and obligations in relation to those around them.

In Western political philosophy, the concept of recognition has roots in Hegel's notion of the "quest for recognition," but the issue has today moved well beyond this early philosophical framework. Hegel's achievement lay in his taking exception to the atomistic and introspective conceptions of the self developed in the work of Descartes and Kant, emphasizing instead that self-identity is a relational and dialogical process shaped by and dependent on the recognition of others. In more recent years, the concept of recognition has been explored further in relation to debates over multiculturalism and recognition in modern Western democracies (Fraser 2000, 2001; Honneth 1995, 2012; Taylor 1994).

As in the works of Axel Honneth and Nancy Fraser, much of this new Western scholarship on recognition is of a prescriptively normative sort, challenging received liberal models of subjectivity, social justice, and human flourishing, and proposing a more intersubjective and dialogical alternative (see Zurn 2000). The approach to recognition deployed in this book builds on these precedents but differs from them in two basic ways. First, rather than arguing that one variety of social recognition is better suited for human flourishing, this book aims simply to examine the varied modes of recognition operative in different Indonesian locales and to assess their implications for citizenship and social coexistence. A second and related way in which the approach used in this book differs from its contemporary Western counterparts is that it seeks to extend the study of social recognition well beyond the confines of Western "liberal" societies, including in this case to the Muslim-majority nation of Indonesia. Although not developed in as explicitly dialogical a manner as in Western philosophy, ideas on and debates over recognition have been a central feature of public life in Indonesia since the dawn of the republic in the 1940s. In the broader Muslim world, questions of how to recognize social fellows in a religiously plural society have been a central concern of Muslim public ethics since the Prophet Muhammad formulated the Medina Charter shortly after his migration from Mecca to Yathrib (known subsequently as Medina) in 622 (Yildirim 2009). The charter extended rights of protection and autonomy to Jewish tribes as well as Muslims, including on matters of religious worship and social organization. Over the centuries that followed, Muslim jurists, theologians, rulers, and mystics devised a variety of ways for recognizing one's fellows in an Islamic manner, not all of them consistent with the Medina Charter (Emon 2012; Friedmann 2003). But the question of how to recognize one's fellows and non-Muslims remains at the heart of Muslim public ethics and is a striking feature of debates across the Muslim world today (Emon 2012; Moosa 2001; Ramadan 2009).

These examples serve to remind us that social recognition is not merely a matter of psychological perception or normative debate; nor is it something that involves only actors' interactions with the state. Instead, and much like the processes of everyday ethical evaluation on which it draws (Laidlaw 2014; Keane 2016), recognition is a pervasive feature of all social life, shaped by the judgments and relationships operative among people in a particular social setting and the "encumbrances" (Sandel 1984) of identity, difference, solidarity, and exclusion to which they give rise. Although in some scholarship social recognition is seen as more or less equivalent to the concept of national citizenship, in fact processes of recognition tend to be more varied and ubiquitous across the whole of social life. They are shaped, not just by actors' vertical relationships with the state and other authorities (although these too are important), but by the lateral relationships in which actors find themselves involved, and the ethico-religious traditions and everyday practices through with which they learn to navigate these social realities.

Processes of recognition in any given society are complicated, however, by one additional social reality. In any society at any given time, there may be not one but several ethico-political frameworks for recognizing one's social others. The feelings and frameworks for recognizing and differentiating societal fellows can be grounded on religion, race, class, ethnicity, gender, sexual preference, national citizenship—or some intersectional combination of several of these. The processes through which these varied registers interact or compete with each other, and by which one among them may become hegemonic in everyday life, are matters that lie at the heart of the approach adopted in this book (cf. Berenschot and van Klinken 2019a; Karsenti 2017; cf. Stokke 2017).

These issues of recognition and coexistence in a plural society, then, were the focus of the project that Zainal Abidin Bagir and I conducted with a small research team over a twenty-month period from late 2015 to late 2017. It is also the concern of the chapters in this book. The project was entitled "Scaling Up Pluralism: Local-National Collaborations for Civic Coexistence in Contemporary Indonesia." The research was funded with the generous support of the Kroc Institute for International Peace Studies at the University of Notre Dame, under the direction of R. Scott Appleby (now dean of the Keough School of International Studies) and in collaboration with Mun'im Sirry, a scholar of Islam and Indonesia also at Notre Dame's Kroc Institute. At its heart, the aim of the project was to explore the public contentions and normative traditions that have shaped the values and practices of social recognition and coexistence in different areas of Indonesia. On the model of recent studies of social recognition and "cultural citizenship" in Europe and the Middle East (Beaman 2016; Bowen 2010; Joppke 2017; Karsenti 2017; Meijer and Butenschøn 2017), the project sought to examine the discourses and practices of recognition operative in each of the research locales, explore their relation to each region's ethnic, religious, and political groupings, and assess their implications for public life and coexistence in Indonesia as a whole.

In the remainder of this chapter, I explain the research rationales and methodologies for the case studies on which the chapters in this book are based. I then step back from the individual cases in an effort to explore the distinctive challenge of social recognition, pluralist coexistence, and citizenship in contemporary Indonesia as a whole. My remarks also seek to situate the Indonesian example in relation to larger theoretical and policy debates over the challenge of social recognition, coexistence, and cultural citizenship (Beaman 2016) in our late modern world.

PLURALITY, RECOGNITION, BELONGING

The research around which this project was organized involved four exercises to investigate the ideals and practices of social recognition and belonging in each of the research locales. The exercises themselves illustrate both the theoretical challenge to understanding recognition and social coexistence, and the distinctive social legacies Indonesians brings to these processes.

The first exercise each researcher was asked to carry out was to create a map of the main currents of practice and public-ethical reasoning with regard to plurality and social recognition in each field setting. From the beginning, of course, we recognized that the map could not be exhaustive. Our guiding principle, however, was simple: each researcher should begin by identifying the most influential organizations, movements, and public discourses operative in her or his region and from there move outward to identify the main rivals or challengers to these dominant groupings and the discourses of social recognition they promote. As the chapters in this book make clear, this first phase of research was premised on two assumptions: first, that neither formal citizenship nor individuals' relationship with the state need be the primary ethico-political referent to which Indonesians look in recognizing, evaluating, and engaging each other in society; and, second, our mapping portion of the project should *not* be limited to actors or associations promoting a democratic and/or pluralist model of recognition and coexistence. Rather than just focusing on "good-guy" pluralists or the formal discourses of citizenship and state, our mapping sought to identify the most *influential* actors and organizations shaping processes of public recognition in each region and to explore the "agonistic plurality" (Mouffe 2000; Hefner 1998) of discursive practice to which they give rise.

Public Reasoning and Coexistence in Agonistic Plurality

After having mapped the dominant groupings and discourses with regard to social recognition and plurality, investigators in each research locale next looked more closely at the content of the discourses deployed by different groupings and their implications for relations among local residents. The features of each recognition discourse we sought to highlight included the *sources and content of its values,* the *extent* or breadth of their application across society, and the ethico-discursive *principles* whereby the tradition includes some categories of actors while excluding or marginalizing others. Thus, for example, in a setting like the Christian-majority city of Manado in North Sulawesi (Larson, chapter 2), we asked: When a local social movement that self-identifies as Protestant presents its views on plurality, recognition, and coexistence, does it justify that discourse solely with reference to Protestant doctrines or traditions? And does it use that religious reference to justify the exclusion of non-Protestants or the creation of a differentiated and stratified model of recognition and citizenship? And what does this pattern of recognition imply for multireligious and inclusive models of civic coexistence, like those associated with Indonesia's official political philosophy, the Pancasila (the five principles)? Among its formal principles, the Pancasila affirms that Indonesia is a *religious* state but *not* an Islamic state and that Indonesians from all recognized religious backgrounds should enjoy equal citizenship rights (Elson 2013). In principle if not always in practice, the Pancasila thus eschews any variety of ethnic or religious supremacism in favor of a religiously *undifferentiated* recognition and citizenship.

To take another example, when a hard-line Islamist movement like Hizbut Tahrir Indonesia (HTI; Ahnaf, chapter 4) enters into public debates over plurality and recognition, does it justify its views solely in relation to the Qur'an, the Sunna (traditions) of the Prophet, and Islamic jurisprudence (*fiqh*)? If it does, and inasmuch as the practice and meanings of Islamic shariah are always socially contingent and epistemologically plural (Daniels 2017; Hefner 2016), on what grounds and by what methodologies does HTI identify and enunciate the Islamic principles said to be derived from these sources? And if the movement claims to ground its views on a putatively paramount shariah law, how do its proponents regard the principles of belonging and coexistence held dear by other Indonesians, such as the ideals of nationhood and religiously inclusive citizenship associated with the Pancasila?

As these examples illustrate, the case studies in this volume were premised on three assumptions with regard to traditions and practices of social recognition: first, that the latter are not static discourses but traditions that coevolve in relation to broader political and ethical changes in society, including for example Indonesia's Islamic resurgence or its recent *adat* revival (see below); second, that practices of recognition in a particular community are *not* necessarily defined in relation to the state or official understandings of citizenship; and, third, that the traditions in question do not exhaustively "constitute" the subjectivity and worldview of all who claim to identify with them. As Talal Asad (1986, 2003) and Alasdair MacIntyre (1984) have both emphasized, and as Timothy Daniels (2017) has recently shown in his study of shariah meanings in contemporary Malaysia, a "tradition" is better understood as "an argument extended through time in which certain fundamental agreements are defined and redefined," with its own standards of rational justification and inquiry, and through which actors come to understand "our own commitments or those of others . . . by situating them within those histories which made them what they have now become" (MacIntyre 1984, 12–13, 350). Equally important, and some-what contrary to MacIntyre's otherwise thoughtful exposition (cf. Laid-law 2014), although actors may claim to base their views on plurality and recognition on just *one* discursive tradition, our research presupposes that in everyday living individuals differ in the degree to which they iden-tify with the tradition with which they claim affiliation and in the degree to which they regard its values as exclusive of other discourses of recog-nition and belonging operative in society (Glenn 2011; Hefner 2016; Schielke 2015).

As this last observation implies, all societies are characterized by a significant measure of ethical and legal plurality, not least with regard to matters of recognition, belonging, and coexistence. In exploring practices of social recognition and coexistence in a particular locale, then, it is more helpful to look first at the plurality of discourses and practices for recogni-tion before engaging in any examination of formal citizenship or even the relationship with the state (formal or informal) as such. In many modern societies, the ideals and practices of formal citizenship may in fact play a lesser role in determining real and existing patterns of recognition, belong-ing, and interaction among residents in society. This fact was tragically il-lustrated in the sectarian violence that swept eastern Indonesia in the early 2000s, as well as many Middle Eastern societies in the aftermath of the Arab uprisings. The fact has also been made painfully apparent in the cul-ture wars raging over immigration and national belonging in the contem-porary West (Brownlee, Masoud, and Reynolds 2015; Hashemi and Postel 2017; Meijer and Butenschøn 2017; Modood 2007; Taylor 1994).

No less significant, even where official citizenship ideals appear well established in a society, their understanding and practice are inevitably in-fluenced by legacies of ethics and recognition derived from other tradi-tions, practices, and power structures operative across society, includ-ing those of religion, ideology, class, ethnicity, and gender (Doorn-Harder 2006; Isin 2008). The resulting pattern of "cultural" (Beaman 2016) or "substantive citizenship" (Glenn 2011) is thus never simply the product of juridico-political principles or even actors' relationship with the state but involves "recognition by other members of the community" (Glenn 2011, 3). That recognition is in turn based, not just on laws or constitutions, but "on a common culture that makes some citizens more or less accepted than others" (Beaman 2016, 852; cf. Ong 1996).

In matters of social recognition and coexistence, then, an agonistic plurality of viewpoints and practices is more or less everywhere the norm, and the resulting plurality of ethical and legal norms in a society may well create "a situation in which two or more legal [and ethical] systems coexist in the same social field" (Engle Merry 1988, 870). The coexistent bodies of law and ethics may in turn "make competing claims of authority; they may impose conflicting demands or norms; they may have different styles and orientations"; the plurality also "poses a challenge to the legal authorities themselves, for it means that they have rivals" (Tamanaha 2008, 375; cf. Turner 2011, 151–74). As highlighted in the anthropology of Islam and the new anthropology of morality (Deeb and Harb 2013; Keane 2013; Marsden 2005; Schielke 2010a, 2010b; Simon 2014; Soares 2005), these other discursive registers may exercise a powerful influence on actors' subjectivities and aspirations, not least with regard to how they categorize, recognize, and otherwise engage people around them. No less important, these discursive legacies inevitably influence the ways actors understand and utilize more formalized public ethical discourses, including, for example, those related to national citizenship. This latter fact has been vividly illustrated in many Western societies in recent years. In these latter settings, the egalitarian and inclusive ideals of formal democratic citizenship have at times been ignored in dealings with new citizen immigrants, not least those Muslim, as a result of an implicit "cultural citizenship" that reserves full rights of recognition only for those residents who share certain traits of race, ethnicity, religion, or gendered lifestyle (Beaman 2016; Glenn 2011).

It was this confluence of ethico-legal and religious discourses on matters of plurality and recognition in post-Soeharto Indonesia, then, with which our research project sought to come to terms. The process whereby disparate normative discourses and registers become the object of sustained social discussion has come to be known in one wing of social and democratic theory as "public reasoning." A few years back in a highly original book, the anthropologist John Bowen (2010, 6) described public reasoning as "the ways in which people deliberate and debate in . . . public settings" and as the "practices of deliberation" in which one justifies one's beliefs and seeks areas of agreement. Bowen also observed that such public reasoning is not static or necessarily derivative of just one ethico-legal or religious tradition. Where there is such a plurality of options, just which ethical discourse an actor finds compelling or resonant often depends on the broader community with which she or he identifies. In the case of French Muslims, for example, Bowen (2010, 24) noted that Muslim activists involved in public debates on ethics and citizenship in France (the focus of his study) who happened to identify with transnational Islamic movements felt a special obligation to develop knowledge and discourses that were "legitimate in transnational terms" as well as being "pertinent to the situation in France." The anthropologist Timothy Daniels (2017) highlighted a similarly contingent variation in the way in which Islamic shariah and national citizenship are interpreted in contemporary Malaysia. In the Indonesian project on which the following chapters are based, we asked researchers to attend to similar situational variation. In particular, researchers were asked to explore the ways in which locals' identification with different social groupings—ethnic, religious, regional, national, or transnational—influences the choice of ethical registers those same actors use in recognizing their fellows in society, and the implications of this choice for patterns of recognition, cultural citizenship, social conflict, and belonging.

Focal Incidents and Dramas of Contention

Having mapped the primary currents of normative reasoning and practice with regard to pluralist coexistence in each research setting, each researcher was asked in the third investigative exercise to identify two or three "focal incidents" that had brought debates over plurality, recognition, and belonging in a particular region into focus in recent years. A focal incident, also known as a "drama of contention" in political sociology and anthropology (Holland et al. 2008; see also Daniels 2017, 150), is some confluence of events, debates, and mobilizations that illustrates the primary social forces and public ethical issues in contention at a particular time and place. In the present project we were primarily interested in those focal incidents that had to do with how different actors and movements propose to recognize and coexist with fellows in local and national society. In exploring each focal incident or drama of contention, the researchers sought to describe the nature of the particular dispute, the ethical frames applied to it by different actors and movements, and the impact of the incident on the local balance of power and public opinion with regard to how to live together and recognize one's fellows. As the studies in this book demonstrate, focal incidents don't simply *illustrate* the state of plurality and recognition in a particular social setting; they serve to *constitute and transform* practices and normativities of recognition operative in that setting.

In today's Indonesia, the importance of such focal incidents / dramas of contention has been seen nowhere more vividly than in the 2016–17 controversy that surrounded the "Defend Islam Action" (Aksi Bela Islam) in metropolitan Jakarta in the aftermath of blasphemy allegations against Basuki Tjahaja Purnama (popularly known as "Ahok"), the Christian Chinese governor of Jakarta (see below and Bagir, chapter 7; and Fealy 2016a; IPAC 2018a, 2019). In these and other instances, focal incidents or dramas of contention provide insights into the public ethical reasoning and contentious politics that different actors and groupings use to advance their viewpoints and programs on recognition, coexistence, and citizenship in a plural social setting.

Scaling Up Models for Recognition and Coexistence

The fourth and last investigative exercise on which the chapters in this volume are based has to do with the ways in which the proponents of a particular practice of recognition and pluralist coexistence struggle to advance their normative ideals and practices by "scaling up" the normativities in question through collaborations or coalitions with other actors in state or society. "Scaling up" is a concept originally developed in the 1990s in studies of social capital, civil society, and the state. The British sociologist Peter Evans (1996) authored several especially useful essays on this concept in its societal or macrosociological sense. However, in a book I wrote almost twenty years ago entitled *Civil Islam* (Hefner 2000), I pointed out that scaling, to be enduringly effective, must have a normative and psychocultural resonance for large numbers of people, similar to that which the psychiatrist and anthropologist Arthur Kleinman (1991) has described as "amplification" in subjective experience. In other words, the image, concept, or discourse in question must assume some degree of centrality in the organization and practice of a person's or group's subjective and shared social experience (cf. Gregg 1998; Simon 2014). In *Civil Islam* and subsequent works (Hefner 2005a, 2005b), I drew on Evans's and Kleinman's work to emphasize that social movements that seek to effect a far-reaching transformation of state and society must work to secure that transformation by anchoring its discursive frames in the ethical and affective experience of real-world actors, so as to make the more abstract discourse resonant with everyday experience.

The concept of scaling used in the chapters in this book builds on these precedents in an effort to explore the ways in which different social movements and associations in Indonesian society seek to collaborate with each other and across the state-society divide to extend the influence of their values and practices beyond the horizons of small social circles or restricted geographic locales. The scaling up requires normative work by certain leaders or actors who seek to legitimate their efforts by situating it within a particular ethical or religious tradition, so as to ensure that the ethical work in question is seen as both compatible and resonant with the tradition itself. Then, in a second-stage effort, these and other actors work to link the emerging normative framework to institutions, organizations, and movements that extend its realm of application well beyond its original field of elaboration. Examples of scaling up include laws that extend certain protections or rights to a broad assortment of actors or spheres (see Swazey, chapter 3; Bagir, chapter 7); civic education programs operated by schools (see Larson, chapter 2) or social movements (see Ahnaf, chapter 4; Tahun, chapter 5); or programs launched by organizations like Muhammadiyah, Nahdlatul Ulama, or Hizbut Tahrir Indonesia that seek to promote values and practices originally formulated in limited circles to broad portions of society (see Anhaf, chapter 4; Qibtiyah, chapter 6; and Bagir, chapter 7). Whatever the mechanism of social scaling, our goal in this project was to look at the agonistic plurality of ethico-religious visions for recognition and coexistence in particular Indonesian settings, and at the social coalitions and scalings that actors use to promote those visions

across broad swaths of society and, at times, into the structures and programs of the state.

These, then, were the core research concerns and methodologies that
the participants in this project brought to their field research and to the
chapters in this volume. As is clear from the choice of settings, our aim
from the start was to decenter analysis away from Jakarta and formal politics out toward the plurality of practices with regard to pluralist coexistence
in different regions of Indonesia. It goes without saying that in a country as
vast as Indonesia a modest-sized project like this one cannot pretend to be
exhaustive. In fact, Zainal Abidin Bagir and I intend a second book project
and six short film documentaries that we are currently preparing (with the
generous support of the program in Religion and World Affairs office at
the Henry Luce Foundation), dealing with the politics and ethics of pluralist coexistence in contemporary Indonesia. Our field sites in the present project—Manado, Ambon, Yogyakarta, and metropolitan Jakarta—
include religiously mixed as well as Muslim-majority areas.

Although religious, ethnic, and regional issues loom large in the chapters that follow, another issue with which we are concerned is gender. The
reason for this will be immediately apparent to most readers of this book:
gender issues figure in virtually every drama of social contention over
plurality and social recognition taking place in the late modern world—
and they have been at the heart of the contentions that have raged in Indonesia since the first years of the *Reformasi* era (see Brenner 2011; Doorn-
Harder 2006; Rinaldo 2013; Robinson 2009; Smith-Hefner 2007, 2019).
During the early years of the *Reformasi* transition that began in 1998–99,
the proponents of gender equity and women's empowerment seemed to
make rapid and impressive headway. But from 2005 onward their campaigns encountered growing opposition from a variety of neoconservative,
hard-line, and even mainline religious groupings. The opponents of LGBT
groups and liberalized notions of sexuality also became more effectively organized during these years, placing the movement for new modes of gender equality and sexual recognition in jeopardy (see Qibtiyah, chapter 6).

Since its first years of independence, Indonesia has always been a complex, plural society, and struggles over competing varieties of recognition
and belonging have marked public politics from the first. Although the

chapters in this book only begin to scratch the surface of the struggles for different varieties of recognition and coexistence in contemporary Indonesia, their particularity, we believe, speaks to issues of fundamental importance in both Indonesia and the broader world.

A PLURAL SOCIETY AT A CRITICAL JUNCTURE

Not surprisingly in light of the crises of recognition and citizenship afflicting large portions of today's world, the present study seeks to speak to pluralities and contentions in societies well beyond the Indonesian archipelago. All modern societies are ever-evolving assemblies of diverse social groupings, political projects, and social imaginaries (Barth 1993; Schielke 2015; Taylor 1994). As noted above and as scholars of law and ethics have also long recognized, every society is also ethically and legally plural, with a variety of ethical traditions and "registers" (Schielke 2015) on offer to provide actors with hope, ambition, and moral clarity—not least with regard to the issue at the heart of the present book, how to recognize and coexist with one's fellows in society. At certain "critical junctures" in their development, however, the dominant groupings and leaderships in society may attempt to impose a more or less paramount "ideological and institutional legacy" that, however widely contested, attempts to establish ground rules and sensibilities for public coexistence and recognition (Kuru 2009; Taylor 1994). If it is to endure, and if its terms are not to be pushed aside by social challengers promoting an alternative register for recognition and belonging, the product of this normative work must be scaled up and maintained over time by the "establishment of institutions that generate self-reinforcing path-dependent processes" (Kuru 2009, 278; cf. Stepan 2011, 2014). No less important, if it is to remain socially consequential, the charter's discourses and practices must influence processes of "social recognition" (Honneth 2001; Zurn 2000) beyond the confines of official state-citizen interactions, so that citizens experience otherwise abstract categories (a religious identity, ethnic solidarity, national citizenship, etc.) as *everyday and lived* realities consonant with a broadly shared way of life (Beaman 2016; Glenn 2011).

As here in *Reformasi* Indonesia, the periods during which civic charters and normativities are established are often accompanied by fierce debates and even violent contentions. Whether on the basis of equality or hierarchy, dominance or marginalization, such social engagements inevitably revive "previous grievances and tensions," to borrow a phrase from the Canadian political scientist Jacques Bertrand (2004, 23; cf. Kuru 2009). In so doing, the social charters and engagements that emerge from critical junctures put in stark relief what a society once was, is now, and aspires to become.

This, then, is the broader background to this project and book on Indonesian pluralities. By all measures, Indonesia today is in the throes of just such a critical juncture, and true to such moments' dynamics, the terms of how a diverse people should recognize each other and flourish are at the center of public debate. A great reassessment of self-identities and social plurality is taking place in this country. As Ward Berenschot and Gerry van Klinken (2019a) have emphasized in a recent and important book, in its more public and formal forms the process concerns state-related matters of constitutionalism, citizenship, party policies, and, most generally, the ways in which people interact with the state. But the processes are also unfolding at the grassroots of society, in patterns of social interaction, evaluation, and recognition more varied than those forged in interaction with the state alone. These processes of social recognition "beyond the state" operate in everyday realities of social recognition like those instantiated when greeting one's neighbors, identifying who is a "fellow-believer" and who is not, or determining just who should and should not be invited to participate in customary celebrations of belonging, ancestry, and remembrance (see Swazey, chapter 3; Maarif 2017).

As the above discussion has already made clear, the changes Indonesia has undergone since the fall of the New Order in May 1998 have not followed a single ethico-political course, particularly with regard to these questions of recognition, belonging, and coexistence (see Hadiz 2016). From the beginning, in fact, the country's progress in democratic reform has been accompanied by a generally worsening pattern of religious intolerance, the form of which has varied greatly by region (Crouch 2014; Fealy 2016b; ICG 2010; Lindsey and Pausacker 2016). The state and its security forces have made good progress toward containing the terrorist fringe operative in the country, in fact to a degree much greater than most Western and Muslim-majority countries (Jones 2013). However, both state and society in Indonesia have shown less ability to deal with the uncivil by-products of the "conservative turn" (Bruinessen 2013a, 2013b; Burhani 2013a) seen in Muslim society in Indonesia since the early 2000s, as well as in, one must emphasize, Indonesia's minority communities. A key feature of the conservative turn has been a striking uptick in interreligious tensions and the harassment of religious minorities by vigilantes from locally dominant ethno-religious groups (Bagir 2013; Crouch 2014; Feillard and Madinier 2006; Human Rights Watch 2013; Pausacker 2013). Again, and as several chapters in this book make clear, these exclusivist trends have not by any means been limited to Islamist circles (see also Schulte Nordholt 2007). In regions like Protestant-majority northern Sulawesi and Hindu-majority Bali, there have been similar attempts to categorize and differentially recognize residents along religious and ethnic lines.

In short, although Indonesia has made great progress toward the long-cherished nationalist goal of creating a significant measure of linguistic, economic, and political integration across its great expanse, its efforts to establish an operating consensus on religion, ethnicity, and social recognition remain something of a work in progress. It goes without saying that the country is not alone in this regard: ours is an age of pluralist trial, including in Western democracies, where many people are increasingly uncertain as to how to engage and recognize immigrants and the new face of citizenship in their own societies (Joppke 2017; Modood 2007; Taylor 1994). This makes the lessons to be learned from a country with the cultural richness and democratic possibilities of Indonesia all the more timely and compelling.

THREE THESES ON PLURALITY
AND RECOGNITION IN INDONESIA

Each chapter in this book presents findings on the state of plurality, recognition, and belonging in a particular part of Indonesia. In an effort to highlight and extend their shared themes, I will in the remainder of this chapter discuss three theses on plurality and social recognition in contemporary Indonesia. Although they are not comprehensive, I present them so as to shed light on the rival varieties of normative work and social scaling that our researchers encountered in their studies, many of which have also marked public-ethical contention elsewhere in Indonesia since the fall of the Soeharto regime in May 1998.

Thesis 1: Ethnicity and Social Recognition

My first thesis has to do with what at various points in Indonesian history has been one of the country's most vexing social realities: ethnicity. Indonesia has more than four hundred ethnic groups, and regional rebellions organized along broadly "ethnic" lines have been a notable feature of politics in republican Indonesia; they played an especially important (but by no means singular) role in the rebellions that broke out in several provinces of Indonesia in the late 1950s (Feith [1962] 2006). Certainly, on the evidence of the chapters that follow, ethnic and regional awareness remains pervasive across Indonesia today, especially at the local and regional level. More strikingly, at the dawn of the *Reformasi* era, ethno-religious tensions seemed to imperil Indonesia's fragile transition to democracy in settings like West Kalimantan (Davidson 2008), Central Sulawesi, Ambon, and Maluku (Duncan 2013; Al Qurtuby 2016; C. Wilson 2008). In these regions, communal violence of catastrophic proportions broke out, taking a heavy toll in human lives and displacement. Although some of the violence soon came to be rearticulated along "religious" lines, its ethnic dimensions did not entirely disappear.

However, and herein lies the heart of my first thesis, grassroots initiatives and national developments since the early years of *Reformasi* have had the welcome effect of significantly damping the ethno-communal tensions that flared up from 1998 to 2001. The result has been partial and uneven but nonetheless notable: the "small town wars" (Klinken 2007) of the early *Reformasi* period have been contained and have not escalated into more extensive and enduring civil wars. Comparing Indonesia with nearby Malaysia, Sri Lanka, or Myanmar, the Australian political scientist Ed Aspinall (2011, 296) has observed, "Indonesia remains a polity in which ethnicity plays a surprisingly minimal role in politics." Aspinall of course intends his observation to apply only to national-level politics. As several chapters in this book make clear, at the regional and local level a "domesticated" ethnic awareness pervades the daily lives of ordinary Indonesians. Moreover, as Erica Larson, Kelli Swazey, and Marthen Tahun make clear in chapters 2, 3, and 5 respectively, ethnic legacies and reinventions often lead to a curious misremembering of history and social belonging (cf. Duncan 2013; Suryadinata 2008). No less important, with regard to the micropolitics of everyday life, ethnic ascriptions and differentiations remain ubiquitous, as seen in everything from business partnerships and philanthropy to language use in social interaction (see Goebel 2010; Suryadinata 2008).

At first glance, even this qualified generalization about ethno-regional tensions in the *Reformasi* era may strike some Indonesia observers as hyperbolic. After all, as Jacques Bertrand (2004), Gerry van Klinken (2007), Chris Wilson (2008), James Davidson (2008), and Chris Duncan (2013) have all shown, during the first three years of the post-Soeharto transition ethnicity was politicized "with sometimes startling speed and ferocity" (Aspinall 2011, 293). In the worst cases the politicization resulted in the "small town wars" about which Gerry van Klinken (2007) has written so insightfully. As Varshney, Tadjoeddin, and Panggabean (2004, 23) have also noted, this politicization proved deadly: the violence of the early transition period peaked in 1999 with an estimated 3,546 deaths. Just four years later (2003), however, the annual death toll had declined to 111 and it has moved lower ever since. All this said, the first years of the post-Soeharto transition were awful enough that some Western analysts likened *Reformasi* Indonesia to Yugoslavia and the former Soviet Union; some warned of the country's imminent collapse. In the end, however, Indonesia's political center and its diverse peripheries reached new accommodations and stabilized. Large-scale communal conflict took place in only eight of Indonesia's (today) thirty-four provinces, in territories hosting just 7.5 percent of Indonesia's population (Aspinall 2011). And for the most part, violence of a broadly communal nature has remained limited to this day (cf. C. Wilson 2008).

Of course, full-blown incidents of communal violence are just one indicator of ethnic tensions, and even if violence has diminished in recent years, other ethnic appeals and politicizations have actually increased. As discussed in the chapters on Ambon and Manado, the civilian vigilantes that have proliferated since the end of the New Order are still often organized along ethnic lines, although (as I will discuss later) some of the largest favor religion over ethnicity in framing their mobilization appeals (see I. Wilson 2008; Bakker 2016; Schulte Nordholt 2007; Talle 2013). Equally important, although ethnic appeals have been largely absent from *national* elections for the presidency (see Liddle and Mujani 2007, 849), the elections of local government heads (known here in Indonesia by the acronym *pilkada*) introduced in 2005 have been accompanied by a marked increase in ethno-regional appeals. Most but not all of the appeals seem simple enough, involving for example the use of local languages in campaign speeches, the wearing of traditional dress, and the trotting out of *adat* (customary) leaders at campaign rallies (see Aspinall 2011, 297; Buehler 2016). Innocuous though they may be, these limited ethnic appeals stand in stark contrast to politics during the New Order period (1966–98), when state policy formally forbade explicit political appeals to ethnicity, religion, race, or *adat*-custom (*suku, agama, ras, antar golongan*, known collectively by the acronym SARA). These developments acknowledged, many would agree with Aspinall's (2011, 298) conclusion that, although ethnic mobilizations figured prominently in the early *Reformasi* period, their "political salience has subsided as a new democratic system has settled in place," at the state level if not the level of micro- and mesosocial politics.

The domestication of ethnic tensions at the national level was the result of a curious mix of legislation, social dealmaking, and ethical scalings, some initiated by state-based actors, others by actors in society. The state-level reforms included the requirement instituted in the early *Reformasi* period that all parties wishing to contest legislative elections had to show that they had effective support across the breadth of the country (a requirement to which the special district of Aceh was granted an exception; see A. Salim 2008). This legal restriction had the welcome effect of compelling national parties to build their coalitions across ethnic and territorial divides, rather than hunkering down within one regional or (as with the Javanese, who make up 40 percent of the country's population) nationally dominant ethnic group. The restriction has had a notably less dramatic effect on regional elections, and it is here that winks and nods to ethnicity still abound.

Another factor that has diminished the salience of ethnic appeals has been the continuing development of Indonesian national culture.

Whether in the near-universal fluency in the national language (Bahasa Indonesia), the national appetite for certain pop musical genres (e.g. *dangdut*, see Weintraub 2010, 2018), or the development of new mass media and programming (see Rakhmani 2016), the creation of a thriving national culture in this country of more than four hundred ethnic groups is one of the more impressive nation-making achievements of our age. Ed Aspinall (2011) also attributes the damping of ethno-communal tensions in the *Reformasi* era to something he aptly describes as the "deep architecture" of Indonesian politics. As a number of other analysts have observed (Mietzner 2009; Ufen 2008), politics in *Reformasi* Indonesia seems no longer steered by the once nationally prominent ideological currents (*aliran*) of the 1950s and 1960s (Feith [1962] 2006; Lev 1966). Today political life is structured by less ideologically grounded networks of patron-clientage and brokerage that extend from the national to the local level. The pervasiveness of patronage ties is often lamented as a blight on Indonesian democracy, and there is no doubt that in its money politics and oligarchical form (see Hadiz 2016; Winters 2013) it does have a deeply corrosive effect. However, as Aspinall (2011, 291) also notes, patron-clientage tends to encourage "a culture of deal making and compromise that . . . has had conflict-ameliorating effects."

Although not typically recognized as such, a "culture of deal making" is a species of recognition and normativity, and it is one that has indeed been scaled up across broad swaths of Indonesian society, including in our project's research sites. But for our purposes it is important to note that this kind of normativity operates in a way different from that we first imagine when talking about norms for social recognition or coexistence; but this very distinctiveness is what makes it noteworthy. In particular, the culture of dealmaking is a background or offstage process rather than a foreground process of public ethical construction. It shapes expectations and social interests among citizens, but, precisely because it can bleed into behaviors that some regard as inappropriate or immoral, it is the subject of little official normativity or supportive public discussion. The culture of dealmaking, then, is *enacted* more than it is discursively *recognized*. No less important, and as Berenschot and Klinken (2019b, 6–7) have rightly emphasized, the fact that so much citizen interaction with state officials is subject to informal and highly personalized dealmaking makes the interactions of less privileged citizens with the state unpredictable; it also makes citizens reluctant to organize collectively in pursuit of their aims. In other words, although informal dealmaking may help keep the peace, it significantly degrades the quality of Indonesian democracy.

The culture of dealmaking's effect on citizens' *lateral* recognition and interactions with one another is also noteworthy, because it sometimes serves to reduce tensions. Where they reach across ethnic divides, dealmaking's norms and practices reduce the incentives to fall back on ethnic and regionalist exclusivity. Equally important, precisely because they are not officially scaled up, dealmaking practices—like the market exchanges that Marthen Tahun (chapter 5) describes for Ambon city—create an interactional space in which ties of a more "bridging" nature may slowly take hold. As chapter 2 by Kelli Swazey on tourism and development in the Banda Islands demonstrates, however, dealmaking does not always work to narrow ethnic divides. In addition, the process sometimes runs up against another social identity and norm-making reality: religion, not least that of a newly revitalized and transregional form.

Thesis 2: Religion and Social Recognition

This book's second thesis with regard to pluralist coexistence in Indonesia has to do with the place of religion in the normative work and institutional scaling of models for recognition, belonging, and coexistence in *Reformasi* Indonesia. My observation here is that, even as Indonesia has made progress at taming ethno-regionalist sectarianism, its progress at scaling up and stabilizing an inclusive civility with regard to *religious* recognition has proved more hesitant, to a degree that suggests that Indonesia today may be at a yet unfinished "critical juncture" (Bertrand 2004; Kuru 2009) with regard to religion, social recognition, and citizenship. The key question at the heart of this juncture has to do with whether Indonesia is to continue with and deepen the religiously inclusive traditions of Pancasila nationalism, which stipulate that citizens of all faiths should enjoy the same rights and see each other as sharing a common national identity, or whether the country's charter for plurality and coexistence will veer toward a *differentiated and stratified* citizenship, in which one religious community is favored over others, in a manner akin to the religiously differentiated and asymmetrical practices of recognition, coexistence, and citizenship found in nearby Malaysia, Myanmar, Thailand, and Sri Lanka (Daniels 2017; Kloos and Berenschot 2016; Moustafa 2013, 2018).

In assessing the crafting and scaling up of normativities for religious recognition in *Reformasi* Indonesia, two facts stand above all others. The first is the sheer ubiquity and contentiousness of the processes, and the second is the fact that much of the normative work has taken place outside of and at times in opposition to state-sanctioned charters and normativities. In other words, one of the ironies of the *Reformasi* transition is that, by comparison with ethnic normativities, there has been a veritable explosion of normative work and institutional scaling of religion-and-recognition norms. Moreover, even within the same religious community, the registers for recognition produced through these processes have varied, sometimes in a starkly agonistic way.

This latter fact is particularly complex and has evolved over the course of the post-Soeharto period. During the early years of the *Reformasi* transition, much of the legal and normative work at the national level (especially in the newly invigorated national assembly) seemed designed to deepen the Pancasila legacy of equal recognition for citizens of all state-acknowledged faiths and to take that culture from the hallways of the state into the interactions of everyday society. Between 1999 and 2002, for example, Indonesian legislators crafted constitutional amendments intended to strengthen the legal environment for religious freedom and Pancasila pluralism in a manner that domestic and international observers welcomed as broadly consistent with liberal-democratic freedoms, as well as the international human rights covenants to which Indonesia was already a signatory (Butt and Lindsey 2012, 19–25). The most important of these amendments were articles 28E and 28(1) to the constitution. Article 28E affirmed, first, that "each person is free to embrace their religion and to worship [*beribadat*] in accordance with his or her religion" and, second, that "each person has the freedom to possess beliefs [*kepercayaan*], and to express his or her thoughts and attitudes in accordance with his or her conscience." Another Reform-era amendment (28I (1)) borrowed language from the Universal Declaration of Human Rights to affirm that the "right to have a religion" (Ind., *hak beragama*) was one among several human rights "that cannot be limited under any circumstance" (Lindsey and Butt 2016, 22).

These initiatives were not just ivory-tower dreams; nor were they without significant social impact. The climate they helped to foster put wind in the sails of other reform efforts, including those that allowed the removal of the military from broad swaths of civilian politics. Earlier, in the final years of the Soeharto regime, an Indonesian military that had long liked to think of itself as standing above religious divisions in society was reported to have developed an internal cleavage between the so-called "red-and-white" or nationalist generals, who wanted to maintain the Pancasila status quo with regard to religion, and so-called "green generals," who advocated a more sustained outreach to Muslim groups—especially conservative Islamists willing to rally to the defense of a Soeharto regime confronting a growing prodemocracy opposition (Hefner 2000; Mietzner 2009). Commentaries on the divide have sometimes exaggerated its scale and overlooked the degree to which it was based on a familiar pattern of personality-centered patronage. But some leading figures *did* use sectarian appeals to rally antidemocratic Islamists to the defense of the Soeharto regime, and inevitably this created tensions in the armed forces command, as well as in society.

During the tumultuous years of the Abdurrahman Wahid presidency (1999–2001), many observers feared that a wing of the Indonesian armed forces might attempt to exploit religious tensions to engineer a political comeback. As Marcus Mietzner (2014) has observed, in July 2013 the Egyptian military used just such a strategy to oust the Muslim-Brotherhood's Mohamed Morsi from power. Up to that time, Mietzner notes, the role played by the military in Egypt's attempted transition had been characterized by "striking similarities" with that of the Indonesian military. But in 2012–13 the Egyptian military did something the Indonesian military would not: it exploited deep-seated tensions between secularists and Islamists to stage a return to power. One of the reasons Indonesians were able to consolidate democracy and implement a new civilian-military relationship was that, unlike their Egyptian counterparts, the civilian elite in early *Reformasi* Indonesia was able to achieve "an intra-civilian consensus on fundamental issues of general governance [and] . . . the most important of these issues has been the role of Islam in state organization" (Mietzner 2014, 436). As the mobilization against the Chinese Christian governor of Jakarta illustrated in 2016–17 (see below), and as some recent national surveys have suggested (Mietzner, Muhtadi, and Halida 2018), it is not clear that this consensus is quite as strong today. But there is also no question that many in the armed forces, the state administration, and society remain determined to defend Indonesia's heritage of Pancasila pluralism (Hefner 2019).

Other developments similarly showed that the national leadership in the early *Reformasi* period had achieved a measure of consensus on an inclusive and Pancasila-based charter for recognition and plurality. One striking illustration of this was the fact that in the period of 2000–2001 the National Assembly rebuffed efforts on the part of several small Islamist parties to change the constitution so as to require the state to implement Islamic law for all Muslim citizens. The effort failed in part because of a striking development in religious society: strong opposition to the proposal from the leadership of Muhammadiyah and Nahdlatul Ulama, Indonesia's two behemoth Muslim social welfare organizations, and veritable pillars of Indonesian civil society (Elson 2013; Feillard and Madinier 2006; Nakamura 2012). The leadership's opposition to the shariah legislation reflected its commitment to the Pancasila model of multireligious recognition and their unwillingness to press for an Islam-first, religiously differentiated citizenship (Elson 2013; A. Salim 2008).

This was not the end of the religion-and-coexistence story, however, and there soon emerged other public proposals of a more religiously differentiated nature; most emanated, not from the state, but from social movements and organizations in society. In the first years of the transition, some religious groupings in society were already pressing for changes that, if implemented, would shift the practice of citizenship away from Pancasila inclusivity toward a religiously differentiated and stratified citizenship. There was no single actor or agency masterminding this citizen-differentiating effort. In many cases, too, the motivation for these initiatives had less to do with norms and scalings for recognition and national citizenship than with the long-standing desire of many religiously observant people, Muslims and non-Muslims, to bring more of their faith into public life. In this latter regard, and as in neighboring Malaysia (Kloos and Berenschot 2016; Moustafa 2018), ongoing changes in popular religious practice and ethics exercised a powerful and evolving influence on ideas and practices of recognition and citizenship.

There were multiple actors, then, but several agents of normative work and scalings for a non- or revised-Pancasila citizenship stand out. One that had a particularly notable influence had to do with scaling initiatives undertaken by the country's foremost association of Islamic scholars, the Indonesian Council of Ulama (MUI). After Soeharto's fall, the new leadership of the MUI concluded that during the New Order period it had compromised its public standing by acting too pliantly toward the Soeharto regime. For most of the New Order the MUI *had* worked closely with the state, and the organization came to be widely seen as "the bureaucratisation of Islam . . . in its most extreme form" (Hooker 2003, 60; see also Mudzhar 1993; Zuhadi 1989). In the more open and competitive religious market of the *Reformasi* era, the MUI leadership realized that it risked losing its public relevance and authority. Faced with this challenge, the MUI leadership set out from 2000 onward to rebrand itself as a boldly independent, nongovernmental organization. At its national congress in that year, the MUI formally announced that its primary role was to be no longer a "servant of the government" (*khadim al-hukumah*) but a servant of the Muslim community (*khadim al-ummah*). Over the next five years, the council extended its authority into several fields, including national education and the lucrative enterprises of Islamic banking and halal certification. The primary role the MUI sought to take on for itself, however, was that of national guardian of Islamic morals and orthodoxy.

As part of its campaign to achieve a new hegemony in the shaping of Muslim practices of public ethics and recognition, the MUI secured its long-standing base among Islamic scholars in Muhammadiyah and Nahdlatul Ulama, but it then also reached out to new Islamist organizations, including small but radical groups like Indonesia's Muslim Brotherhood, Hizbut Tahrir Indonesia (see Ahnaf, chapter 4; Ahnaf 2011; Osman 2018), and the Majelis Mujahadin Indonesia (Hefner 2005b, 2019). Liberal and progressive Muslims like those associated with the Network of Liberal Islam (Jaringan Islam Liberal, JIL; see Feillard and Madinier 2006; Nurdin 2005) were conspicuous by their absence from the MUI's list of invitees (Ichwan 2013, 64; Hasyim 2014; Olle 2009). Equally notable, militants in hard-line groups like Hizbut Tahrir Indonesia were not simply admitted to MUI circles but rewarded for their affiliation by being given strategic positions on the MUI's all-important commission for the formulation of fatwa rulings (religious rulings based on Islamic jurisprudence) and *tausiyah* (jurisprudentially grounded recommendations).

Consistent with its new role as a defender of Sunni orthodoxy, the national MUI also called for the banning of the Ahmadis, curbs on Christian church building, and measures to prosecute "deviationist" groupings on charges of religious defamation (Ali-Fauzi et al. 2011; Bagir 2013; Crouch 2014; Fenwick 2015). To consolidate its grassroots networks and build a mobile force for enforcing its rulings, the MUI also reactivated the Forum for Islamic Unity (Forum Ukhuwah Islamiyah; FUI). The FUI had been established under MUI auspices in 1989 but then allowed to go dormant. The revitalized FUI recruited heavily from among the local Islamist militias that had proliferated since the early *Reformasi* period, many of which were opposed to Indonesia's new democratic system and advocated a religiously differentiated citizenship (see Bamualim 2011; Burhani 2013b, 197–98; Hasan 2006; I. Wilson 2006, 2008).

It is important to note that even in MUI circles there were exceptions to these trends, and today, especially in the aftermath of the anti-Ahok mobilizations, the exceptions have become greater in number. In several districts I visited from 2014 to 2019, including Ambon, Manado, Central Java, and metropolitan Jakarta, local chapters of the MUI have begun to distance themselves from earlier MUI policies and discourage collaborations with vigilante groups. Marthen Tahun discusses some of these developments in chapter 5 on Ambon, where the regional director of the MUI in 2016–18, Abidin Wakano, and the rector of the State Islamic Institute (IAIN), Hasbollah Toisuta, have become courageous spokespersons for Pancasila pluralism. However, in other areas of the country the cooperation of local MUI councils with hard-line militias remains common, albeit at levels typically below those of the early 2000s.

Where the MUI-militia alliance remains operational, it is often deployed in campaigns against individuals and groups deemed religiously deviant or otherwise threatening to the religious majority. In 2005, the national MUI issued several fatwas that clarified just what the council regarded as its priorities with regard to Muslim morals and orthodoxy and showed that, even if this was not their intent, the rulings were destined to have implications for recognition and sociability across religious divides (Gillespie 2007). Among other things, the MUI reiterated its ruling banning interreligious marriages. It also prohibited Muslim participation in interreligious prayer services, activities that had become popular in multifaith peacebuilding in the early *Reformasi* era.

Two among the MUI's 2005 rulings, however, proved especially consequential for efforts to build an inclusive and pluralistic recognition of religious identities in the public sphere. The first was the declaration mentioned above, which renewed the MUI's 1980 call for the government to ban the Ahmadiyah movement outright. The issuing of this appeal was not unexpected. A few years earlier, at its National Congress in 2000, the MUI had released a statement that signaled its determination to struggle against thirteen varieties of "reprehensible acts" (*munkarat*); religious "deviation" sat at the top of the list. From 2002 onward, militias associated with the FUI had invoked the MUI declaration to justify their harassment of Ahmadiyah in their mosques, offices, and homes. On July 9, 2005, less than three weeks prior to the MUI congress, a crowd of some five thousand to ten thousand men, led by the Islamic Defenders Front (FPI) and a small organization known as the Islamic Research and Study Institute (Lembaga Penelitian dan Pengkajian Islam, a group long involved in "antiheresy" campaigns), launched an attack on an Ahmadiyah campus in Parung, Bogor, south of Jakarta. Although the police eventually succeeded at pushing the attackers back, the incident was seen as a signal to the MUI congress that it should escalate the campaign against the Ahmadiyah by reissuing a fatwa condemning the small community as heretical and non-Islamic (Human Rights Watch 2013; ICG 2008, 2).

Over the next few years, officials in provincial and district offices of the MUI worked with local vigilantes to press this campaign, not just against Ahmadis, but against Muslim liberals, out-of-the-mainstream Sufis and syncretists, and other designated deviants. On several occasions, local MUI officials pressured police and prosecutors to take action against people accused of defamation or deviationism under Indonesia's Defamation Law (Fenwick 2015). Through these and other actions, an influential wing of the MUI has largely succeeded in turning itself into an institution that this country has never had—an "official national mufti" (Lindsey 2012, 124)—

and one with street-smart militias to scale up and enforce its antipluralist positions.

In short, whether by design or happenstance, the normative work and hegemonizing scalings of the MUI and its mobilizational allies have had a decidedly differentiating effect on recognition and coexistence in *Reformasi* Indonesia. Zainal Abidin Bagir's chapter at the end of this book focuses on one of the most dramatic examples of this effort, the FPI-coordinated campaign against the Christian Chinese governor of Jakarta in late 2016 and early 2017, culminating in his defeat in the elections of April 19, 2017, and his subsequent imprisonment on charges of religious defamation (see also IPAC 2018a). Observers have rightly noted that a major new player in the antipluralist camp was a coalition of ostensibly "moderate" Salafists (IPAC 2019). A key ingredient in their newly moderated public proposals was that, rather than calling for the replacement of the Indonesian nation with an "Islamic state," the neo-Salafists and their Islamist partners accepted the legitimacy of the nation-state but with the understanding that its charters for social recognition and citizenship must be "Islamized" in a manner consistent with Salafi understandings of Muslim supremacy (Chaplin 2018). All this is to say that, if Indonesia's neo-Salafists and Islamists have now reached a new accommodation on the ideals and practices of nationhood, they have done so in part to challenge and remake these with regard to public recognition, with the aim of creating a citizenship differentiated and stratified along religious lines (Chaplin 2019; Hefner 2019).

These and other developments show that the early *Reformasi* era laid a solid but unfinished foundation for Pancasila pluralism and religiously inclusive recognition. During these same years, however, and culminating in the "Defend Islam Actions" of 2016–17, other developments have pressed public recognition and citizenship in a religiously exclusive and stratified direction. National opinion polls carried out in 2017–18 indicate that the latter antipluralist mobilizations have had a notable impact on Muslim public opinion (Mietzner, Muhtadi, and Halida 2018). However, the national elections of April 2019 led some Indonesians and international observers to wonder whether the campaign for a less inclusive practice of recognition and citizenship had at long last not generated a pluralist countermobilization.

Thesis 3: What Variety of Recognition?

This brings me to my third and last thesis with regard to this book's research findings. Thesis 3 is that, rather than being the simple product of anti-Pancasila populism or patronage scheming, the contentious plurality about which the book chapters speak has been exacerbated by a broad shift in the categories of religious recognition normalized in Indonesian public discourse since the 1950s. The shift has to do with the growing popular acceptance and normalization of the *agama-kepercayaan* ("religion" vs. "spiritual beliefs") distinction promoted by Muslim reformists and (on a less pervasive scale) Christian missionaries since the early 1950s (cf. Ramstedt 2004 and Picard 2011 for Indonesian Hinduism). The binary extends full recognition and legitimacy only to *agama*, which is to say, revealed "religions" with a prophet or seer, a *kitab* or holy scripture, a more or less standardized body of doctrine and worship, and international recognition (Maarif 2017; Picard 2011; Ropi 2012; Stange 1986). Earlier, and in particular in Indonesia's 1945 constitution, *kepercayaan* or "spiritual beliefs" had in principle enjoyed near-equal standing and legal protection with *agama*. However, with the growing public acceptance of a starker and more stratified distinction between religion and spiritual beliefs, from the late 1970s onward such non-*agama* traditions lost their legitimacy and many of their legal protections (Atkinson 1987; Mutaqin 2014).

This development was neither inevitable nor unchallenged. In the 1950s and 1960s, a significant minority of Indonesians still practiced local religions and/or new religious traditions of a *kepercayaan*/spirituality nature. An even greater number—probably the majority among the ethnic Javanese who at the time made up 50 percent of the country's population—practiced nonstandard or "localized" varieties of Islam. Like the Alevis in Turkey (Hurd 2014), the latter "nonstandard" varieties of Islam combined recognition of Allah as God and the Prophet Muhammad as his messenger with ritual traditions that included the presentation of incense, offerings, and ritual veneration to various guardian and ancestral beings. There were many local variations on this "mystic synthesis," as Merle Ricklefs (2006, 2012) has put it, and they were found not just in Java but (on a much smaller scale) in Lombok, South Sumatra, and South Sulawesi.

However, for reasons that Merle Ricklefs, Ismatu Ropi (2012), Bambang Pranowo (1991), Jamhari (2000), Julia Day Howell (2008), and many others have explored, a combination of state policies, rapid social change, urbanization, new youth cultures, and the categorical shift associated with the normative supremacy of *agama* over *kepercayaan* ensured that, since the 1980s, these localized religious traditions have steadily declined, in some regions (including Java) quite precipitously (see also Cederroth 1996; Ricklefs 2012; Hefner 1987, 2011b).

Notwithstanding these developments, the struggle for religious recognition and self-determination is by no means over. With the implementation of an ambitious program of political decentralization after 1999–2000, some *kepercayaan* groups and some practitioners of local or indigenous religions—now increasingly referred to as *agama leluhur* or "ancestral religions" (Maarif 2017)—have mobilized and reasserted their right to recognition on par with Indonesia's officially recognized religions. For most of the history of the republic, officials in the Ministry of Religion and the MUI have steadfastly opposed recognition of ancestral religions and *kepercayaan*-spiritual traditions as "religions" (*agama*). However, and in contradistinction to the "conservative turn" seen in so many other areas of religious life in Indonesia in the 2000s, opinion in both institutions began to soften in the early 2010s. The relaxation was in part a reaction against the global ascent of transnational Islamist movements like al-Qaeda and the Islamic State in Iraq and Syria (ISIS), which reinforced the desire in many state and societal circles in Indonesia to manage religion in a manner consistent with the moderate and inclusive image of the country that government officials sought to promote on the global stage (Hoesterey 2018). However (and as Zainal Abidin Bagir discusses in chapter 7), the shift was also supported by two startling legal developments: first, the Constitutional Court's ruling in April 2010 that both *agama*-religion and *kepercayaan*-spiritualities are equally protected under the constitution; and, second, the no less momentous high court decision in November 2017 affirming (for the first time in Indonesian history) that the members of traditional religions and spiritualities should be allowed to list *kepercayaan* on their citizen identification cards rather than being obliged to list one of the six recognized religions (*agama*; see Maarif 2017, 107).

These court-based influences on religious recognition were in turn buttressed by no less remarkable developments in civil society. Some of the long-marginalized local religions—like West Java's Agama Djawa Sunda (Java-Sunda religion; see Mutaqin 2014)—buttressed their appeals for recognition by attempting to tether their religious traditions to the larger body of territorially linked customs and properties identified in much of Indonesia as *adat* ("custom" or "territorially based traditions and properties"; see Bowen 2005; Henley and Davidson 2008). The linkage was consistent with another important trend in the early *Reformasi* period: the efforts of regionally based ethnic minorities to assert claims to a broad range of local properties and heritages, including rights of ownership over forest lands long regarded as part of their *adat* properties. During the New Order period, access to the latter had been blocked by state authorities who preferred to extend rights of access to forest tracts to multinational timber companies or well-connected oligarchs (Li 2014; Winters 2013). The mobilization of long-marginalized indigenous populations into movements demanding both land rights and religious recognition has been one of the more remarkable, if deeply unfinished, developments of the *Reformasi* period (Maarif 2017; Henley and Davidson 2008).

In the post–New Order period, this effort to buttress appeals for the recognition of local religions by linking them to claims of indigenousness and *adat* heritage, however, has itself had varied effects. As Swazey and Tahun show in chapters 3 and 5 on the Banda Islands and Maluku respectively, the ideals and recognitions implicit in *adat* practice in some parts of pre-*Reformasi* Indonesia, not least eastern Indonesia, had once been sufficiently encompassing to allow people from different religious traditions (e.g., Christians and Muslims) to participate in shared ritual performances, which served to affirm their common identity and joint ownership of *adat* properties. Swazey's vivid description of Christian and Muslim Bandanese participation in *adat* rites of ancestral memorialization once had counterparts in many parts of Indonesia where a shared *adat* tradition and identity were seen as ethically superogatory to membership in a "world" religion.

Swazey's account of the way in which in the aftermath of the 1999–2000 violence in Banda (in which few people died, but the entire indigenous Christian minority was driven from the islands) the Christian minority has lost its once pivotal role alongside Muslims in *adat* rites of ancestral and territorial memorialization, however, also has parallels elsewhere in Indonesia. In particular, in many regions a concept of *adat* once capable of accommodating people of diverse religious faiths in a shared *adat* community has declined or been rearticulated in less inclusive ways. The latter change often involves *adat*'s being redefined in relation to just one religious identity, rather than its inclusively bridging religious divides. In an article some years ago on normative plurality in Indonesia, the American anthropologist John Bowen (2005, 158) noted that the concept of *adat* in eastern Indonesia often worked in a way that neutralized more exclusive assertions of religious identity. By contrast, he observed, in western Indonesia, especially among peoples like the Acehnese and Minangkabau of Sumatra or among Malays in the Riau archipelago or West Kalimantan, the categories of Islam and *adat* tended to merge in a manner that was so mutually reinforcing as to be singular and exclusive: to be Minangkabau, Acehnese, or Malay was, quite simply, to be Muslim (Bowen 2005, 167).

The situation that Swazey observes among Muslim Bandanese and that Larson finds among Christian Manadonese in North Sulawesi thus reflects a deeper and more troubled trans-Indonesian history. Its recent genesis has involved the emergence in many regions of "ethnic" identities grounded on a more singular and exclusive religious identity, and a concept of *adat* identity that is exclusive rather than accommodating of multiple faith traditions. As Birgit Bräuchler (2009a), Christopher R. Duncan (2009a, 2009b, 2013), and Sumanto Al Qurtuby (2016) have all shown, and as Marthen Tahun discusses in chapter 5, there are exceptions to this narrowing of *adat* recognition. In places like Tobelo in North Maluku some local actors have bravely attempted to revive *adat* practices in an effort to promote reconciliation between Christians and Muslims by effectively shifting "people's focus of identity from their religion . . . to their ethnicity" (Duncan 2009b, 1077). However, in some other postconflict regions, what Duncan (2013, 170) has described as a "war-induced essentialism" has converged with revivalist religion to undercut these efforts at religiously inclusive recognition.

HORIZONS OF RECOGNITION AND BELONGING

In an otherwise brilliant third volume in his trilogy on Islamization in Java, the historian Merle Ricklefs (2012) concludes that the processes I have described here are an inevitable aspect of the "Islamization" of Indonesian society. More specifically, Ricklefs argues, the consequences of "Islamization" will be a growing segregation of Indonesian society, a diminution of interreligious tolerance, and a steady erosion of religious freedom. Ricklefs does not cite the work of James Liow (2009), Timothy Daniels (2017), Tamir Moustafa (2018), or David Kloos and Ward Berenschot (2016), all of whom have written eloquently on the corrosive effects of ethno-religious polarization on efforts to build an inclusive practice of recognition and citizenship in Malaysia. It is nonetheless striking that the processes that Ricklefs describes in Java and Indonesia so visibly resemble those in post-colonial Malaysia, where we have seen the emergence of two or three "parallel societies" segregated and stratified along ethno-religious lines (Liow 2009, 191).

However, whether in Malaysia or Indonesia, I do not think the corrosion of national identity and the undermining of a religiously inclusive citizenship are by any means inevitable results of "Islamization," as Ricklefs argues. Islamization is not a single or unitary process but a family of processes organized around plural and sometimes contradictory understandings of Islam and the higher aims of Islam and shariah (*maqasid al-shariah*; see Daniels 2017; Moosa 2001; Hefner 2016). Recently this point has been vividly highlighted by Shahab Ahmed (2016) in his encyclopedic survey of the past one thousand years of Islam and culture in the huge expanse of the Muslim world stretching from the Balkans to Bengal. Ahmed's conclusion also applies here in modern Indonesia: the specific form that Islamization takes, and its consequences for social recognition and fellowship, are contingent upon the normative work and scaling in which socially influential Muslim intellectuals, leaders, and ordinary people engage, with regard to both their own traditions and their engagement with other ethical communities (cf. Feener 2007).

As the late and great Alfred Stepan noted in a 2014 essay on Muslims and toleration, what is so remarkable about Indonesia is that, from the

1990s onward, a growing number of influential scholars, activists, and politicians have concluded that democracy and Indonesian traditions of multireligious recognition are consistent with Islam and the higher aims of God's law (Stepan 2014; see also Abdillah 1997). In the early 2000s, the leadership of the Muhammadiyah and NU threw their support behind constitutional amendments and political reforms consistent with these inclusive ideals. Indonesia still today has an impressive network of Muslim intellectuals and civic organizations committed to multireligious recognition and a plurality-accommodating coexistence (Feener 2007; Kersten 2015; Sirry 2004; see also Hefner 2018a). The chapters in this book show that, at the grassroots of society, the country also has an impressive array of non-Muslim activists committed to similarly pluralist visions.

Notwithstanding these inclusive legacies, one of the most significant developments in *Reformasi* Indonesia has been the consolidation of non-governmental networks linking quasi-official religious authorities to populist and religiously exclusive militias in society, in collaborations intended to promote a religiously differentiated and stratified practice of recognition and citizenship. One must emphasize again that the phenomenon is not unique to conservative Islamist circles but has become a major force in Christian, Hindu, and even *adat*-based communities. However complex their histories, it is clear that none of these sectarian and polarizing forces is subject to democratic control and that none reinforces the culture of inclusive recognition and civility on which any formal practice of multireligious citizenship depends. No less seriously, where these currents have taken a populist turn (Hadiz 2016; IPAC 2018a, 2018b, 2019), they have coarsened public discussion, deepened divisions in society, and tempted populist politicians to make common cause with ethno-religious exclusivists to advance their political interests. Over the past few years, my own United States of America has provided a stark example of the dangers of such pluralism-destroying instrumentalism, one that has resulted in the stigmatizing and segregating of citizens from Muslim and immigrant backgrounds.

As this book went to press, Indonesia in April 2019 held another round of presidential and parliamentary elections. Their outcome did not greatly deviate from the pattern seen in previous election cycles, with Islamist parties winning only a small share of the total vote. However, two trends did appear stronger. The two-year mobilization campaign that preceded the elections (in the aftermath of the 2016–17 campaign against the Christian Chinese governor of Jakarta) indexed a growing determination in Islamist circles to differentiate citizens along religious lines and to make faith the core criterion in the selection of regional and national leaders (Chaplin 2019; IPAC 2019). National surveys show that prior to the anti-Ahok mobilization Islamist attitudes on matters of recognition and citizenship had actually been moderating for several years. However, in the aftermath of the campaign's repeated demands for the exclusion of non-Muslims from political office, attitudes on non-Muslim leadership hardened—even though on other matters of interfaith relations (such as allowing non-Muslim houses of worship in Muslim neighborhoods) there was no significant uptick in exclusivism (Mietzner, Muhtadi, and Halida 2018).

Most proponents of this religiously differentiated and stratified citizenship claim to have given up on the idea of replacing the Pancasila state with an "Islamic" one. But their commitment to a religiously differentiated and stratified citizenship amounts to a repudiation of a long-cherished ideal of Indonesian democracy and nationalism. The commitment also often includes a relative indifference to the rights of religious and sexual minorities. In this regard, the single greatest challenge to the Indonesian heritage of a religiously inclusive practice of recognition and citizenship is not so much an Islamism dedicated to the establishment of an "Islamic state" as an Islamist populism leveraged by ambitious political entrepreneurs—a phenomenon similar in some regards to majoritarian-minded, "alt-right" conservatives in Western democracies, including the United States (Joppke 2017; Laclau 2005; cf. Hadiz 2016).

The second trend visible in the 2019 elections is no less important: the pro-Pancasila, pluralist camp appears to have achieved a greater measure of organization and determination in the two years since the mobilizations against the Christian Chinese governor of Jakarta. At the state level, the Jokowi administration has mounted a bitter legal campaign against the procaliphate HTI, culminating in the organization's legal proscription in two legislative steps carried out in July and October 2017 (see Anhaf, chapter 4; Bagir, chapter 7). Many Western analysts and more liberal-minded activists in Indonesia regarded the decree as undemocratic, but it has proved popular in, among others, NU circles. However, the single most striking feature of the April 2019 elections was the degree to which the national and Java-based leadership of NU threw its weight behind the Jokowi candidacy—and did so under the banner of defending Pancasila inclusivity and the integrity of Indonesia against anti-Pancasila forces, not least those of "transnational Islam." Although some observers have spoken as if the ideological dynamics expressed in the elections represent a return to the bitter polarization of the 1950s, such a conclusion is too simple. The contest today does not pit Muslim parties against secular nationalists and the communist Left, but rather sets Islamists and their allies against Muslim supporters of multireligious recognition and citizenship. What is in contention, then, is the very definition of how to be a Muslim in Indonesia and what the profession of that religious ethic means for the project of Indonesian nationhood.

Although the results of Indonesia's national elections continue to indicate that radical Islamist policies do not sell well in the electoral marketplace (but cf. Fealy 2016b; Mietzner, Muhtadi, and Halida 2018), religious publics in Indonesia appear to be still grappling with the question of how to balance the aspiration for personal and public religiosity with an inclusive practice of recognition and citizenship. This public ethical uncertainty is, of course, an attitude they share with national publics in much of the late modern world, including those in contemporary India (Hansen 1999) and the liberal democracies of the West. In light of the crisis of recognition and coexistence raging in so many nations of the world, the outcome of Indonesia's struggles will be of global and not just national significance. The contributors to this volume hope for an outcome that affirms an inclusive recognition and citizenship, one that might yet allow Indonesia to serve as a model of civic decency and coexistence in a plural and troubled age.

TWO

Scaling Plural Coexistence in Manado

What Does It Take to Remain Brothers?

ERICA M. LARSON

The majority-Protestant province of North Sulawesi, with its popular motto "We Are All Brothers" (*Torang samua basudara*), is often praised as a model of plural coexistence for Indonesia. In 2015, the province's capital city of Manado was named the fourth most tolerant city in Indonesia, but by 2017 it had moved up several positions to be designated the most tolerant city in the country, according to the Setara Institute for Democracy and Peace. Manado's reputation as an exemplar of coexistence is related to the ability of the city to remain peaceful even as conflict broke out in other regions during Indonesia's process of democratization and decentralization that started with the *Reformasi* movement in 1998. In the early 2000s, nearby Central Sulawesi, Maluku, and North Maluku became embroiled in ethno-religious conflicts, and significant numbers of Christian and Muslim refugees fled to Manado (Duncan 2005a, 2005b). Tensions ran high, and many feared that conflict would spread to majority-Christian North Sulawesi. The ability of the region to ultimately remain peaceful during such a turbulent time, made possible through the proactive attitude of the local government and its cooperation with police and community and religious leaders (Panggabean 2017), was an important affirmation of coexistence across ethnic and religious lines. This historical trajectory has played a role in shaping current public debates about issues of religious plurality in Manado, but the social and political situation remains dynamic, and maintaining coexistence requires continuous work.

In this chapter, I focus on the normative work that is being done by various organizations, actors, state officials, ethico-religious communities, and educational institutions relevant to religious plurality in Manado. By paying specific attention to the kinds of "public reasoning" (see Hefner, chapter 1; Bowen 2010) in which these various actors engage, as well as the potential mechanisms of scaling they use to communicate their positioning on issues relevant to coexistence, I locate the contested frames of plurality and cultural citizenship. In Manado, North Sulawesi, a public discourse of religious harmony has become hegemonic to the extent that actors with a range of agendas invariably invoke the discourse and indicate their praise of and general agreement with the principle. Yet rather than signaling a general consensus about how to enact religious coexistence, the uses of this discourse and the stances that accompany it actually reflect varied and contested responses to the question of how to live together in religious difference. A closer examination of several focal incidents and their local impact on ideas about plurality and lived citizenship will serve to outline the various normative frames applied by different social actors, the ethical currents on which they draw, and the processes through which different interpretations of the discourse are scaled up.

The ongoing public debates in Manado demonstrate the varied approaches to managing plurality in a context where a discourse of commitment to religious harmony is required for legitimacy in the public sphere. Manado is building up an identity focused on being both a majority-Christian city and a place of religious harmony and tolerance. In some interpretations of this vision for the city, clear societal limits of inclusivity and tolerance have become apparent. Some organizations and individuals who appeal to religious pluralism do so under the assumption that the province will remain majority-Christian, with a broad Christian influence in the public sphere. Focal incidents involving significant discussion about living in religious plurality have occurred in recent years when the status of Christians as a dominant majority in the province or the rights of Christians in other areas of Indonesia have been perceived to be threatened.

I begin the chapter with an introduction to major institutions and organizations in Manado. Then I analyze these ethico-religious communities and the public reasoning in which they engage about religious diversity through the discussion of several focal incidents. These incidents include responses to national cases where houses of worship in other provinces were destroyed: a mosque burning in Papua in July 2015 and a church burning in Aceh in October 2015. I also include discussion of a local focal incident in Manado beginning in 2015 related to city officials' plans to build a religious theme park in the city to enshrine its commitment to religious harmony, and how the future of a local mosque ended up at the center of the debate. Then I consider the mechanisms of scaling to understand the avenues used by institutions and organizations to make their normative work public. Recognizing the potential of educational institutions to provide normative frames for living in plurality, I focus on three different high schools in Manado and their approaches to religious diversity. Finally, I consider the major issues at the heart of these public debates and contrast the approach of Minahasan (the majority ethnic group in North Sulawesi) traditional organizations and women's organizations in the principles they appeal to and the avenues they use to scale up their positions on living in religious difference.

MAPPING ETHICO-RELIGIOUS COMMUNITIES IN MANADO

Manado is a coastal city and the provincial capital of North Sulawesi. As of 2014, the population of Manado was 423,257 (BPS Kota Manado 2016a). The city is known for being both religiously and ethnically diverse. According to the 2010 census, 62.6 percent of the city's inhabitants are Protestant, belonging to various denominations discussed below. Muslims make up 31.5 percent of the city's population, and Catholics account for 5.1 percent. The rest of the city's population is Buddhist (0.5 percent), Hindu (0.2 percent), and Confucian (0.1 percent) (BPS Kota Manado 2016b). Ethnically, the majority of Manado's inhabitants are Minahasan (which comprises several subethnic groups). Other ethnic groups represented in Manado include Sangir-Talaud, Bolaang-Mongondow, Gorontalo, Chinese, Bugis, Ternate, Maluku, Batak, and Javanese (Pomalingo 2004, 58). Ethnic Mina-hasans are generally assumed to be Christian, although ethnic and religious identifications do not always neatly overlap, and the conjunction of ethnic and religious identities is significantly more complex.

Interreligious Organizations

In Manado, branches of two major organizations for interreligious di-alogue mediate between religious communities and the government in North Sulawesi. While the existence of these institutions certainly does not guarantee interreligious tolerance, it does provide institutional support for interreligious communication about social issues.

One major organization that is specific to North Sulawesi and often cited as a contributor to the peace is the Committee for Interreligious Co-operation (BKSAUA—Badan Kerja Sama Antar Umat Beragama). In 1969, North Sulawesi governor H. V. Worang founded the BKSAUA as an inde-pendent body to act as his adviser on religious and social issues (Pomalingo 2004, 64). The history of the BKSAUA is significant because it was a locally driven initiative that predated similar national interreligious initiatives. The organization includes representatives from five official religions (Prot-estantism, Islam, Catholicism, Hinduism, and Buddhism) and is organized from the provincial to the village level, connecting a network of influential and well-respected religious figures. In 2000, the BKSAUA was awarded the status of an official advisory board for the governor (Swazey 2013, 115).

The BKSAUA currently exists alongside the Interreligious Harmony Forum (FKUB—Forum Kerukunan Umat Beragama), a semiofficial gov-ernmental interreligious body that was created in each province of Indone-sia as a result of joint ministerial decrees from the minister of religion and the minister of home affairs in 2006. The FKUB differs from the BKSAUA in that it goes down only to the city/regency level, allocates representatives on the basis of the proportion of religious followers in the population, and includes representatives from the Confucian religion. As discussed below, the FKUB is also required to give its recommendation to the local govern-ment on the allocation of building permits for houses of worship.

Both the FKUB and the BKSAUA currently act as mediators between the government and religious communities in Manado. They are geared toward mediating social issues, rather than engaging in theologically driven dialogue. When local or national issues have the potential to incite conflict, representatives often make official statements reminding the public not to be provoked by these issues and to allow legal action to be carried out by the proper authorities.

Religious Communities and Organizations

The Christian Evangelical Church in Minahasa (GMIM—Gereja Masehi Injili di Minahasa) is the largest Protestant denomination in North Sulawesi and in 2015 claimed 791,807 members in its area of ministry (GMIM 2017).[1] The GMIM was founded as an indigenous Protestant denomination in 1934 after the synod gained independence from the Dutch-controlled Indische Kerk, the Protestant Church in the Dutch East Indies (de Jonge Parengkuan, and Steenbrink, 2008). The GMIM, a member of the national ecumenical organization of the Indonesian Communion of Churches (PGI—Persekutuan Gereja-gereja di Indonesia), is active in the social and educational sectors and politically influential in Manado and North Sulawesi. The private Christian university UKIT (Universitas Kristen Indonesia-Tomohon) is affiliated with the GMIM and trains pastors and religious education teachers, but it also has several other faculties and fields of study.

Because of its size, influence, and significance in the community, representatives from the GMIM are active in interreligious organizations, and in 2015 GMIM pastors held the positions of chairman in both the BKSAUA and the FKUB. Despite this involvement, several GMIM pastors who are active in interreligious dialogue express concern that as a whole the church is becoming increasingly isolationist and less active in ecumenical and interreligious dialogues. GMIM pastors are active not only through the church but also in the political sphere and are involved in both women's organizations and mass organizations, all of which embrace varying normative frames on the question of how to live in a religiously plural society.

In addition to the other indigenous Protestant denomination in North Sulawesi, the Union of Minahasan Protestant Churches (KGPM—

Kerapatan Gereja Protestan Minahasa), there are numerous Pentecostal and Evangelical denominations active in Manado. These include the Pentecostal Church in Indonesia (GPdI—Gereja Pantekosta di Indonesia), Indonesia Bethel Church (GBI—Gereja Bethel Indonesia), and the Assembly of God Church (GSJA—Gereja Sidang Jemaat Allah), among others. Many of these denominations have seminaries or religious institutions of higher education to train pastors or religious education teachers in North Sulawesi. The Seventh-Day Adventist Church (Gereja Masehi Advent Hari Ketujuh) also has significant membership in Manado, and Universitas Klabat, an Adventist university, is located in North Sulawesi. In Manado, there is also a state-run Christian institute of higher education (STAKN—Sekolah Tinggi Agama Kristen Negeri) with students and professors from various Protestant denominations. Participation in the FKUB and the BKSAUA is one way in which representatives from some of these Pentecostal and Evangelical denominations have been involved in strengthening ecumenical and interreligious relationships in North Sulawesi (Tahun 2014, 166).

The bishop of the Catholic Diocese of Manado, as part of the ecclesiastical structure of the church, is a member of the national Conference of Indonesian Bishops (KWI—Konferensi Waligereja Indonesia). The KWI has formed a Commission on Interreligious and Interfaith Relations (Komisi HAK—Hubungan antar Agama dan Kepercayaan), which also exists at the diocesan level. The Komisi HAK of the Diocese of Manado is involved in locating and training potential Catholic representatives for interreligious organizations like the BKSAUA and the FKUB. Several highly regarded Catholic schools are located in Manado, attended not only by Catholics but also by Protestants and students from other religious backgrounds, in part because of the prestige and quality of the institutions (Steenbrink 2003, 273).

Islamic institutions in Manado include local branches of the largest religious associations in Indonesia, Nahdlatul Ulama (NU) and Muhammadiyah. Local figures from both organizations are active in the city- and provincial-level FKUB and BKSAUA, and also in the local branch of the Indonesian Council of Ulama (MUI—Majelis Ulama Indonesia; see Hefner, chapter 1). Other active Islamic organizations present in Manado are Sarekat Islam, Mathla'ul Anwar, and youth associations such as the Muslim Students' Association (HMI—Himpunan Mahasiswa Islam) and the Islamic Youth Movement (GPI—Gerakan Pemuda Islam). The state-run Islamic institute of higher education in Manado, IAIN (Institut Agama Islam Negeri), provides education in several different fields, including religion, education, and economics. In Manado, Muhammadiyah runs a training institute and degree program for health professionals (STIKES—Sekolah Tinggi Ilmu Kesehatan Muhammadiyah). Many Islamic organizations in Manado, especially NU and its suborganizations, have been involved in promoting discussion about the relationship between Islam, national values and principles, and the promotion of social harmony in a plural society.

Minahasan *Adat* Organizations

Many groups that have been visible and vocal in the public sphere on the question of religious coexistence are relatively new Minahasan organizations labeling themselves as *adat* organizations.[2] The proliferation of these organizations in Manado and North Sulawesi beginning with the *Reformasi* era can be understood in part as related to the general national trend of "*adat* revivalism" during this same period (Henley and Davidson 2008). Many *adat* organizations in Manado were initially formed as paramilitary organizations in the early 2000s when there was significant fear that interreligious conflicts in nearby provinces could spread to the region. In particular, concern that radical Muslim organizations, such as Laskar Jihad or Abu Sayaaf, might infiltrate the region and incite violence was one major factor that triggered the formation of local militias (Jacobsen 2004, 84). Many of the organizations formed at that time have since disbanded. But many new ones have also been created, and those still existing have rebranded themselves in the context of the *adat* movement (Swazey 2013, 174). Several promote a Minahasan identity strongly intertwined with Christianity, though none currently have official affiliations with Christian churches or denominations.

Brigade Manguni was formed in 2002 as a regional organization that some have labeled as a paramilitary group or a Christian militia.[3] Since its establishment, it has undergone organizational changes that have included the development of a quasi-national structure, Brigade Manguni Indonesia (BMI). BMI now exists in several provinces of Indonesia and touts nationalist goals; its membership now is not restricted by religion (Swazey 2013, 174). It is also considered an *adat* organization, and some of the members do perform traditional Minahasan rituals. Another organization, which was formed in 2002 and still exists, is Milisi Waraney;[4] it has rebranded itself through the frame of *adat* and restricts itself to Christian members. The group's logo features a Minahasan owl superimposed on a Star of David and a cross, providing a visually symbolic linkage of Minahasan identity and Christianity.

Many other groups formed in the early 2000s have dissolved or no longer exist, while other new organizations continue to be formed or fracture. In early 2016, Laskar Adat Manguni Indonesia (LAMI) formed as a splinter group from BMI. Aliansi Makapetor was formed in 2015 as an alliance drawing together members from other major *adat* organizations and has been quite vocal in local politics.[5] Membership in all of these groups is both fluid and variable in number. Individuals may take part in activities of multiple *adat* organizations but may not be officially registered as a member of any.

The nationalist frames employed by *adat* organizations in public debates about plurality and citizenship typically focus on Indonesia's national ideology, the Pancasila, or principles of religious freedom. However, in many cases their discourse and actions also reinforce the linkage between Minahasan *adat* and Christianity, sometimes conflating ethnic and religious identity. Both *adat* and Christianity as normative frames are central in the ways in which social actors respond to focal incidents leading to public discussion about the limits of tolerance in religiously plural Manado.

NATIONAL FOCAL INCIDENTS: HOUSES OF WORSHIP

Houses of worship are often the focal point of practical public discussions about managing religious plurality and preventing conflict in Indonesia, and cases can quickly achieve a national profile because of their sensitive nature. In 2006, joint ministerial decrees from the minister of religion and the minister of home affairs provided new regulations for building houses of worship. These new requirements were presented as a reform to the previous 1969 regulations, which had been opposed by Catholics and Protestants as discriminatory on account of practical difficulties they raised to establishing churches in Muslim-majority areas (Crouch 2014, 25). In addition to requiring approval from the local government and the district representatives of the FKUB (whose creation was mandated through the same ministerial decrees), the 2006 law requires signatures from at least ninety congregation members and sixty surrounding community members who support the establishment of the place of worship.

In practice, these requirements introduce significant difficulties in establishing houses of worship for religious groups who are local minorities (Lindsey 2012, 55). When religious tensions rise, accusations about the existence or validity of building permits for houses of worship, especially churches, have been a strategy for hard-liners to mobilize support and threaten minority religious groups. Following the transition to democracy, interreligious disputes, including over houses of worship, have become increasingly judicialized (Crouch 2014, 171), rendering them more visible and susceptible to becoming national-level issues.

Here, I compare the local responses in Manado to two major national focal incidents regarding the destruction of houses of worship: the burning of a mosque in Tolikara, Papua, in July 2015 and the burning of a church (and closing of several others) in Aceh Singkil in October 2015. Both of these incidents occurred in relatively remote areas of the Indonesian archipelago but quickly escalated to national-level news. Although tensions over houses of worship are relatively common, the actual destruction of houses of worship is not. While the Tolikara case was not discussed among the broader public in Manado beyond a few localized dialogues and public statements made by Islamic organizations, the church burning and closings led to significant public outrage and demonstrations that made use of a nationalist frame and appealed to the values of religious freedom and anti-discrimination. Public leaders and interreligious organizations became involved, imploring the people of North Sulawesi not to become provoked by the burning of a church in a distant province, as it would only endanger local religious harmony. In contrast, Minahasan *adat* organizations highlighted the position of Christians as a national minority, with some groups going so far as to also leverage their position as a local majority to implicitly but publicly threaten local mosques. The way in which these actors shifted between regional and national frames is key to understanding how *adat*-based groups were able to become so audible in the public sphere.

Manado's Response to the Tolikara Mosque Burning

On July 17, 2015, the day of the Muslim Idul Fitri holiday, a dispute broke out between residents of Tolikara, Papua, as Muslims gathered for prayer in the field of a local military command center, worshipping using loudspeakers (IPAC 2016, 9–10). The local Protestant denomination Gereja Injili di Indonesia (GIDI) had circulated a letter on July 11 forbidding public celebration of the end of the fasting month and forbidding women to wear headscarves in public during the church's own youth revival conference at that time (IPAC 2016). GIDI youth reportedly threw rocks at the worshippers, and the police responded by firing warning shots. While the remaining sequence of events is disputed, an unidentified shooter fired a second round of shots that left wounded twelve GIDI youth, one of whom later died. A group of GIDI members subsequently set fire to nearby kiosks and the local mosque (IPAC 2016, 10–11).[6] News of the incident spread rapidly on social media platforms and through various national media outlets. The national government appeared to respond quickly to condemn and try to contain the event, and the Ministry of Religion quickly assembled a team to send to Papua to investigate the conflict.

In Manado, there was little audible response to the Tolikara mosque burning from the government, religious communities, and other social actors. The head of the North Sulawesi provincial branch of the national Islamic organization Mathla'ul Anwar released a statement to local press condemning the incident, encouraging the government and police to take action against those responsible, and asking Muslims not to be provoked. Similarly, the provincial leader of a national Islamic organization for youth, BKPRMI (Badan Komunikasi Pemuda Remaja Masjid Indonesia), condemned the incident, asked the government to take action, and issued a reminder that the constitution guarantees freedom of worship.

Following the incident, the mayor of Manado, Vicky Lumentut, promptly met in private with several religious leaders and asked them to take steps so that their congregations would not respond to the incident in a way that might incite a local religious conflict. The meeting was not publicized and did not lead to any official statements from the provincial or city government or from the provincial FKUB or the BKSAUA. In other words, there was little public response to the event from the government and religious communities in Manado, though certainly steps were taken by political and religious leaders, organizations, and communities to discourage provocation. National religious organizations with local branches or members in North Sulawesi, including the Muslim organization NU and the Indonesian Communion of Churches (PGI), gave official statements condemning the events in Tolikara and calling for official investigation and a peaceful resolution.

By itself, the mosque incident was hardly "focal," as there was little public response in Manado, and it did not trigger public debates about living together in religious plurality. If anything, the public statements about the event localized it as a Papuan separatist issue in which religious communities in Manado need not become involved. However, the lack of response becomes much more significant when compared to the local reaction to the burning of a church in the province of Aceh several months later, which brought up serious questions and challenges for managing religious diversity on a local and national level.

Manado's Response to the Aceh Singkil Church Burning

On October 6, 2015, demonstrators in Aceh Singkil Regency from the Islamic youth organization PPI (Pemuda Peduli Islam) renewed protests against the existence of nineteen churches and chapels without proper building permits.[7] The protesters gave local government officials an ultimatum that either the government had to take action and demolish the churches, or the protesters would tear down the churches themselves (Kamal 2016, 130). The local government signed an agreement on October 12, 2015, committing to tear down ten of the nineteen churches without proper permits starting on October 19 (US Bureau of Democracy 2015). Despite this promise from local officials, protesters still gathered on October 13, 2015, armed with bamboo spears, knives, and Molotov cocktails, and proceeded to set fire to one of the churches slated for demolition. Police and military personnel formed a blockade as protesters attempted but did not succeed in advancing toward a second church guarded by local villagers (Kamal 2016, 135). A group of more than four thousand Protestants and Catholics temporarily fled the regency in the aftermath of the incident (Amnesty International 2016).

News of the church's destruction spread quickly across Indonesia. On a national scale, President Joko Widodo, Muslim religious leaders from the mainstream Islamic organizations Muhammadiyah and Nahdlatul Ulama, Christian religious leaders, and various civil society organizations issued public statements condemning the incident (US Bureau of Democracy 2015). Despite these statements, the local government in Aceh Singkil continued with its controversial plans to close and tear down the remaining churches (Kamal 2016, 139). In contrast with Tolikara, the incident in Aceh sparked strong reactions from groups and individuals in Manado and led to public debates about the limits of religious coexistence in North Sulawesi.

Nearly one week after the incident, the interim governor of North Sulawesi, Soni Sumarsono, met with BKSAUA representatives. On the same day, the representatives publicly released a statement requesting cooperation from religious communities in the province to continue strengthening religious harmony and not to become divided by groups seeking to disrupt it. Sumarsono, who is Javanese, publicly expressed his concern as a Muslim and as the interim governor of the province about the potential of the incident to destabilize Indonesia. BKSAUA representatives also met with the provincial FKUB and released a statement stressing the importance of protecting North Sulawesi from the threat of conflict, asking the people of North Sulawesi to avoid provocation and preserve religious harmony for the sake of national unity. The response of the FKUB and the BKSAUA was more an attempt to manage the local situation and to discourage any negative reactions than a response to the incident itself.

The local press reported on the official meetings and statements made by politicians and the FKUB and the BKSAUA, but the coverage given to them was minimal compared to coverage given to local protests led by Minahasan *adat* organizations. On the day of the governor's meeting with the BKSAUA, hundreds of protesters from a loose alliance of *adat* organizations gathered at the North Sulawesi governor's office and the regional parliament to protest the church burning in Aceh and the government's lack of response. The protesters came from a range of Minahasan *adat* organizations, including Aliansi Makapetor, Brigade Manguni Indonesia (BMI), Milisi Waraney, and Waraney Puser in Tana. Dressed in red and black, they conducted a motorcycle procession around the area, waving their organizations' flags and shouting the Minahasan war cry "I yayat u santi!"

Aliansi Makapetor had posted photos of their members at the provincial police office to gain permission for their protest the day before the demonstration. The commentary of the post invoked the ideal of national religious harmony: "Together, let's condemn the actions that have occurred in the archipelago; let's guard Pancasila and the Constitution as the foundation of interreligious harmony in the Republic of Indonesia."[8] In contrast to the Tolikara response, which had focused on the need to preserve local religious harmony, a national frame was used throughout the Aceh church-burning protest to draw attention to the situation of Christians as a national minority in Indonesia and to call for action. During the protest, the organizations also leveraged their position as a local religious majority as they threatened to close any local houses of worship lacking proper building permits, a threat implicitly understood as directed at local mosques. After the demonstration, Aliansi Makapetor summarized its position on its Facebook page: "Minahasa rejects discrimination. If in Aceh churches are destroyed because they don't have a building permit, then we will do the same in Minahasa!! Minahasans will close all houses of worship that don't have a building permit."

The demonstrators shifted the normative frame by using the argument of national unity to advocate for Christians as a national minority, leveraging their position as a regional majority to take action. This response clearly differs from that of the interreligious bodies, which appealed to nationalist principles and religious harmony to deter the spread of conflict and its potential provocation rather than focusing on addressing the incident itself. In addition to threatening to take matters into their own hands, Minahasan *adat* organizations asked the provincial government to take an active role in rejecting discrimination against minorities in Indonesia. The organizations were seeking some form of justice in making sure that the government would attempt to investigate the situation and condemn the perpetrators as they had for the Tolikara incident. One group, Waraney Puser in Tana, gave statements echoing those of Aliansi Makapetor, calling for an end to discrimination against minorities and an end to discrimination against Christians with regard to building houses of worship and gathering to worship.

While the protesters' declarations attempted to underscore their alignment with national values, they also appeared to question the commitment of Muslims to these same values by arguing that Muslims were not being active enough in condemning the destruction of Christian churches. The demonstrators were received by two members of the regional parliament, who reminded them not to be provoked by the incident in Aceh and stated that proper legal action from the government and police must be taken against those involved in the church burning. Otherwise, there was no direct public response from politicians or other organizations to this mass protest. On this point, it is important to note that politicians' lack of response to protests is not exclusively due to the appeals to nationalist ideals that are made by organizations for interreligious dialogue; it is also due to the unofficial patronage that many of these organizations enjoy from local politicians. Ultimately, the *adat* organizations did not conduct the "sweeping" of (Muslim) houses of worship to check building permits that they had previously threatened.

In both of these national focal incidents, it was the local religious minority whose house of worship was destroyed. However, in responding only to the church burning and reacting to discrimination against Christians (framed as a national minority), groups publicly threatened the houses of worship of the local Muslim minority in Manado, without any audible public response or rejection of their argument. The chairman of Milisi Waraney, an *adat* organization that limits membership to Christians, later explained that the protest had been about ensuring that legal action would be taken against those who were responsible, just as it had been taken in the Tolikara case. Framing their protests in terms of justice based on national principles, these groups demonstrated in a way that was ultimately threatening to local religious coexistence, going against the appeals of the BKSAUA and the interim governor, but received no clear public response to their actions.

Following these incidents, there were additional demonstrations, such as the one from GMIM youth, who called for the national government to revoke the 2006 ministerial decrees regarding the building of houses of worship and to rebuild the destroyed church. Such protests were on a smaller scale and did not receive significant media attention compared to those of the *adat* organizations. Another response, which came from university students who were already active in promoting interfaith initiatives, was an interreligious dialogue among university students to discuss the local impact of the incident. The dialogue, which brought together some twenty-five participants, took place before the major demonstrations at the governor's office in Manado. At this particular event, students and the invited speakers linked the Tolikara and Aceh Singkil cases as evidence of a larger systemic problem of growing religious intolerance in Indonesia. During the dialogue, the students struggled to come up with an action plan to combat religious intolerance. Although activism was encouraged, and an invited speaker called on all of the participants to be "provocateurs for peace," the main call for action was for the participants to continue taking part in interreligious dialogues and to invite others to join.

One of the thematic foci of the chapters in this book is the process of sociocultural scaling, or the normative and organizational mechanisms that various groups utilize to advance their ethico-political positions and the kinds of social resonances and consequences these have. In this particular debate, *adat* organizations were extremely visible and vocal, advancing their views in local news reports and actively sharing their views and actions on social media. By this measure, it is clear that the demonstrators were much more effective in having their voices heard than the university students participating in interreligious dialogue. The BKSAUA and the FKUB gave public statements calling on the people of North Sulawesi to remain calm and not be provoked, but they also engaged in less visible but significant scaling through collaboration with religious leaders and communities in Manado to communicate this message to their congregations.

After the church-burning incident in Aceh, social media were an important avenue for people in Manado to seek information. At the interreligious dialogue, several university students expressed concern about the incendiary posts they had seen on social media in the event's aftermath. While the public events and statements employed a mostly nationalist frame and emphasized the rights of citizens and religious minorities, many Facebook posts took a more sectarian tone. Criticism of the central government for its slow response to this incident was also widespread in social media and was contrasted with the government response to Tolikara, portrayed as a quick and concerted effort to serve justice and punish the perpetrators.

LOCAL FOCAL INCIDENT: A RELIGIOUS THEME PARK

An incident regarding a local house of worship in Manado has also become the center of a public debate about living in plurality. Al-Khairiyah Mosque in Manado was thrust into the spotlight in early 2015 after Mayor Lumentut indicated he would continue with long-discussed plans to build a religious theme park on government-owned land to celebrate the religious harmony of Manado, on a site where the mosque also stands.[9] The religious theme park, an intended tourist site, was planned to include miniature houses of worship for the six official religions in Indonesia, although there was significant confusion as to whether they would be built around the already existing mosque or whether the mosque would require rebuilding (possibly on a smaller scale). While the mayor had moved forward with the project in 2012 with the request for the required permits, the project had stalled since then, apparently because of competing claims over the land from the mosque officials. In early 2015, tensions rose again over allegations that the mosque had expanded in a way that was inconsistent with the plans for the theme park, and without the proper permits. The escalation of these debates, detailed below, is turning into a test of the multiculturalism that Manadonese claim as part of their vision for the city and that, ironically, the theme park is meant to enshrine. While the BKSAUA and the FKUB have been closely involved in the search for a peaceful solution, the issue remains unsettled as of July 2018.

One religious theme park already exists in North Sulawesi: the Hill of Love (Bukit Kasih) monument in Minahasa Regency, with five miniature houses of worship built on the side of a volcano in 2002 as a government project undertaken by North Sulawesi governor A. J. Sondakh. The theme park was part of the agenda for the "Year of Love," declared by the government with support from the GMIM Church upon recommendation from JAJAK (Jaringan Kerja Kasih). JAJAK was a network of journalists in Manado (with the support and participation of Muslim and Christian religious organizations) advocating for peace at a time when surrounding provinces in eastern Indonesia were experiencing violent conflicts (Thufail 2012, 364). The sentiment behind these types of religious theme parks remains popular in its public affirmation of what most people in Manado see as an integral part of their identity: peace, "a norm believed by the activists of Minahasan culture to have lasted for centuries and constitute the core value of Minahasan identity and subjectivity" (Thufail 2012, 366).

The location for the planned religious theme park is near the center of Manado in an area formerly known as Kampung Texas. In 2007, Mayor Jimmy Rimba Rogi began the project to "clean up" the area by evicting those who had settled on the government-owned land and tearing down the buildings in the area, with the exception of the mosque. This work was undertaken with plans for a religious theme park in mind and with the intention that other houses of worship would be built next to the mosque. Mayor Vicky Lumentut continued the project, and by 2012 the local government had applied for the land certificate for the area and necessary building permits. The project slowed to a standstill for several years until early 2015, when controversy emerged after Al-Khairiyah Mosque was accused of expanding beyond the land allotment officially set for each house of worship.

A meeting between the mayor and representatives from the BKSAUA and the FKUB on March 10, 2015, produced a new plan that would make use of the existing mosque by turning its ground floor into a library for all religions and the top floor as a place of worship for Muslims. With the remaining land, they planned to build a multistory tower, according one floor to each religion and one additional floor for the BKSAUA and the FKUB.

By March 2015, the Minahasan *adat* alliance Aliansi Makapetor had mobilized largely in response to the Kampung Texas issue. On March 23, 2015, dozens of its members came to demonstrate at the regional parliament building in Manado, shouting "I yayat u santi!" until they were received by parliamentary representatives. The organization called for the land to be used for its originally "intended function," referring to the religious theme park, and for all construction of buildings without proper permits to stop, a clear reference to the mosque. The rally coordinator threatened that the group would take matters into its own hands and stop construction of any building without proper permits if the government did not take action. The group reassembled for a demonstration and traditional ritual on March 29, in the center of the city, although police prevented the group from advancing toward Kampung Texas. The city government intensified meetings with the BKSAUA and the provincial FKUB, as well as with important Islamic institutions, including the Manado office of the MUI; eventually the meetings culminated in the agreed plans to move forward with the multistory religious tower.

The city government held an official groundbreaking ceremony for the new tower on June 8, 2015, sparking renewed demonstrations from Aliansi Makapetor. They called once more for realization of the original plans for a religious theme park and "destruction of the building that is not in accordance with the land allotment in ex-Kampung Texas," referring implicitly to the mosque. By June 25, 2015, the mayor's office had announced that it would stop construction on the religious tower, pending further discussion with the regional parliament and police.

From the standpoint of the BKSAUA and the FKUB, the two major bodies involved in interreligious dialogue and mediation, the handling of the Kampung Texas case in late 2015 was seen as a success. The outcome was cited as proof of these organizations' ability to mediate between the government, local religious communities, and organizations like the Aliansi Makapetor. The head of MUI Manado cited the incident as a test of Manado's religious harmony but one that, as a result of their intense communication with and support from the government, they were able to mediate. The MUI became involved in discussions with government officials and the FKUB and the BKSAUA to clarify the situation and find a reasonable solution.

However, the Kampung Texas debate flared up again as Aliansi Makapetor, working with LAMI and other *adat* organizations, organized a demonstration with hundreds of protesters on October 26, 2016. Members from the groups condemned the "illegal buildings" that were impeding progress on the religious theme park. However, the ambiguous reference to "illegal buildings" left the local media speculating over whether they were referring to Al Khairiyah Mosque or to the cafes that had started to pop up on the perimeter of the land intended for the park. The sudden revival of the debate about the religious theme park was almost certainly influenced by national political events, in particular the accusations of blasphemy against Jakarta's Christian and ethnic Chinese governor Basuki Tjahaja Purnama (Ahok; see Bagir, chapter 7) and the sectarian religious and political displays that followed. The connection between national and local events was publicly discussed at an event held by the provincial Lesbumi (a suborganization of NU) on October 31, 2016, at which several invited speakers talked about regional tensions related to Jakarta's gubernatorial race, including Al Khairiyah Mosque, and how the ethics of Pancasila can help to meet these challenges (Syafieq and Alawi 2016).

In November 2016, Mayor Lumentut held meetings to address issues related to the religious theme park with leaders of the mosque and officials from Manado's Department of Religious Affairs, and later with the governor of North Sulawesi. As the case gained more national attention, the Indonesian National Commission on Human Rights (Komnas HAM) came to Manado in November 2016 to meet with the mayor and representatives from several *adat* organizations in an attempt to work toward a consensus about the future of the intended religious theme park and Al Khairiyah Mosque.

This case demonstrates the strong impact that the protests had on rejecting a decision that had been reached by the government in conjunction with the interreligious bodies of the city, and the lack of public voices in response to the demonstrations. However, the perceived silence following the protests and demonstrations of the *adat* organizations reflects the refusal of religious organizations and leaders to engage in public debate with these groups for fear of increasing tensions and upsetting the religious harmony of the city.

The case of the religious theme park in Manado aptly demonstrates the existence of a hegemonic normative frame that requires social actors to indicate their agreement with religious harmony as an important ideal in order to be taken seriously in the public sphere, even as the practical ends these groups pursue might challenge these dominant ethical norms. After the protests in June 2015, Aliansi Makapetor held a press conference in Manado, in which their leader Decky Joice Tumar attempted to clarify the goal of his organization. He claimed that far from trying to cause conflict or bringing up issues related to SARA (*suku, agama, ras, antar golongan,* an acronym referring to discrimination based on ethnicity, religion, race, or social affiliation), their organization was dedicated to protecting religious harmony in Manado from those who tried to destabilize it. While the group was effectively calling for the dismantling of a mosque, the aim was expressed, not directly, but by way of a more legalistic reference to "the building that is not in accordance with the religious theme park design." Using this frame, they positioned themselves as the defenders of religious harmony struggling so that the religious theme park could be realized and, as they saw it, equal importance could be accorded to all religions.

Though the group's name Makapetor, which stands for "Minahasans who care about tolerance," highlights its official commitment to tolerance, the group's strategy clearly also pushes a normative frame that represents threats to local tolerance as necessarily originating from "outside." The group's strong focus on Minahasan *adat* (and its assumed links to Christianity) also implicitly defines Islam as foreign to Manado. The fear that Manado and North Sulawesi are becoming increasingly Muslim is often invoked to encourage Christians to take action. The organization Aliansi Makapetor, like many others, has publicly voiced objections to North Sulawesi as a potential destination under the government's transmigration program, which brings large numbers of indigent settlers from Java and other central Indonesian islands to less populated territories like North Sulawesi. Many Christians, not only those belonging to more radical organizations, privately express their fear that a government transmigration program to North Sulawesi would mean the end of a Christian majority in the province. A clear limit to tolerance is often drawn when the future of Manado and North Sulawesi as a majority-Christian place is seen as threatened.

SCALING MODELS FOR PLURALITY: INTERRELIGIOUS ORGANIZATIONS

These focal incidents have provided a window on the varied positions groups have taken in public debate regarding how to live in a religiously plural society. In addition to the positioning and public reasoning of these actors, it is necessary to evaluate the mechanisms of scaling these normative frames.

The FKUB and the BKSAUA are charged with promoting interreligious dialogue, mediating between religious communities and the government, and helping prevent conflict in North Sulawesi. These organizations have a strong potential for scaling frameworks on how to live in a plural society and are in a position to mediate between state and society on such issues. The local and national focal incidents discussed above all launched the FKUB and the BKSAUA into discussions and dialogue with the local and provincial government. Representatives from both bodies stress the importance of their roles in communicating information to their religious communities, especially to discourage their congregations from becoming provoked by local, national, and international events that could raise interreligious tensions.

Critics of the two interreligious organizations claim that their actions are merely symbolic and ceremonial, lacking substance. Another general concern about the effectiveness of these bodies is the dominance of the GMIM Protestant Church, not only within these organizations, but also in its ability to work around them through close connections with local and provincial government officials. While the FKUB and the BKSAUA do have strategic positions for scaling, it cannot be assumed that religious communities will follow what their elite representatives say and do as members of these organizations. Furthermore, it is clear from the focal incidents that *adat* organizations bring a significant challenge to the authority of the interreligious organizations and their ability to negotiate public conflicts in a way that will be accepted as legitimate by all major public actors.

SCALING VIA CIVIC AND
RELIGIOUS EDUCATION

One of the most important existing institutions for scaling frameworks for coexistence is the educational system. Civic education and religious education are both required subjects for Indonesian students and provide a potential forum for dialogue regarding social debates on living in plurality. Robert Hefner's (2009, 71) analysis of Islamic schooling in Indonesia demonstrates its resemblance to a social movement because of its ability to "draw social actors into organizations and projects that extend well beyond the school yard." In my analysis of the kind of scaling and normative work entailed in civic and religious education in several of Manado's high schools (Muslim, Catholic, and public), I focus on how schools are arenas for debates about plurality and citizenship. I also indicate the ways in which they are shaped by the larger public conversations taking place about religious diversity, as well as their potential to feed back onto these issues.

First, it is important to provide some background information about significant changes in civic and religious education in the Indonesian educational system. During the authoritarian New Order regime (1966–98), civic education through indoctrination in an especially conservative interpretation of the national ideology of Pancasila was part of the state's strategy for maintaining control, emphasizing national unity and suppressing difference. As Indonesia began a democratic transition in 1998, the educational system underwent significant changes in developing new material to teach democratic attitudes and values. The national ideology, Pancasila, was deemphasized not only in the new curriculum developed for democratic civic education but also more generally in the public sphere (Lindsey 2012, 45). Although changes to the civic education curriculum during the early *Reformasi* era tended to deemphasize Pancasila, it survived and in fact has been revived as one of the components of the civic education curriculum in operation today.

A major challenge, therefore, has been to reinvent and reinterpret the meaning of Pancasila to make it a suitable basis for a democratic citizenship education (Gaylord 2007, 48). All students are required to have at least two hours per week of both civic education and religious education in accordance with their official religious affiliation. In this context, religious education is also linked to the project of forming pious citizens and has the potential to provide ethical frames for making sense of religious diversity in Indonesian society. Moreover, socializing youth into views of the nation depends on how messages in the curriculum are delivered and contextualized by teachers in the local situation.

In high schools in Manado, teachers and administrators use both religious and nationalist reasoning to talk about the importance of mutual respect and tolerance toward those of different ethnic and religious backgrounds, consistent with the national curriculum for both religious and civic education. When these subjects are discussed in Manado schools, teachers proudly remind students that the city is a role model of religious harmony for the rest of Indonesia. However, the focal incidents discussed above are rarely if ever brought up in the school environment by teachers, likely because of their sensitive nature. The avoidance of discussion about current local events is also due to the way in which religious and civic education classes tend to treat topics such as "respect for diversity" in rather abstract terms. While the importance of avoiding religious or other social conflicts does come up in classrooms, the axiomatic response for avoiding conflict is to "respect and value others," a discourse that most students seem readily able to use but are rarely asked to explain concretely.

However, this does not mean that Indonesian youth are unable to grasp the meaning of respect for diversity, or that they are unaware of the broader social and religious situation of Manado and of Indonesia. When speaking casually with Muslim students at the public school, I brought up the topic of the church burning in Aceh. One of the students active in the Muslim students' club quickly explained that any such conflict was troubling for them because it was troubling for the unity of the nation as a whole. In other words, some students are well aware of the high stakes of these issues and their potential impact on the future of Indonesia.

Manado's Public High School

The religious makeup of Manado Public High School students is broadly reflective of that of the population of Manado, and the school prides itself on being a diverse public institution dedicated to religious education and worship. The overall dynamic of the school also reflects the tensions present in the broader public sphere: an ideal of religious diversity and coexistence that is important and even a source of pride, but also a feeling among Christians that the public sphere should remain visibly and audibly Christian. The way in which the majority of teachers and administrators take steps to accommodate other religions while effectively maintaining a Christian atmosphere at the school is itself an example of a certain kind of normative work also visible from groups and actors in the focal incidents described above. In the classroom, some teachers preach the importance of religious harmony and tolerance in the abstract, but when faced with concrete questions they propagate ideas and opinions that go against or have a different interpretation of these ostensibly public ethical norms.

In a Protestant education class I attended in April 2016 at the public high school, a discussion about living in a religiously diverse society involved students drawing on a discourse about the importance of respecting and valuing difference. The teacher launched into a lecture about both the good intentions of all religions and the importance of love in Christian teachings. The topic of the lecture prompted a student in the front row to ask about a Facebook post she had recently seen about demonstrations in Java against the construction of a church, wondering what had motivated the protesters and how she should respond to them in a Christian way. In addressing this concrete example, the teacher explained that Christians were continually taught about love but that "they" (Muslims) were taught that Christians were *kafir,* unbelievers. She lamented how difficult it was for Christians to worship in Indonesia where they were a minority and their neighbors might report them just for clapping their hands in worship, while Christians tolerated Muslims yelling "Allahu Akbar" early in the morning. This example demonstrates how teachers can play a role in scaling, not only the official discourse of religious harmony and respect for difference, but also assumptions about Christian love and tolerance that attribute the religious harmony in Manado to its majority-Christian population and see those defined as "outsiders" as potential threats.

The line of reasoning this particular teacher used is quite common in Manado. It resonates with the broader discourse of Manado as an example of religious harmony but attributes this achievement to the fact that the majority of people in Manado follow Christianity. One GMIM pastor affiliated with the Manado FKUB cited Manado's position as the fourth most religiously tolerant city in Indonesia at the time as proof that religious harmony in the city was decreasing. He argued that increasing the level of tolerance would be difficult so long as Muslims remained opposed to the building of churches in other regions of Indonesia. Suspicion of Muslims was thus framed as a reasonable response and was justified using essentialized portraits of both religions.

Previous studies in Indonesia have shown the importance that extracurricular religious clubs can have in schools as a public sphere where students debate ideas about coexistence, and how they can also be used by various social actors to gain influence among youth and spread ideas antithetical to plural coexistence (Salim, Kailani, and Azekiyah 2011). At the public high school studied in Manado, there are several active religious clubs, including the Islamic students' club, ROHIS (Kerohanian Islam), which is found at schools across Indonesia, and a locally established Protestant students' club, PELSIS (Pelayanan Siswa Kristen).

PELSIS is a province-wide organization active in identifying and recruiting Christian students with leadership potential. The club is most active at public schools in North Sulawesi and is founded on the principle that Christian students must be aware of their ministry to preach the gospel everywhere, including in their respective schools. The organization's leader intends to expand the organization to the national level. He appeals to both Pancasila and Christian teachings of love in order to affirm the dedication of Christians in North Sulawesi to nationalist principles. He claims that although Indonesian Christians are seen as *kafir*, they nonetheless continue to work for the unity of the country. The number of students actually participating in PELSIS from any one school may be small because those participating are typically identified as leaders. Part of their training in PELSIS encourages them to take initiative within their schools to become leaders in other Christian activities as well.

Schools themselves can and do become the objects of debate about accommodation of religious difference in public space. In Manado, this often relates to campaigns to maintain a public religiosity that is visibly Christian. When discussing his calling to contribute to PELSIS in the 1990s, the organization's leader recounted that he had been living in Jakarta when he heard about a plan to build prayer rooms for Muslim students in public schools in Manado. This convinced him to come back to Manado and petition that if prayer rooms for Muslim students were to be built in public schools, Christian churches or chapels should also be built; this argument effectively put a halt to the construction of most of the prayer rooms. More recently, at one public high school in Manado, the principal was rumored to have told the admissions committee of the school not to accept too many Muslims at the school, especially girls who wore a headscarf. These incidents again speak to the prevalence of fear of Islamization among Manado Christians, and desires to maintain a Christian environment in public spaces, including schools.

Private Catholic Boarding School

A Catholic boarding school near Manado is owned by a private foundation and is not registered as an official Catholic institution but enjoys many informal ties to the Catholic Church. Its highly prestigious boarding school program is geared toward character education and has been able to attract students from different provinces and from different ethnic and religious backgrounds to study there. The cofounder of the school has stressed this as part of the "curriculum based on life" that he developed in order to teach students respect for diversity in a multicultural setting.

The student body is majority Protestant, though with a large Catholic minority and some non-Christian students (including Muslim, Buddhist, Confucian, and Hindu). In Indonesia's public schools, students receive religious education according to their professed religion, but all students at this private school take Catholic religious education classes and attend Catholic prayer and mass at the school. Requiring all students to join Catholic education classes is a common practice among private Catholic schools across Indonesia, typically asking parents to sign a form indicating their agreement with this arrangement at the time of their child's enrollment (Hoon 2014, 512). In North Sulawesi, this practice is not considered controversial at private institutions; however, at the national level, it has been the subject of bitter debates since the very beginning of the republic (Crouch 2014, 20–21).

The private Catholic school clearly has a different approach to dealing with religious diversity than the public school, as can be seen in its policy requiring all students to attend Catholic religious classes and worship. However, the religious education teachers are aware of the religious diversity in their classroom and stress the importance of teaching the "universal values" that can be learned from Catholicism, such as solidarity, justice, and love, so that the class may be relevant to all students. The Carmelite priest who acts as the spiritual director for students explained that Catholicism is a universal teaching and also supported the school's policy of being respectful toward other religions on the basis of the recognition in the Second Vatican Council (Vatican II) that there are seeds of truth in other religions.

A major part of the Catholic religious education curriculum, taken from materials from the KWI, focuses on the importance of interreligious dialogue. The textbook's approach features a theologically based dialogue, under the assumption that one must understand the basic teachings of a religion before entering into meaningful dialogue with its followers. In the classroom, teachers discuss the importance of interreligious dialogue and respect for diversity in terms of religious, nationalist, and humanitarian rationales. In one class session on interreligious dialogue, the Catholic religious education teacher supported such teachings through reference to specific Bible verses, teachings in Vatican II, diverse humanity as God's creation, the national ideology of Pancasila, and the national motto, "Unity in Diversity." In civic education class, the material and class activities are more formalistic in practice but also emphasize the importance of mutual respect on the grounds of Pancasila, national integration, and human rights.

Public Muslim High School (Madrasah)

Manado's public Muslim high school implements the standard national curriculum but also requires its students, who are all Muslim, to take additional hours of religious education. While students at the public school or private Christian school receive approximately two hours per week of religious instruction, students at the public madrasah receive a total of nine hours of religious education per week, divided among six different subjects. At the madrasah, there is an emphasis among teachers and administrators on building character and instilling moral principles based in Islamic ethics. While the topics of religious diversity and respect for religious freedom do come up in classroom encounters, the topic is more often discussed in civic education than in religious education, through the frames of Pancasila and human rights.

Teachers at the madrasah express agreement that Manado is an exemplar of religious coexistence and that religious teachings in Islam support such coexistence. For example, one religious education teacher drew on Islamic teachings to explain that in addition to building a strong vertical relationship with God, it is important to build a strong horizontal relationship with people in society, regardless of their religious and ethnic background.

Students are often encouraged to participate in extracurricular activities, such as sports, scouting, science Olympiad, and religious clubs. These extracurricular activities are also important instances of scaling because of their potential to bring students in contact with students from other schools with different religious backgrounds. For example, the scouting troop organizes camping trips with troops from other area schools, and the sports teams at the madrasah on occasion have the chance to invite students from other local public and private (Christian and Muslim) schools to participate in sports tournaments.

Civic and religious education courses do still directly address the topic of living in a diverse society, as they did in all three schools. In one religious education subject that students are required to take on the Qur'an, the tenth-grade curriculum has a unit about respecting all human beings as God's creation; the twelfth-grade curriculum has a unit specifically about the importance of respecting non-Muslims. However, there is a general assumption among teachers and administrators that students will learn about tolerance through their daily experiences outside the school in their diverse communities and that it does not need to be specifically emphasized other than what is already in the curriculum. This viewpoint is consistent with the assumption that building students' foundations as pious Muslims will also contribute toward making them tolerant and respectful of others. In other words, while the madrasah teachers support the idea of teaching tolerance, the school is seen primarily as a place for teaching Islamic ethics that will lead students to act in a tolerant way if they correctly apply religious principles in their daily life outside the school.

Religious "Exchange" Program in Manado

One active attempt at scaling pluralism by educational institutions in Manado is a local initiative coordinated among several religious institutions of higher education. The participating universities, all of which have programs to train religious leaders and teachers, support students in planning and implementing an annual student religious "exchange" program. This program allows university students studying to become religious leaders and/or teachers to spend a week at a different religious university, attending and observing religious activities and classes at their host university. The goal is that students will begin the lifelong process of dialogue with those from different religious communities, so that as future religious leaders they will be motivated to continue building relationships with other religious leaders. Rather than focusing on a theologically based or even exclusively religious dialogue, the goal in the exchange program is to build dialogue through spending time together in daily activities, referred to as a "life dialogue" (*dialog kehidupan*).

The exchange program was started in the 1970s, initially between the GMIM-affiliated Protestant university UKIT and the Catholic seminary STF-SP. Over the past decade, the program has expanded to include the state-run Muslim institute of higher education IAIN Manado, the state-run Protestant institute STAKN Manado, and the Pentecostal theological school STT Parakletos. The exchange program is a local initiative for scaling up approaches to religious coexistence geared toward building the foundation for interreligious relations among the future generation of religious leaders.

MINAHASAN ADAT REVIVAL:
SCALING THROUGH MOTORCYCLES AND MUSCLE

In its numerous permutations across Indonesia, one of the notable characteristics of the contemporary *adat* revival has been the flexibility and paradoxical nature of the concept of *adat*, deployed in ways that are "by turns progressive and reactionary, emancipating and authoritarian, idealistic and manipulative" (Henley and Davidson 2008, 835). In Manado, *adat* politics have become increasingly visible in the public sphere during the post-Suharto era and have emerged in locally specific ways based on the strong association between Minahasan *adat* and Christianity. The paradox, however, emerges in the simultaneously inclusive and exclusive claims put forth by various *adat* organizations and the ambiguity of what actually constitutes *adat* from their perspective.

In this case, it is interesting to compare the current *adat* movement in Manado, which was able to remain peaceful in the early 2000s, to the nearby provinces of Maluku and North Maluku, where violent conflicts broke out and evolved to take on a religious frame and narrative, pitting

Muslims against Christians. Birgit Bräuchler (2009a, 888), who has written about the postconflict reconciliation process in Maluku, argues that *adat* and the village alliance system it enshrines can provide the integrative push necessary for reconciliation by encompassing the entire Moluccan society and overcoming religious divisions. Christopher Duncan (2013, 15), who has conducted research on the conflict in North Maluku, has noted that the religious framing of the conflict itself has led to a tendency of some local organizations to seek reconciliation and the prevention of future violence through the promotion of an *adat*-based identity, "one that forefronted cultural identities rather than religious ones." In the search for cultural practices that have historically supported coexistence in these postconflict regions, the potential of *adat* to overcome other kinds of social divisions has been recognized.

In North Sulawesi, there is an ongoing public debate about Minahasan *adat* and religious identity that is proving significant for the future of the region and its ability to accommodate plurality. The range of actors mobilizing in the name of *adat* is large, with numerous understandings of what *adat* means and different methods of scaling. Kelli Swazey (2013, 24) has argued that the contemporary movements dedicated to rediscovering Minahasan *adat* have opened up space for its conceptual separation from Christianity, and the potential to reshape regional notions of Minahasan ethnic identity and regional belonging to be more inclusive. For example, prominent GMIM pastor and BKSAUA chairman Richard Siwu explains that the Minahasan ethnic group was formed through the uniting of different subethnic groups, which provides a framework that can be elaborated to serve the purpose of accommodating diversity in contemporary society. Reiner Emyot Ointoe, an active Muslim intellectual and cultural observer, sees the relationship between Minahasans and the Muslim Javanese who were exiled to North Sulawesi by the Dutch colonial government as a historical model of coexistence that can be harnessed to avoid the sectarian-bent present in North Sulawesi today.[10] There are movements in Manado to harness the integrative potential of *adat*, seeking out local cultural frameworks to address the challenges of living in a religiously plural society.

On the other hand, many of the *adat* organizations that have been visible and vocal in the public sphere actually have little consensus on what constitutes Minahasan *adat*. They define their organizations' goals in relation to national ideologies and principles, such as Pancasila and religious freedom, which are effective in mobilizing followers and legitimizing these organizations in the public eye. However, as a result of their concern for the place and freedom of Christians in the country, their actions tend to reinforce the link between Christianity and Minahasan *adat* and may ultimately threaten the position of local Muslims. Sven Kosel (2010, 292) has remarked in regard to Minahasan *adat* organizations, "Paradoxically, the ethnically and religiously exclusive ways chosen to make a plea for pluralism tend to undermine tolerance and alienate minorities within the province." In looking out for Christian interests and religious freedom, these groups often advance exclusivist claims that ultimately threaten local religious minorities and religious harmony.

Strengthening the link between Minahasan *adat* and Christianity, and conflating Minahasan ethnic identity with religious affiliation, has the effect of positioning Muslims as outsiders. In doing so, the *adat* organizations reinforce the common assumption that religious harmony in the region is guaranteed by the Christian majority. However, many of the *adat* organizations define their role as "protecting the Minahasan homeland" and lack a framework for addressing diversity and social complexity. Most groups continue to define their social mission in terms of protecting the region from outside threats, particularly hard-line Muslim organizations. For example, both BMI and Milisi Waraney justify their existence by referring to the need to protect the region from groups like the Islamic Defenders Front (FPI—Front Pembela Islam), a hard-line Muslim organization known for its vigilante-style violence (C. Wilson 2008; Bamualim 2011). BMI also held a "show of force" demonstration in Manado in April 2015 to denounce ISIS and demonstrate BMI's readiness to protect the region from terrorism.

The focal incidents discussed above demonstrate the growing strength and influence of *adat* organizations, which often take on a religious tone and use religious symbols in their logos. Many of the organizations have a reputation for being made up of drunken motorcycle "gangsters" (*preman*), an image that some of the groups have tried to change through their claims of dedication to religious freedom and harmony, their sponsorship of debates, and the inclusion of women in their ranks. Local opinion on these groups varies greatly, and while some praise their existence as the reason why the FPI has not been able to establish itself in North Sulawesi, others privately remark that the groups amount to the Christian version of the FPI.

The influence of groups like BMI and Milisi Waraney is bolstered by their strong ties to local politicians. Although they are not official or public political links, they often involve financial patronage by particular individuals rather than parties. Because of the ability of these organizations to mobilize thousands, they constitute core support groups for particular candidates during election time. While the actual impact of *adat* organizations on the regional elections in December 2015 may have been minimal (Jaffrey and Ali Fauzi 2016), the analysis of focal incidents demonstrates their enormous influence in the public sphere on matters related to plural coexistence. The response of *adat* groups to both the church burning in Aceh and the local Kampung Texas issue dominated local media. Also, in the Kampung Texas case, the organizations have thus far succeeded at stalling the plans that were agreed upon by the city government in conjunction with the BKSAUA and the FKUB. Although they have been involved in a somewhat ambiguous deployment of *adat*, lacking a framework for addressing local religious diversity, their public reasoning positions them as defenders of religious harmony, making it difficult for other groups to speak directly against their agendas.

The highly polarizing Jakarta gubernatorial race and the trial and sentencing of the former Christian governor Basuki Tjahaja Purnama (Ahok) for blasphemy against Islam (see Hefner, chapter 1; Bagir, chapter 7) have raised uncertainty among Minahasans about the position of Christians in Indonesia's future. This fear has further emboldened Minahasan *adat* organizations to express their opinions publicly through demonstrations (Pinontoan 2017). In May 2017, several days after a peaceful public vigil was held on the streets of Manado in solidarity with Ahok, *adat* organizations led a protest at the airport. The demonstration was against the scheduled visit of Fahri Hamzah, deputy speaker of the Indonesian People's Representative Council. Hamzah, a member of the Islamist Prosperous Justice Party (PKS), had been openly supportive of the demonstrations against Ahok in Jakarta during the election. *Adat* groups publicly condemned Fahri Hamzah as an intolerant figure and refused his visit on the basis of rumors that he was coming to North Sulawesi to attend the induction of

FPI leaders in nearby Bitung. The protesters, some of whom were dressed in traditional clothing and armed with swords, overwhelmed airport security and succeeded in making their way to the runway. By that time, Fahri Hamzah had already arrived and been received by the governor of North Sulawesi and was able to leave Manado that same evening without incident.

The protest at the airport, which made national news, indicates that *adat* organizations have been invigorated and emboldened in the highly polarized identity politics that have emerged following Jakarta's gubernatorial race and Ahok's trial. The political climate has allowed these organizations to appear as strong advocates for the rights of Christians, using nationalist rhetoric about Pancasila and religious freedom to legitimate their appeals.

WOMEN'S ORGANIZATIONS: APPEALING
TO SOCIAL JUSTICE

Several women's organizations in Manado have foregrounded an approach to working toward plural coexistence by addressing issues of social injustice affecting the broader society. The leaders of Swara Parangpuan (Women's Voice), a locally founded women's NGO, and PERUATI (Persekutuan Perempuan Berpendidikan Teologi di Indonesia, the Indonesian Women's Theological Education Association), a national Protestant organization for women educated in theology whose current leader is from Manado, have taken similar approaches to promoting inclusivity and religious coexistence by attempting to address humanitarian issues and inviting collaborations across religious lines. These groups scale up their ideas about coexistence (not only across religious lines, but also across gendered ones) through commitment to social justice and broader social issues that affect everyone.

The founder and leader of Swara Parangpuan, Lily Djenaan, is Muslim but recognizes that social issues cut across religious lines. Accordingly, she believes that the organization needs to be prepared to respond to victims of domestic and/or sexual violence from varying religious backgrounds. The founder works with a religiously diverse staff and strives to build her organization's reputation for working toward social justice in helping all women who have become victims of violence and abuse. In addition, Swara Parangpuan has collaborated with various religious organizations and communities for educational and preventative programs, including the Catholic KWI, the Protestant PERUATI, and university students active in the Muslim students' organization HMI. They have also worked with the national Indonesian Women's Coalition (Koalisi Perempuan Indonesia), and have implemented antiviolence educational programs at several local public high schools. Swara Parangpuan's mission encourages its members to collaborate with leaders from different religious communities and as-sociations in order to have a broader impact. The organization also does normative work through cross-cutting partnerships in state and society and their social impact on local women's issues.

PERUATI is another women's organization that has sought to make a difference by tackling humanitarian issues, including women's issues (in collaboration with Swara Parangpuan), and environmental issues. The head of the national PERUATI, Ruth Wangkai, a GMIM pastor from North Sulawesi, argues that an effective way for religious communities to mobilize the grassroots and model plural coexistence is to work together to solve pressing social issues. While these groups do not receive the same amount of local media attention as the *adat* organizations, the normative work they are promoting through collaborations across the state-society and religious divides is an alternative approach to scaling frameworks for plural co-existence.

As this chapter's discussion of focal incidents in Manado illustrates, public debates in the region are characterized by a broad and consistent ap-peal to the normative discourse of religious coexistence. These appeals to coexistence are given shape by varied ethical currents, some of which look to religious and nationalist principles to support a working model of coex-istence. However, a more exclusive frame put forth by many *adat* organiza-tions positions ethnic Minahasans as "insiders," whose Christian religion above all else guarantees the peace of the region. The same discourse im-plicitly positions Muslims as "outsiders" whose loyalty to nationalist princi-ples is suspect. The debate taking place about the nature of Minahasan *adat* and its relation to Christianity demonstrates vividly the tension between the desire to maintain the reputation of the area for its peaceful interreligious relations and the desire to safeguard the province's Christian majority. Some respected religious figures have sought to develop the integrative potential that *adat* could serve in supporting some measure of religious coexistence in the region. The majority of *adat* organizations, however, reference national principles of religious freedom to advocate for the position of Christians within the national framework, pushing an exclusivist version of *adat* that has the potential to endanger local religious coexistence. The local developments following Ahok's trial and sentencing have thrust existing tensions into further relief as Minahasans negotiate their position within a highly polarized national scene while still advocating for the religious freedom and equality of Christians within the nation.

Although this chapter has been more focused on Christian actors and organizations, it is important to note that most Muslims in Manado also take pride in the region's reputation for tolerance, and many Muslim organizations also promote interreligious dialogue and strive to maintain religious harmony. Despite recent incidents, the ideal of religious harmony continues to garner widespread support among Christians and Muslims alike in Manado. There is general agreement on the positive aspects of the region's stability and its reputation for religious harmony. However, as the focal incidents discussed above indicate, there are competing frames on how this reputation has been secured, how to maintain it, and where its limits lie. A major limit appears when the influence of Christianity in the public sphere is questioned and when the future of the province as majority Christian is perceived as threatened.

This chapter has focused on mechanisms for normative scaling, as these are critical for understanding how some frameworks for recognition and plural coexistence have become especially prominent in the public sphere. One of the primary examples of scaling seen here is the *adat* organizations' promotion of a Minahasan identity strongly linked to Christianity and their framing of goals through a nationalist lens, ultimately reinforcing local exclusion. Religious communities and religious organizations also play an important role in public ethical scaling, as they formulate and communicate narratives on plurality and citizenship to their congregations. Further, it is important to highlight the role of women's organizations in

Manado because of their ability to cut across religious lines by foregrounding matters of social justice, and to work across religious divides in implementing their programs. Civic and religious education represents another
important instrument for public ethical scaling, particularly in the context
of the Pancasila revival and the use of religious teachings to provide frameworks for understanding diversity. As the case studies indicated, however,
the transmission of these messages is constrained by the local situation of
Manado, the atmosphere of the school, and the interests and worldviews
of teachers.

Certainly, significant challenges to inclusive recognition and religious
coexistence in Manado remain. However, there is an ongoing and vibrant
effort by religious leaders, interreligious organizations, schools, and local
and national humanitarian organizations to provide models and practices
for religious recognition and coexistence capable of meeting the challenge
of living in a plural society.

NOTES

1. The GMIM's area of ministry includes three cities (Manado, Tomohon,
Bitung) and four regencies (Minahasa, North Minahasa, South Minahasa, and
Southeast Minahasa).

2. Derived from Arabic, *adat* is a term used throughout Indonesia to refer to
"customs" or "traditions," typically of particular ethnic groups.

3. *Manguni* means "owl," a sacred bird in Minahasan tradition.

4. *Waraney* is a Minahasan term referring to a warrior, or "someone elected in
the Minahasan cultural order to guard or protect" (Tambayong 2007, 359).

5. *Makapetor* serves as an acronym for Masyarakat Kawanua yang Peduli Tol-
eransi (Minahasans Who Care about Tolerance).

6. It remains unclear whether the building had the legal status of a *musholla* (a
prayer room) or a *masjid* (a mosque). The IPAC (2016, 7) report contains a more
detailed discussion of a history of GIDI attempts to prohibit houses of worship
from other Christian denominations or religions from being built in Tolikara.

7. As in the previous case, there is disagreement about the legal status of the
buildings as either churches (*gereja*) or chapels (*undung*) (Kamal 2016, 127–29).

8. Unless otherwise noted, all quotations are the author's translation from the
original Indonesian.

9. Because the religious theme park issue is still unresolved at the time of writing, there are still many competing narratives about the history of the mosque and the religious theme park project.

10. Kampung Jawa Tondano, where Kyai Modjo and his male followers were exiled by the Dutch colonial government in the 1830s and married local Minahasan women (Babcock 1981).

THREE

Reimagining Tradition and Forgetting Plurality

Religion, Tourism, and Cultural Belonging in the Banda Islands, Maluku

KELLI SWAZEY

Wandering through the villages of Nusantara and Dwiwarna on the island of Banda Neira conveys the curious sense of being in a half-finished colonial theme park. Colonial-era buildings that were once renovated but now languish in various states of disrepair line the sleepy streets, interspersed on the main road leading away from the harbor with small shops and restaurants with menu offerings written in English. Leaving the main port of Banda Neira, the administrative center of the small chain of islands in the center of the Banda Sea known as the "Spice Islands," one passes a large mosque with contemporary architecture, a Chinese temple nearly invisible behind a wall and locked gate, and a resplendent colonial-era church. Turning to the left past the town square and offices of the subdistrict head (*camat*) affords a view of two colonial forts. At the foot of Fort Nassau is a recently erected hotel, a recreation of a colonial mansion complete with a wrought-iron gate bearing the Dutch East Indies VOC (Vereenigde Oostindische Compagnie) logo. On one side of the hotel, the

verandas of the rooms face the Parigi Rante monument, which commemo-
rates the slaughter of the forty-four *orang kaya* or "chiefs" by Dutch forces
in 1621, an act that heralded the start of a period of definitive colonial domain over the islands with the slaughter and displacement of the majority
of the island chain's native population.

Beyond this hotel, the village of Dwiwarna is the former center of the
Dutch colonial presence in the islands, including the Istana Mini, a long
colonial building with a columned veranda facing the sea, the former
home of the governor-general of the Dutch East Indies. Many of the colonial homes are empty, although signs of habitation are visible from the
street: clothes hanging on a line in a window, fishing nets being repaired in
a heap on the floor next to an empty chair. Yet the village retains a feel of
being unused, especially as you move toward the more recent residential
area beyond the colonial complex; there a burned-out church is over-
grown with weeds, and in between the well-kept lawns of the inhabited
houses shells of burnt residences sit empty. A tourist would be forgiven for
thinking that the brutal history of the colonial domination of the islands
that is the focus of tourism narratives had been recreated here, along with
other reconstructions of the presence of the Dutch East Indies Company,
who controlled the cultivation and trade of spices, most importantly nutmeg, which is endemic to the islands.

These spaces are reminders of a much more recent conflict, however,
one that is not memorialized or discussed in the same way as the well-
publicized historical narrative of the murder and expulsion of an estimated 90 percent of the population of Banda in the early seventeenth century. In April of 1999, the Banda Islands were drawn into the waves of
sectarian conflict that moved outwards from Ambon, Maluku's provincial
capital. The arrival of Christian refugees to the islands of Hatta and Neira
exacerbated local Muslims' fears of being overwhelmed as a religious minority in a Christian-dominated province. Despite historical practices of
intermarriage and shared cultural identifications between the predomi-
nantly Muslim population of the Banda Islands and Christian locals, a
killing on the island of Hatta on April 19, 1999, sparked a violent interlude
of interreligious conflict that led to the expulsion of almost all of the
Christian residents from the islands within the space of a few weeks.

The forced migration of Christian Bandanese and the in-migration of Muslims fleeing from the conflict in other regions of Maluku shifted the religious demographic of the Banda Islands, leaving it with an almost entirely Muslim population. As the Central Maluku Regency Government has recently renewed efforts to return Banda to the status of an international tourist attraction in postconflict Maluku, they have focused on the practical concerns of restarting abandoned infrastructure projects and repairing historical sites that were damaged in the course of the conflict. These efforts seek to fill the vacuum left after the death of Banda-born Indonesian diplomat "Des Alwi" Abubakar in 2010, the most significant stakeholder in the region's tourism industry and the driving force behind efforts to reclaim and reconstruct the history and *adat* (customs) of Banda that was lost under colonial domination.

The question of whether Christian inhabitants of the Banda Islands can ever resettle in their former homes remains largely unaddressed by government officials. Yet the main areas that are accessed by tourists, and those being eyed for further development on Hatta Island, are the lands and villages formerly inhabited by Christians who played a significant role in the revitalization of culture in the Banda Islands for tourism envisioned by Des Alwi. As investment in tourism is focused on the areas formerly inhabited by Christians who have resettled in Ambon and other parts of Indonesia, former Christian residents of the islands also seek opportunities to participate in the renewal of the tourism industry, even as the link between religion and local identity is being reassessed. Despite an enduring identification with Islam as part of the ritual and social practices of the islands, the impact of the near-total colonial interference with the island chain's population and its social economic system necessitated that the requirements for being Bandanese (*orang Banda*) are based in consocial relations, territorially based systems of natural resource management, and ritual concerns that link people and communities to land, all practices associated with the realm of *adat*. Aspects of Islam represented in local myths, ritual practices, and folk histories that mediate people's relationship with sacred places on the islands have not been perceived to belong exclusively to the realm of religion, facilitating the inclusion of non-Muslim inhabitants in frameworks of ethno-local identity.

In this case study, I examine how Christians are being remembered as outsiders in the Banda Islands, particularly on the islands of Banda Neira and Hatta, both sites of the islands' returning tourist trade. A developing normative understanding that those who have a valid claim to being Bandanese are Muslim is an effect of the widespread patterns of displacement and segregation that are the legacy of communal violence affecting many areas of Maluku from 1998 to 2001. I argue that this emergent normative framework is also an unintended effect of the renewed efforts to promote the area as a tourist destination. The loss of the Christian communities goes unremarked in the official history of the island that is presented for tourists, one that focuses almost exclusively on effects of colonialism and the island's role in the global spice trade, as well as on stories about the Indonesian nationalist figures Syahrir and Hatta, who were exiled to the region during the nascent Independence period. Although the official history portrays the island as a microcosm of diversity where belonging is based not on descent but on participation in a culture that emerged from the island chain's protracted and transformative period as a "plantation colony" (Loth 1995, 28), stories of contemporary challenges to that inclusive model of Banda society are absent from the narrative of the past presented to tourists.

In theorizing how tourism activities in Indonesia reproduce and intersect with dominant narratives about the relationship between religion, culture, and *adat* as a tool for communal harmony, this chapter will examine how those practices overlap with local institutional practices and narratives that focus on *adat* relationships as a strategy to overcome religious divisions in postconflict Maluku, and the political concerns surrounding the promotion of the islands as a revitalized tourism destination in Central Maluku.

The term *adat*, which can be loosely glossed as "custom" or "tradition," refers to a method of conceptualizing identity reliant on participation in cultural practices imagined to belong to the past and corresponding to cosmologies and communities associated with particular places. In post-*Reformasi* Indonesia, discourses of cultural revival in much if not all of the country have increasingly been framed in reference to *adat*, and organizations that have gathered under the banner of *adat* have promoted the preservation of culture as a nationally protected right, as well as a normative reference point for political struggle. However, as *adat* has increasingly become a mode of representation in the politics of recognition and difference that defines insiders and outsiders (Henley and Davidson 2008, 840), it is also employed in debates about what is representative of local culture that are linked to competition for recognition and resources.

In Maluku, the revitalization of *adat* as a frame for peaceful plural relations between Muslims and Christians depends on the imagination of a shared history and territory that serves as a locus for restoring relationships. *Adat* has been utilized in many parts of eastern Indonesia as an inclusive framework for cooperation or reconciliation between communities under the aegis of a shared culture and moral orientations that exceed religious difference (Duncan 2009b, 1079). In this sense, the cultural approach to reconciliation used in many postconflict areas of Maluku seeks to elide or minimize narratives of religious conflict for the sake of moving past the negative events of the past. The case of the Banda Islands demonstrates, however, that widespread displacement of communities on account of their religious identity poses extreme challenges for cultural recognition and reconciliation based in concepts of *adat*, and in some cases displacement and segregation have the potential to strengthen an exclusive tie between religious identity and cultural belonging. It also demonstrates the semantic ambiguity of culture and *adat*. *Adat*'s basis in atavistic extension of one group's sovereignty over territory (Acciaioli 2001, 108) means that invocations of culture or *adat* as a mode of representation can just as easily support forms of cultural exclusivism as they can serve as a point of unity for diverse actors in a given locality.

Members of the Christian community who were expelled from Banda during the violence that erupted on the islands in April of 1999 are today being represented and remembered as *pendatang* (variously translated as migrants, outsiders, or newcomers), where they were previously accepted as members of the cultural community despite being a minority religious population in the islands. This is shaping the development of a new normative understanding of how religion demarcates the right to identify as part of the community, one that has unintentionally emerged in the processes of representing, remembering, and forgetting that are linked to ideas about how the Banda Islands should be represented for the tourist's gaze.

Christians who left Banda Neira and Hatta seek to maintain their claims to being accepted as *orang Banda* through the need for their cultural competency to perform *adat* rituals from their former *negeri*, cultural realms that roughly correspond to village administrative boundaries in the islands. This form of participation and representation is particularly important as their ability to reclaim former lands diminishes over time. Additionally, efforts to document and package the Banda Islands' history and culture for the consumption of tourists overlap with institutional approaches to rebuilding a postconflict society that seek to minimize acts of remembering connected to interreligious violence through reconciliation. Both the reconciliation movement, which enacts national ideals of harmony through a cultural frame, and the representation of the Banda Islands in the tourism industry, which focuses on decontextualized cultural symbols and colonial history, promote performances of culture that leave little space for the continued participation of former Christian inhabitants of the islands or for narratives addressing the loss of the Christian community.

POSTCONFLICT TOURISM AND POLITICS IN THE REPRESENTATION OF THE SPICE ISLANDS' CULTURE

Development for tourism has been central to the "revival" of Banda's cultural practices since the 1970s, when charismatic local leader Des Alwi set out to rediscover the island chain's history. This rediscovery of the past was framed as a method to distill colonial history and selected precolonial practices into a narrative fit for the consumption of tourists. The reinterpretation of the past, and its representation, were therefore linked to the ideology of development and desires for national recognition. They also presented the role of the islands in the colonial spice trade as the main attraction of the islands for tourists. Des Alwi, a former Indonesian diplomat, writer, and amateur historian, returned to his home in Banda Neira with the hope to develop a tourism industry there. This included efforts to record and reconstruct cultural rituals related to *adat*. Alwi sought to rebuild knowledge and revive practices that could be displayed for visitors, performances of culture that were inclusive of both Muslim and Christian inhabitants of the

Banda Islands. Adopting a previously unknown title of *Orlima Besar* and positioning himself as the highest authority on local *adat,* he envisioned Banda Neira as a premier destination for elite tourists that would come to bear witness to the forgotten role these tiny islands had played in the history of world trade. More importantly, the people of Banda themselves would be able to read the codes embedded in their revitalized practices, such as the *cakalele* dance, and properly understand them as a form of resistance against the Dutch rather than just a locally contextualized ritual practice (Kenji and Seigel 1990, 64).

The kind of cultural tourism attractions that Des Alwi created in Banda Neira can be characterized as a form of postcolonial tourism, reminiscent of the imperialist nostalgia for imagined "traditional" cultures and ways of life that were intentionally transformed during the colonial period (Rosaldo 1989, 108). Alwi rediscovered what he presented as the true history of the Banda Islands in archives in the Netherlands, locating the islands within a narrative of global history and trade. He then set out to reeducate the people of Banda about their own past, one that promoted the singular historical view of the islands' central role in the spice trade and the islands' importance as the temporary home of exiled nationalist figures Hatta and Syahrir. Local cosmologies and understandings of how people are linked to the landscape, and the stories of the role that religion played in social and cultural relations, were sidelined to the grand historical narrative of the islands as a center for colonial trade and the source of spice.

In addition to investing in tourism infrastructure and building the island's first hotel near the harbor in Banda Neira, Alwi revived two practices that continue to be emblematic of Bandanese identity: *belang* (*kora-kora* canoe) races and the *cakalele* dance. These are the two activities most often featured in tourist advertising as the visual representation of Spice Islands' culture. Although *kora-kora* canoe races were a Dutch innovation, and the *cakalele* dance is now presented to tourists as a secret code of resistance against colonial powers, both activities are accompanied by *adat* rituals that express the sacred and mystical aspects of people's connection to particular territories. This includes the creation of *tempat siri,* betel nut offerings for sacred spaces in the landscape known as *kramat.* The offerings are prepared for an event called a *buka kampung* (opening of the village) that should be held before the *cakalele* dance or the use of the *kora-kora* canoes. This *adat* "work" involves members of the various *negeri* who prepare offerings and participate in the ritual activities under the advisement of a ritual expert called the *kepala adat* (*adat* expert).

Since Des Alwi's death in 2010, the tourism industry in Banda has remained in the hands of a few powerful stakeholders who run tourism facilities on the island. The Maulana Hotel, as well the Banda Naira Culture and Heritage Foundation, is managed from afar by Des Alwi's descendants, who do not currently reside in the islands. Much of the advertising and development planning for the promotion of the islands as a tourism attraction for Maluku is undertaken by the Central Maluku Office of Tourism and Culture and by those with business interests who live in Jakarta. Many islanders expressed frustration with their lack of involvement and the perceived lack of benefits they received from the tourist trade. This also extended to a sense that local histories and cultures that did not fit within the overarching narrative of Banda as a former colonial center were not valued by those who sought to utilize culture as a tourist attraction. As a 1999 report on tourism development in Banda Neira notes, this precedent may have originally been set with Alwi's domination over all aspects of the tourism industry and the *adat* revival. Alwi's interpretations, based on colonial archival material, were presented as the authoritative explanations of *adat* symbolism in materials created for the tourism industry, despite the existence of several alternative interpretations of practices like the *cakalele*. The report concludes that this domination of the narratives about *adat* "has had the effect not only of reducing its diversity, but also runs the risk that European colonial discourse will subsume the independent historical consciousness which has survived so long" (Wrangham 1999, 114).

Limited opportunity for local participation in the tourism industry is one of the reasons that local residents support a proposal for the Banda Islands to become a New Autonomous Region (DOB) combined with a designation as a Special Economic Region (*kawasan ekonomi khusus*) for tourism. Proponents of the proposal note that the islands' status as a subdistrict (*kecamatan*) under the regency of Central Maluku has hampered the ability for the region to become a major tourist attraction, as well as efforts to be accepted as a UNESCO World Heritage Site (Berita Maluku

Online 2015). The recent push for tourism development across Maluku is also a way of indicating the region's stability and counteracting the stigma of violence. Societal harmony is seen as a prerequisite for the success of tourist development and national recognition for the region. In a 2016 article entitled "Tuasikal Abua: Let's Tell the World That Central Maluku Is Safe," Central Maluku regent Abua Tuasikal described the need to convince people that religious conflict is something of the past in order to promote tourist attractions like Banda Neira (Jaringan News 2015).

The idea that tourism can be a field for reconciliation was indicated in media coverage of the speech made by the governor of Maluku Province, Said Assagaf, for the the 2017 Banda Neira Community Festival (Pesta Rakyat Banda Neira), the new incarnation of the annual tourism festival funded by the Central Maluku Office of Tourism and Culture. Assagaf, who called for the participation of the local community, also cited a program event "Banda Calls Home" (Banda Pangel Pulang) that called on former residents living outside the islands to return and participate in the region's development and efforts to improve the welfare of local residents (*Indonesia Timur* 2017).

Despite these positive evaluations of tourism as a space for development and an expression of reconciliation, I would argue that the type of performative culture that is being produced in efforts to construct and promote the Banda Islands as a site of historical tourism also inadvertently contributes to the processes of forgetting—in the sense both of moving past the conflict and of forgetting the role of Christian community members in practicing and protecting particular *adat* traditions in individual *negeri*. Ritual practice in the Banda Islands, particularly in tourist areas like Banda Neira and Hatta, is undergoing a new phase of change through contact with the tourism industry. As was the case with the revival of *adat* in the 1970s, *adat* rituals that embody knowledge tied to specific territories and the social relations of individual *negeri* communities are now undertaken in conjunction with events that are primarily performed for the tourism industry. The loss of Christians knowledgeable in the work of *adat* for individual *negeri* and the pressures to create cultural objects for use in tourism that are free from ritual obligations are changing the social practices of *adat*. These trends are also narrowing one avenue that Christians living outside the islands have to continue to claim their cultural belonging as Bandanese, their continued participation in *adat*.

CHRISTIAN *NEGERI*: CHRISTIAN SPACES AND PARTICIPATION IN *ADAT*

Prior to 1999, it is estimated that Protestant Christians represented approximately 25 percent of the population of the Banda Islands, although that number likely included small communities of Catholics and Pentecostals on Banda Neira. Christian communities were found on the islands of Banda Neira, Banda Besar, Lonthoir, Ai, and Hatta. In 2015, the Office of the Subdistrict Head reported that one hundred Christians were living in the islands, including twelve families on the island of Ai. The majority of these Christians were not residents of the islands prior to the conflict but civil servants, police, or other government employees who were relocated to the subdistrict to fill vacant positions. Two congregations of the Protestant Church of Maluku are active on Banda Neira and Ai, led by a single pastor who commutes between the islands. These congregations are part of the Protestant Church of Maluku Synod's *klasis* Banda that includes the congregation of Banda Suli, the village outside Ambon where many Christian former residents of the Banda Islands settled after they were forced to leave in 1999.

Prior to 1999, Christian presence in Banda Neira was centered in the villages of Dwiwarna and Nusantara, areas that contain the majority of the island's tourism infrastructure, including the main port for the Pelni passenger ships and Banda Neira's hotels, homestays, and dive centers. These villages correspond to the culturally designated boundaries of the *negeri* of Namasawar and Ratu, with their individual *rumah adat* (houses for ritual objects) and *adat* experts in charge of safeguarding sacred items and overseeing the fulfillment of ritual obligations connected to cultural activities, including performances of the *cakalele* dance and use of the *kora-kora* canoes. The village of Nusantara also includes Banda Neira's only Chinese temple, although it was not in use in 2015. According to a local Chinese family, it was opened only for the observation of Chinese New Year once a year.

Since the displacement of Christian families from the two villages, the positions of the ritual experts known as *adat* experts for Namasawar and Ratu have been filled by Muslim individuals who were chosen to replace Christians responsible for overseeing the *adat* for these *negeri*. In describing how these areas had been recognized as Christian spaces on the island, the current *adat* expert of *negeri* Namasawar recalled Des Alwi's role in facilitating Muslim-Christian relations in lobbying for the construction of a new mosque on the island built near the harbor in the formerly Christian area:

K: In this area, Namasawar, there aren't any Christians left, since 1999? They all already fled?

Namasawar *adat* expert: Yes, there aren't any. Previously around here everyone was Christian. This place, this *rumah adat,* was built by Christians. We only had a little space down there [towards the harbor]. We Muslims who wanted to build a mosque were scared. They didn't want it. In Namasawar, I mean Nusantara now, Namasawar is the *adat* name, you see? In Kampung Baru [the bordering Muslim village] they didn't give us a good space to pray, without a mosque it's wrong. It was because there were so many Christians here and they didn't want it. "Go and pray there, or in Merdeka Village or Rajawali Village, but here you can't." Then Des came, Des was here. He came to develop this *negeri*. He asked the permission of the Christians here, and when he came back he built the mosque.

Christians played an active role in the reconfiguration of *adat* rituals for tourism in Banda Neira in the two *negeri* they inhabited on the island. The former *adat* experts of Nusantara Village (Negeri Namasawar) and Dwiwarna Village (Negeri Ratu) were Christian, and Christian contemporaries of Des Alwi were involved in the processes of recovering culture for the development of Banda tourism in the 1970s and 1980s. Ceisar Ruipassa, a Christian guide from Hatta Island who facilitates tourist visits to Banda Neira and to a homestay he runs on Hatta Island, recalled his father's role as a former *adat* expert and his dedication to recording the *adat* practices passed down through his family as part of Alwi's efforts to reconnect the people of Banda with their history. Christians involved in Alwi's project of reviving local culture even developed theories reading cultural symbols as a proof of how the arrival of Islam had transformed the *adat* traditions of the islands into a system of peace (Wrangham et al. 1996, 29).

Christian inhabitants of Banda have historically been involved in *adat* practices, although some villagers from Banda Neira described limitations on Christian inclusion in ritual practice when elements of the rituals were seen to be too overtly Islamic, such as the recitation of Islamic prayers at sacred sites. Other Muslim inhabitants claimed that Christian villagers were included in Islamic-influenced veneration practices, reciting Arabic phrases used as part of the ritual of placing betel nut offerings at sacred sites called *kramat*. In his autobiography on growing up in Banda in the early twentieth century, Des Alwi describes a cosmological system followed by all Bandanese regardless of their religious affiliation. Inhabitants of the Banda Islands acknowledged different types of spiritual entities, including the *orang halus* (protector spirits), *orang kaya* (deceased Bandanese leaders), and *orang lima* (deceased warriors) that were associated with natural features of the landscape, as well as with the established *kramat* sites (Alwi 2010, 122). Des Alwai recalls that both Muslims and Christians visited the *kramat* and left offerings, stating that practices of veneration at the sites had mixed Hindu, Muslim, and Christian influences (Alwi 2010, 123).

The *adat* expert of Namasawar described the *kramat* as spaces belonging to *adat* and therefore not exclusive to Islamic practices, even those *kramat* that were thought to contain the remains or relics of figures credited with bringing Islam to the islands: "Yes, it wasn't just Muslims but whoever wanted to go, if the Christians wanted to, if the Chinese wanted to, it belonged to the community. It belonged to the village community. It belonged to *adat*. It was up to them. If they wanted to come. Once we got to the burial place it was Muslims who worked [undertook the ritual activities]."

In his examination of the moral domain of resource management practices on Banda Besar Island, Phillip Winn states that the spirits that inhabit the *kramat* are not understood as ancestors. These spirits draw their authority from association with particular places, not from relations of descent with the population of Banda. Some consider the *kramat* as sites once inhabited by the original Bandanese (*orang asli Banda*) who fled from Dutch persecution in the 1600s, or as the resting places of individuals who journeyed to Mecca and returned to the islands to spread the teachings of Islam, so that these locations "combine the themes of autochthony and precedence with being Muslim" (Winn 2002, 279). Despite the association between these spiritual figures and Islam, the ritual activities related to the veneration of sacred sites in the landscape and the spiritual presences associated with them are one example of how *adat* in the Banda Islands emphasizes particular ties to place over religious affiliations. Winn (2010, 383) notes that "contemporary Bandanese envisage local identity in terms of a necessary obligation for newcomers to adapt to the customary practices associated with the islands as a locale, rather than those linked to places of ancestral origin elsewhere. This is seen as especially imperative for those born in the islands."

Participation in *adat* practices was once not only a signifier of local identity but also central to relations across religious communities. Jenny Abidin, a Muslim teacher at the Hatta-Sjahrir Fisheries Academy, which is run under the auspices of the Banda Naira Culture and Heritage Foundation, is a resident of Dwiwarna whose parents were involved in stewardship for the *adat* houses after the conflict. She recalled families standing at the harbor the day their Christian neighbors boarded the military ship to leave the islands, crying "as though someone had died." The departure of Christian residents of Dwiwarna, as she described it, involved not just familial loss but a "vacuum" of knowledge, since Christians had always been active in *adat* affairs; she added that in 2008–9 former residents were invited back to assist with the proper procedures for the ritual to open the village.

For the *adat* expert of Ratu who is entrusted with caring for the *adat* house of the *negeri*, the displaced Christian inhabitants continue to be the rightful holders and most competent practitioners of the *adat* specific to the *negeri*. Now in his seventies, he has been involved in *adat* practices with Christian villagers in Ratu/Dwiwarna since the 1960s.

K: The population in Ratu, the religious population, were they Muslim or Christian, or was it it mixed?

Ratu *adat* expert: That lived here? You've heard of the conflict? When the conflict happened, those who held it [the *adat*] here were Christian, but that's over. The Muslims and Christians all left, and they called me. Maybe because they believed in me, they turned things over to me. Now there is no one, and I have to revive it; if there isn't anyone left and I don't revive it, what then?

In his efforts to preserve *adat* knowledge disrupted by the conflict, this expert has sought the consultation of former Christian residents, even at the cost of creating some strain between him and current Muslim inhabitants who seek to participate in *adat*-related activities:

It's like this. They've all left. But as the head of *adat* here, I've organized meetings. So I've made an *adat* organization, and I've already sought the advice and protection of all of the *orlima* and *mama lima*, the *bapak-bapak lima*, the *mai mai* [designations of different roles in *adat* rituals], all of the older men and women. . . . Now when I talk to my fellow Muslims they'll say I want to help the Christians. It's because I worked with the Christians that I feel like this. Do you understand? But with Muslims I feel like I'm in a bind.

His position exposes the tensions that displacement of the Christian community has left in the transition of these *negeri*, and the question of the transmission of cultural practices in the light of lost knowledge. Furthermore, he feels that Muslim residents of the village who now participate in *adat* rituals and performances do so insincerely with an eye to the financial benefits entailed in developing rituals for tourist events like the *kora-kora* races. He explained that financial support provided by former Indonesian president Susilo Bambang Yudhoyono to build a "national" *kora-kora* allowed for ritual practices associated with the handling of the boat to be bypassed, symptomatic of the way that those taking on the mantle of *adat* in *negeri* Ratu were prioritizing religious identity over *adat* concerns:

When the [financial] assistance came from SBY [President Yudhoyono], he [the head of Dwiwarna Village] was the one who received the money. They said it was to make a "national" canoe. . . . This is why the rights to possess *adat*, this is why there are so many who don't understand *adat*, they want it but they are only playing with it. But I was so happy working with the Christians . . . but these Muslims, they just want to cause a row. They ignore *adat*, they just want to quarrel.

The innovation of a national *kora-kora* canoe that does not require ritual preparation for use is part of the dynamic nature of *adat* on the islands that has been influenced by shifting politics and tourism policies. In some cases, this has allowed villages that are not recognized as possessing *adat* to participate in cultural tourism activities. The 2015 canoe race for the Festival Budaya Banda Neira was divided into two competitions; one for the seven *adat* canoes (*belang adat*) and the other for the ten villages racing national canoes (*belang nasional*).[1] In the 1990s, only six of the villages in the Banda Islands were considered *adat* villages, but the sub-desa of Waer campaigned for and later received recognition as an *adat* village. For villages that do not have claim to an *adat* tradition, ritual obligations are not required for cultural performances. This is seen in the village of Rajawali, where the Terang Bulan dance and the Pa' Joge dance associated with Butonese communities are not considered *adat* practices, although this is contested. Though Hatta was considered an *adat* village, its canoe was not in use throughout the 1990s. It is now being used with the accompanying *adat* rituals by the inhabitants of the village of Kampung Lama. These changes underscore the dynamic nature of *adat* as "imaginative and adaptive, serving as a living and evolving body of agreements, rights and rules" (Tyson 2011, 655); in short, *adat* is a concept of place-based "tradition" that is vulnerable to shifting politics and demographics, and that reflects evolving normative frameworks of who can make authoritative claims of belonging.

Christians who were evacuated in 1999 refer to the possession of *adat* as proof of being Bandanese, although it has been nearly twenty years since they have lived in the place from which they continue to draw their identification. For those living in the village of Banda Suli, located approximately fifteen kilometers from the city of Ambon, continued participation in *adat* is key to their continued identification as Bandanese. As the name implies, Banda Suli is a settlement of those who fled from Banda and settled in Suli, carrying their territorial identity with them into exile. These displaced Bandanese are part of a wider community of Christians who left the islands in 1999, some settling as far afield as Jakarta and Bali. They organize rotating visits to the islands to engage in volunteer activities and to check on the harvest of nutmeg and other crops that are managed by contracted laborers or former neighbors on cultivated lands they left behind. During these visits and activities, they hold *adat* practices like the launching of the community *kora-kora* canoe and the associated rituals to open the village.

Residents of Banda Suli from Hatta Island cited *adat* as the proof of their undisputable claim to being indigenous Bandanese:

A: If you are talking about newcomers in Hatta Island, it's the Butonese who are the newcomers. We were the original inhabitants; they were the ones that came after. My father-in-law was once the *raja* [community leader] there. Their houses were in the jungle. They didn't live in the village, they lived in the jungle behind it. Then they came from out back and settled in the village, that's why it's called the New Settlement. In Hatta there is the New Settlement and the Old Settlement. If they didn't get any place to live, what then? They were told to live in the forest because they were newcomers. If you mean who were the original inhabitants, well, as I said earlier, in Banda there aren't any original inhabitants, but if you want to say anyone it's Kempa, Kempa were Christian inhabitants. They were the original ones. Because when it comes to the ritual to open the village, they are the ones who are the *orang tua adat* [*adat* authorities]. The Kempa people, they were the ones who were the *orang adat* [people with *adat*].
B: When we talk about *adat*, Kelli, that's the *cakalele* dance.
A: Yes, and the ritual launching of the canoe. No, they're the ones who opened the *adat*, they were the old ones of the *adat*.

As Christians are recognized as the custodians of knowledge for particular *negeri*, their displacement from their former villages has led to a disruption in *adat* rituals, which in the opinion of one of the current *adat* experts must be performed correctly. This has facilitated displaced Christian residents' continued ties to their former homelands, as the *adat* expert of Namasawar explained: "Yes, they come back, they take turns. They come here, for things like our ritual for opening the village. They come and they are involved. We welcome them. They used to be the old authorities on the *adat* here." The involvement of displaced Christians is seen as appropriate to their status as the former authorities of *negeri* traditions; however, there are indications that their long-term displacement is beginning to change the perception that their presence is necessary for the correct execution of *adat* ritual obligations. The *adat* expert of Ratu described a shift in the status of returning villagers to one as guests, as the ongoing work of *adat* has stalled in their absence:

> K: Do the Christians still come here often?
> **Ratu *adat* expert:** Yes, they come. Just at the time of the *adat* rituals they are involved in things. But when they are here, it's like they are just here as guests, whereas in the past they were part of it too.

Christians in Banda Suli also remark on changes to *adat* that indicate new limitations on their participation in practices and rituals associated with their former villages, as the responsibilities for performing *adat* rituals have been taken over by Muslim villagers or kin:

> K: Some of the Muslim *adat* experts have told me that they ask Christians to come back to provide information about the *adat* there because they lack knowledge, is that right?
> A: Especially in Ratu, if they want to do a ceremony for opening the village, they come here to call us and tell us we must attend. For the work that needs to be done. In Hatta, they continue the *adat* practices. I don't know if it's the true *adat* or not, but ever since we were there the *adat* expert was Christian from the family Kempa.
> K: The *adat* expert now? Did he convert to Islam?
> A: Yes, he did. It's his [the former *adat* expert's] son. He took the position when his father died.

RELIGION AND THE QUESTION OF
IDENTITY IN THE BANDA ISLANDS

The role of Islam in the Banda archipelago is often the focus of historical inquiry into the islands' precolonial profile, as part of a focus on the region as the center of the spice trade. The earliest recorded mention of Islam in the islands comes from Tome Pires in 1512 (Cortesao, 1943, 206, in Lape 2010, 5), who reported that the presence of "Moors" had been known in the islands for thirty years. The arrival of Islam to the archipelago is enshrined in local mythology that links the particular landmarks around the islands with stories of conversion.

Archaeologist Peter Lape's work in the islands identifies the presence of non-Islamic communities that existed in the precolonial and early contact periods. He notes that early colonial documents are an unreliable source of ascertaining the religious demography of the region, as initial European contact with traders in Banda was facilitated by guides from Malaka, who would have directed them toward the Islamic trading networks in the islands. His work provides evidence that some communities in precolonial Banda did not convert to Islam after its arrival in the archipelago, or at least that some communities that displayed non-Islamic food practices persisted in their practices after the arrival of Islam. He locates one of these communities in the harbor area on Banda Neira, the location of one of the villages whose Christian residents left the island because of the conflict (Lape 2010, 10).

The religious life of precolonial communities in Banda Neira and the surrounding islands is obscured by the brutal impact of the onset of Dutch colonial rule in the islands that nearly eradicated the population in the early 1600s. On May 8, 1621, the Dutch East Indies governor-general Jan Pieterzen Coen led a massacre of local leaders known as the *orang kaya* (lit., "rich" or "great people") and the island's inhabitants. Estimates vary as to how many of the archipelago's inhabitants survived the calculated attack, but the event marked the peak of a systematic depopulation of islands that enabled Dutch control of the region and the cultivation of spices.

Those inhabitants who were not killed in the attempt to eradicate the local population were spread across the Indies. Approximately eight hundred individuals were transported to Banten as prisoners of the company, others were taken to Batavia, and an unknown number escaped and fled to other islands in the Moluccas including Seram, Tanimbar, Kei Besar, and Kei Kecil (Thalib and La Raman 2015, 97). One narrative of local identity is that a small group of the "original" Bandanese inhabitants escaped the massacre and fled to the Kei Islands, where their descendants live in a village called Banda Eli. This Muslim village is considered by some to represent the true indigenous Bandanese, lending credence to the association between Islam and a "pure" Banda identity.[2]

The decimation of the islands' population was accompanied by the institution of a system of nutmeg cultivation called *perkeniersstelsel* (plantation system) that divided nutmeg-producing areas into individual estates or *perks* run by the colonial administration and powered by slave labor. The emptied islands were repopulated with Dutch burghers and slaves drawn from other islands in the region including Seram, Halmahera, Tanimbar, Aru, Papua, and South Sulawesi, as well as from Java and Bali. Individuals from Banda captured in 1621 were later returned to the islands to utilize their cultivation skills (Winn 2010, 369). By 1794, nearly three-quarters of the recorded population were listed as slaves, but the reconfigured society embodied the islands' previous history as a center of trade, with nonslave inhabitants including Europeans, Batavians, Chinese, Ambonese, and freed slaves from around the archipelago (Winn 2010, 371).

The mixed character of the inhabitants of the Banda Islands prior to colonial intervention meant that frameworks of identification based in biology or genealogical descent were generally ineffectual in determining localness. Although religion played a role in local mythologies and origin stories, being Bandanese was more reliant on social relations and affiliation with place. Thalib and La Raman (2015, 51) describe contemporary Banda society as a "metropolis community" whose identity has been shaped by the environment in which they live. Their mixed heritage dictates that they prioritize associative social processes over the importance of ethnic origins. Anthropologist Philip Winn (2010, 367) theorizes that the nature of contemporary identity in Banda, which recognizes inhabitants' diverse origins while allowing for flexible participation in identifying as *orang Banda*, is attributable to the legacy of the *perk* system, which incorporated precolonial inhabitants, Europeans, and other migrants into a shared process of "culture building."

One contemporary exception to this pattern of place-based integration in the Banda Islands is the exclusion of Butonese inhabitants, who trace their descent to the island of Buton. Butonese in Banda are normally perceived as a distinct community not connected to local landscapes and *adat* practices. The perception that Butonese constitute a separate community is widespread in Maluku, since they are perceived as migrants because of their inability or limited opportunity to obtain *adat* rights in the places that they settle (Bräuchler 2017, 12), and are viewed as having economic advantages that they achieved in their position as middlemen in trade networks throughout the region (Kadir 2019).

In historical narratives utilized in the promotion of Banda as a tourist destination, the influence of Christianity is downplayed in the story of Islam, trade, and nationalism presented for tourist audiences. The role of the Dutch Reformed Church as an authoritative institution in the islands and an important source of social cohesion for converts from different sectors of society (former slaves, native spouses of Dutch settlers, and female slaves adopted into Dutch households among others; Loth 1995, 25) is rarely discussed in tourist materials or historical attractions on the islands. Although colonial objects fill the small museum in the center of town supported by the Alwi family's Banda Naira Culture and Heritage Foundation, and the colonial-era church is one of the best preserved of the island chain's historical tourist attractions, tourism narratives provide little information about the influence of Christianity or the role of Bandanese Christians in the cultural life of the island.

In the version of history used in the promotion of Banda Neira for tourism, the focus is on what was lost as a result of colonial aggression. The recuperation of the true meaning of *adat* practices is achieved by applying an outside perspective that analyzes the practices with the addition of the colonial-era knowledge recovered by Alwi's historical research. Yet this totalizing narrative that recounts the history of the islands from a global perspective is refuted by some locals. For some, the claim that the original Bandanese have been settled elsewhere since the early colonial period contradicts the more inclusive frames for Bandanese identity that recognize contemporary inhabitants' mixed origins. An *ustad* (Islamic

teacher) from the village of Rajawali who heads efforts to revive other traditions from Banda Neira that are sidelined by the cultural performances
for tourism cast doubt on the narrative of loss that characterizes the authoritative version of Banda's history: "If we are talking about the issue of
Bandanese and history, we're talking about the eleventh generation on.
Where's the history from the beginning until the tenth generation? The
descendants of the Bandanese are mixed, there are Javanese descendants,
Bugis descendants, many. There's many ethnic groups here. If we say that
the original people of Banda are the people of Banda Eli, we can't verify
that yet."

His version of history also relies on *adat* as an indicator of belonging,
one that does not exclude local Christians as part of the history or identity
of the islands, but instead sees them as central to concepts of the origins of
the traditions of the islands. He referred to kinship across religious lines as
evidence that *adat* is not exclusive to one religious identity:

M: Usually would they [the Christians] participate in the performances like we saw earlier?
Ustad: Yes, including those who are in the *negeri* that is in Ratu. They
are Christian. The *adat* house below, the one in Dwiwarna, they are
ethnically mixed and it's from the *adat*, the ones who created and
made the meaning for the *adat* for the *kora-kora* canoes are from two
lines of descent, from the descendants of Clan Kempa and the descendants of Clan Abraham. There were Muslim Kempas and Christian
Kempas, and Muslim Abrahams and Christian Abrahams, from two
different ethnic groups. The Muslims and the Christians had the same
dances.
M: So the Muslims and the Christians were from different ethnicities?
Ustad: From Christian and Muslim, but it all comes from one founda-
tional pillar . . . meaning that they are intermingled. If you ask if they
have "history," well, not everyone has it. They don't necessarily have
it . . . but it can be seen in their *orang adat* [people with adat] who
made the first canoe here in the lands of Banda, on Pulau Hatta. From
the two family clans of Abraham and Kempa. It was they who made
the canoes. Then Islam and other things emerged, but it was learned
from there. Meaning the oldest *adat* is from Hatta Island.

The *adat* expert of Namasawar also presented an alternative to the historical narrative that sees Christianity as part of the religious history of the islands:

> In Ratu they are all Christian, those of us in Banda, in the old days the oldest people were all Christian. So our story about the religion of Islam, the ones who came here first were slaves. It was the slaves first, and then the representatives of Islam who came, five people, it was them who came and made things here.
>
> They made the *negeri*, they taught the slaves so that there was Islam. All of a sudden the Dutch came, couldn't be turned back, and couldn't be mixed, so what could be preserved of Islam was preserved, but what remained was only partial. Some people joined with the Dutch. Became Christian. Many of them fled, they went to Banda Eli.

In other conversations, competing frameworks for identity were expressed that were more exclusive, with religious identity demarcating the boundary between "newcomers" and others who saw themselves as part of more established communities. This was despite the candid admission from many of these informants of their own mixed backgrounds, including ancestors of European descent. The son of the leader of the oldest mosque on Banda Neira identified Christians as newcomers, although he also noted that despite this designation they had been integrated into Banda society:

> M: The Christians from here, where are they from?
> Om A: The Christians are from Hatta, from TNS, and from Saparua.[3] They are newcomers. The police saved them [at the time of the conflict], the police put them all at Des Alwi's place. Those Christian names are from the Netherlands. When we meet them now, everything is fine with them. We regret what happened. They invite us.
> K: So you mean the Christians that lived here during the colonial period, they were from Hatta or from the Netherlands?
> Om A: Many from Saparua, from Ambon, there's a lot of them, the newcomers. They have descendants. In these *marga* [family lines] there

are those from Christianity and those from Islam. They've already mixed in.

Participation in *adat* practices and intermarriage are two ways in which the exclusive tie between Islam and an indigenous religious identity is challenged by frameworks of kinship (fictive or otherwise). However, competing versions of who are considered the original inhabitants (*orang asli*) versus newcomers or migrants (*pendatang*) still circulate in historical narratives and discourses on belonging. How the past is perceived to affect who and to what degree people can be considered Bandanese is part of the evolving state of how plurality is perceived and practiced in the Spice Islands. Renewed interest in representing the region's history and culture as tourist attractions brings questions of the relationship between religion and culture to be played out on a public stage. The cultural practices that have been designated as representative of the Bandanese are linked to *adat* as a system of social participation that is part of a normative inclusivity in the islands, one that Christian inhabitants see as central to their claims that their religious identity doesn't exclude them from being Bandanese.

NARRATIVES OF CULTURE FOR RECONCILIATION

In postconflict Maluku, *adat* is utilized in the promotion of the ideology of harmony across religious groups. As anthropologist Birgit Bräuchler (2009a, 873) notes, local concepts of culture and tradition were central to rebuilding social ties between Muslims and Christians in postconflict efforts toward reconciliation, rooted in the ideal of a shared identification as *orang Maluku* (Malukan people) that could overcome the divisiveness of religious identity. However, in her examination of the reconstruction or revitalization of how *pela*, a cultural institution for creating alliances between villages, can serve as a local frame for reconciliation between Christians and Muslims, she also notes that the invocation of tradition was part of the development of communal memories that supported violence. In the postconflict era, little attention has been given to how the widespread displacement that resulted from the violence, as well as institutional pressures that direct the expression of how the conflict should be memorialized, has affected the development and expression of public memory, and the development of postconflict identities in individual communities.

Reconciliation efforts in postconflict Maluku have focused on *adat* rituals as a way to rebuild relationships between religious communities on the basis of relations of fictive kinship (Klinken 2001, 10) and the assumption of a shared cultural framework that exceeds religious identity. Simultaneously, institutional approaches to reconciliation in the region focus on forgetting past misdeeds for the sake of moving forward (Duncan 2009a, 432). This leaves little space for remembering or reflecting on the displacement of religious communities due to conflict, and the loss of whole communities in particular regions. For displaced groups, the "revival of *adat* has a territorial interpretation" (Adam 2008, 228). Although returning to a former village may not be realistically achievable, narratives about returning are part of the discourse of *adat* as an expression of community harmony that posits a common ground across religious differences (Adam 2008, 234).

Reconciliation in the terms of the repatriation of former lands to former Christian inhabitants of the Banda Islands was viewed as impractical, however, without government intervention. Exhortations of brotherhood and enduring ties between Muslim families and displaced Christian communities were not deemed sufficient by either side to facilitate the return of displaced communities. That Christians would not return to Banda Neira was seen by many as a foregone conclusion because of the difficulty of reclaiming land left or sold after the conflict:

> K: If they want come back and live here, would they be received or no?
> **Ratu *adat* expert:** Those who have land. If it's their land there aren't any Muslims that would take it and live there. Maybe they want to come back. But I think coming back would also be hard. Some of them have sold their land. They can come back. But to live across [on another island] because everyone is Muslim here now.

On the island of Hatta, the part of the village known as Kampung Lama (the Old Settlement) was Christian save for two families. All of the Christian community of the island left, entrusting their lands to Muslim neighbors. Two guesthouses on former Christian land are also run by the Muslim families left in Kampung Lama, who manage the business with Christian guides who bring tourists from Ambon or from Banda Neira.[4] A former villager from Hatta explained the system that has been set up in their absence:

> The majority of the lands the Christians had were in Banda, but you could say that some of them have been sold, it's true some people have sold. But in Hatta, it can't be denied that all of that land belongs to us. It's just we left, when we first left we gave the land over to their guardianship. To protect our area, because since 1999, 2000, 2001, the nutmeg there was harvested three times, but then for three or four years we haven't gotten anything, so we've contracted the land out. Even if we just get the cheapest parts of the harvest at least we still get something. We contract to the Muslims there for about 1 million Rupiah [US$74] a year.

Land ownership and control over dispossessed properties was still a sensitive topic in interviews conducted in 2015. Muslim residents on Banda Neira often expressed nostalgia for the time when their Christian neighbors lived on the island but also underlined that in order for them to return, the government would need to ensure their safety. Christians in Banda Suli recalled an attempt in 2003 to organize an event to discuss the possibility of return with a similar result; concern over safety led local authorities to insist that return was possible only if facilitated by military protection.

These anxieties over land rights were exacerbated by discussions of plans for tourism development. The land that many of the former colonial buildings are on was purchased by the Alwi family during the early years of tourism building on the island, and some have now been taken over by the national government heritage management institutions (*cagar budaya*). Many Muslim residents in Banda Neira have heard that they will be granted land rights to properties after twenty years of habitation on properties that have been vacated. Several informants were upset to learn of a plan by a former resident of Hatta who had purchased two properties in Banda Neira with the intent to open guesthouses. Plans to widen the runway on Banda Neira's small landing strip, as well as to resettle residents who have built homes and run small businesses on the grounds of the historic Fort Nassau that is slated for rehabilitation as as a national heritage site, have increased tensions over questions of land ownership and control, as well as the economic implications of increased tourism to the islands.

Despite these concerns, tourism planning and development by local and regional elites continue to promote the narrative of Banda as a destination that embodies the harmonious diversity enshrined in Indonesia's national motto. This is also reflected in attitudes toward culture or *adat* as a mechanism not just for relegating previous conflict to the past, but also for moving it out of communal memory. The idea that cultural reconciliation can potentially erase memories of past conflict between Muslims and Christians was reflected in a conversation with the regent of Maluku Tengah, who has been actively involved in efforts to promote the Banda Islands as a premier tourist destination. In response to a question about the current status of interreligious relations in the promotion of the region as a cultural tourist destination, he explained that the *pela gandong* relationship had been created hundreds of years ago between Muslims and Christians as a cultural institution for unity that functions as a guarantor against provocations from outsiders: "If we rely on [the traditions of *pela gandong*], we can get along as if the conflict that befell us never even happened."

In analyzing practices of memorialization for those who died in the conflict in Maluku, Christopher Duncan (2009a, 433, 430) writes that graves for martyrs and others are a response to the discourse of forgetting espoused by officials, regional scholars, and institutions involved in reconciliation efforts who argue that the conflict was about something other than religion. The focus on culture in reconciliation work also reinforces the dominant narrative that religion was subsidiary to the real causes of the conflict. *Adat* provides a stable ground for discussing interreligious relations that does not upset the hegemonic discourse aimed at forgetting and moving forward. Such discussions limit, however, opportunities to address ongoing tensions in postconflict communities. They also curtail the ability of individual communities to express their memories of the conflict in public.

The territorial associations that continue to link displaced peoples to particular places express the ongoing connections between land, a sense of shared history and cosmology, and social relations to which the concept of *adat* refers when invoked in public narratives. However, when rights to land cannot be recuperated, reconciliation is a more difficult task, one that the remaining community might be uninterested in engaging with. Displaced communities can seek to reaffirm their identification with certain places through participation in cultural activities that display their affective ties to the land and the traditions that they have carried from the place they left. For Christians displaced from Banda, continued participation in the rituals associated with particular *negeri* is a strategy of asserting continued inclusion in the communities they have been displaced from. It also validates their continued claims to particular territories to which they have lost or relinquished rights of land ownership. As time passes, however, changes to *adat* practices through the influence of increasing tourism in the islands indicate that opportunities for Christians to participate in cultural events and rituals may be narrowing as *adat* practices evolve to reflect the interpretations of the majority-Muslim population in the Banda Islands.

CONTESTED BOUNDARIES OF CULTURE
AND RELIGION IN TOURISM PRACTICES

In Indonesia today, *adat* is a framework through which the national ideology of harmonious religious relations is applied to specific communities. Although *adat* is a concept that is ontologically associated with the realm of the *cultural* and therefore should not be the exclusive domain of any one religion, in practice religious identity can align with place-based cultural cosmologies so that *adat* and *agama* combine to serve as a coterminous boundary for a community. The use of *adat* as a term that encompasses moral concerns means that it can easily overlap with religious morality in such a way that religious orientations and *adat* are indistinguishable in practice and in some cases can be seen as an essential characteristic of place-based identities.

In his examination of Indonesian forms of normative pluralism in Indonesia, John Bowen (2005, 158) theorizes that the type of identification based in local social norms and embeddedness in local contexts that modern *adat* communities represent possesses variable relationships to concepts of peoplehood, ethnicity, or language and therefore provides a different basis for legitimacy than is seen in Western forms of multiculturalism. In eastern Indonesia, concepts of *adat* have been seen to embody this potential to serve as a flexible category inclusive of various actors who participate in a shared sociocultural context, often in distinction to more exclusivist frameworks of ethnicity or religious identity. However, Bowen (2005, 167) notes that a third type of normative pluralism in Indonesia is one in which Islam and *adat* norms converge. Historically, this merging of religion and *adat* can be seen in several regions where reformist varieties of Islam or Christianity were integral in the development of a distinct regional identity. In these cases, local norms rooted in a sense of place-based identity fused with religious concepts in such a way that religion became a distinguishing characteristic of regional identity and a normative requirement for membership in cultural communities.

Despite the contemporary revival of *adat* as a category of representation in local politics, or as a basis for inclusive regional communities, religious identity remains a powerful normative framework that shapes the perception of difference as well as an increasingly important source of symbolic capital in the Indonesian public. As Chantal Mouffe (2013, 47) notes, the work of establishing normative practices of pluralism depends, not on overcoming differences between those who belong and those who do not, but on the different ways in which that difference is established. As debates over who can legitimately speak for (and therefore define) *adat* communities often focus on disputes over the nature of the social groups being represented (Bowen 2005, 158), exclusivist formations of identity that position religion as a marker of cultural authority may emerge more often as a method of establishing difference in the pursuit of claims for legitimacy or control over resources.

This potential can be seen not only in the increase in public displays of religious identity but also in the increasing use of religious identity as political capital in Indonesia. In some cases, regional politicians defend their application of religious morality at the local level as part of cultural distinction and the expression of the right to regional autonomy. This has resulted in a type of ethno-religious exclusivism that portrays *adat* as indistinguishable from religion. In several cases linked to the advent of political decentralization in the early 2000s, local leaders positioned the religion of the majority as part of the region's cultural tradition that arguably should serve as the appropriate basis for independent local governance. In some cases, the idea that religious identity is part of the particular characteristics that designate ethno-local identity has led to the codification of religious norms into law at the regency (*kabupaten*) level through the creation of regional regulations (*peraturan daearah*).

The politics of piety and the trend toward concern over the "purification" of religious practices also contribute to anxiety over cultural rituals and their impact on religiosity. Religious institutions of a purist persuasion urge practitioners to police not only their practices but also their intentions in performing cultural rituals, or, at the most extreme, to stop participation in cultural practices because these are seen to conflict with religious principles. Concern over piety and orthodox behavior has also been seen in the tourism industry, ranging from debates over appropriate behavior at burial sites that have historically hosted a range of practices to the development of a national program of shariah tourism. These issues are also often expressed in relation to the way that certain localities are associated with particular religious identities and therefore the kinds of tourists (and tourism activities) they host.

One of the evolving tensions in the postconflict tourism industry in the Banda Islands hinges on moral concerns over the behavior of tourists. Local informants recounted incidents of tourists being harassed and in a few cases, pelted with stones for walking through village centers skimpily dressed. In focus group discussions with the mostly male cadre of young guides in Banda Neira, concerns over the moral temptations thought to be introduced through the behavior of Western tourists were discussed as a threat to *adat,* which they referred to as overarching rules of social interaction with little sense that different religious communities might have different attitudes toward these issues.

Anxieties over religious morality and policing of the lines between religion and culture are a concern for the *adat* experts, who see the increase in religious orthodoxy as part of the general diminishment of cultural knowledge enshrined in *adat* and a shift in the moral order that governs cultural mores. The increasing convergence of Islam and *adat* is also a concern for displaced Bandanese Christians, who worry that it further displaces them from contributing to the social and cultural environment of their home territory. Representations of *adat* as reflecting Islamic moral concerns are problematic both in how outsiders are received and in the possible political implications for developing the special legal status for the islands as a Special Economic Zone (*kawasan ekonomi khusus*) or a New Autonomous Region (*daerah otonomi baru*). In Banda Suli, residents discussed stories they had heard about the treatment of tourists who visited the few guesthouses operating in Kampung Lama on former Christian-owned lands and the representation of *adat* promoted by young Muslim guides:

> A: I worry a little because when I ask them about the tourism industry, I said to them, almost all of the guides are young Muslim men, right? They have this perception now that for the political reconfiguration there needs to be a policy from the government that if tourists go to Banda Neira they must adhere to *adat* or local values, meaning women need to be covered and maybe they can't sell beer. I asked them, is that *adat* or Islam? They said, "This is *adat* here." But if you ask around a little more, ask the Christians there, it's no problem if women are wearing bikinis. . . . But now that we've gone, why is it that previously *adat* didn't say anything like that but now it suddenly does? What model of *adat* is that?

The Islamic teacher (*ustad*) from Rajawali also complained that simplification and standardization of cultural practices for tourism had prevented the preservation or revitalization of other traditions and had also shifted perceptions about who had the authority to participate in displays of culture and *adat* practices. He discussed efforts in Rajawali to bring cultural practices forth to be recognized as part of the island's *adat* system:

> The dance we saw earlier is just like the dance in this village, meaning that culture is just a few things, history just a few. There are over seventy-five dances that are still lost here, and only a few emerge; it's a mistake to make it that new way. We're looking for something to change this new way of doing things; we feel that with this issue we have the capability to change things, the truth is we are making something not in conflict with other groups [*etnis*], because if we are talking about the issue of culture there are so many cultural practices

we need to bring forth in a good way. . . . We have to change the customs [*adat istiadat*] totally, for example like the dances. For example, those who dance the *cakalele* have to be persons of Muslim descent, but *adat* says something else. Even when someone is a descendant of *adat*, if they don't understand about *adat* then they shouldn't be used.

Displays of culture are part of the processes of identity negotiation that have great potential to change intergroup perspectives (Adams 2006, 9), even as they often fail to embody the lived realities and social expectations of people living together in a particular locale. The version of *adat* that is presented for tourists in Banda Neira is contrasted with people's experience of socially embedded rituals that define authenticity through the enactment of practices rooted in particular social relations, a way of extending authority from the past into the present. New forms of authority are developing because of the disturbance of previous social relations and the loss of knowledge related to *adat* rituals resulting from the forced migration of Christians from *negeri* in Banda Neira and Hatta. Cultural performances for tourism that display identity or adhere to the standard forms of representation that make culture palatable for tourism are arenas where authority rests on who gets to define the community being represented and who is being addressed (Erb 2003, 130). The development of cultural displays and narratives for tourist audiences has played a major role in the revitalization and imagination of the identity of contemporary Bandanese. As tourism activities continue to be a significant site for the development of collective identity and processes of cultural preservation, they will inevitably continue to influence how the past is represented and who will be invested with the authority to define the boundaries of cultural communities in the future.

REPRESENTING HARMONY, FORGETTING CONFLICT: TOURISM AND SPACES FOR DIVERGENT MEMORIES IN BANDA NEIRA

On a walking tour for a small group of tourists led by the proprietor of one of the three hotels on Banda Neira, we stopped at the monument to the murdered chiefs. Their names, preserved in archival documents, are rein-scribed on a plaque that memorializes not only the massacre but also the narrative that real Bandanese culture was lost and is in need of recupera-tion. This is the center of the story recounted in the authoritative version of history Des Alwi uncovered in the Netherlands that is retold in tours, films, performances, and the halls of refurbished colonial buildings. "These are the original Bandanese," the tour guide told us.

"Are there any Christians listed there?" I asked.

"There weren't any Christian original Bandanese," he replied.

"You mean they were all Muslim?"

"Yes, the original people of Banda were Muslim. Christians were brought from other regions by the Dutch to cultivate nutmeg."

In narratives for tourists, Islam is part of the authentic version of local identity lost to history. For the former residents of Kampung Lama on Hatta, these kinds of statements invalidate their identification as Ban-danese. Christian informants saw these kinds of statements as attempts to "cover up" traces of their history in the islands. However, tourist objects, as well as memorial sites, are often ambiguous and multivalent, "vehicles for articulating ideas concerning contrasting identities" (Adams 2006, 27) that can be narrated and understood in various ways. The historical char-acterization of Bandanese identity rests in the authority of a chronologi-cal, factual retelling of the island's past that situates Islam and Christianity on separate sides of a society divided by colonialism or, at the very least, presents Islam as more authentic given its earlier arrival to the islands. For many in the Banda Islands, *adat* is a system that emphasizes knowledge and cultural competency over a historical reckoning of identity. Islam's ar-rival to the islands earlier than contact with Dutch Protestantism doesn't preclude the ability for people to be Bandanese through their knowledge and participation in social expressions of *adat*.

At other tourism sites, opportunities to represent local Christian his-tories in the island are silenced because of their connection to the 1999 conflict. The Old Church (Gereja Tua) in Banda Neira is one of the most evident symbols of the legacy of Christianity in the islands. Still serving a small population of Christian civil servants, the church is both an active religious site and a historical tourist attraction. It is located a short walk from the harbor in the central town square, and tourists can enter the building when the church is not holding services. The building is one of the best-preserved historical sites in the region, especially in comparison to other colonial-era buildings nearby that are in various states of disrepair.

Over the course of interviews in 2015, several Muslim families brought up the church as an example of the close relations between the two religious groups on the island, claiming that it had been protected by local Muslims during the violence in 1999. This was striking, as the Catholic church behind the colonial waterfront area was burned along with Christian residences in Ratu and remains a burnt-out shell, as do some of the other buildings that were the former homes of Christian residents of Ratu. Accessing the church in low tourism season was problematic because there was no regular system in place to open the doors when it wasn't being used by the Christian congregation for worship.

The small Christian congregation that now worships there told a different story than that recounted by Muslims we interviewed. One of the distinct characteristics of the church is thirty-four VOC headstones of deceased colonial nobles that line the center aisle between the pews, set into the floor when the church was rebuilt after an earthquake in 1865. Behind the altar, out of the view of visitors, a few of the headstones show signs of fire damage. The headstones were moved behind the altar when the church was reopened in 2007 after being closed for several years because of damage sustained during the 1999 conflict. In the memory of Christians in Banda Suli, the restoration of the church was a poignant moment for many of them who had returned to work on the project with the protection of local police. One individual recalled the surrounding community gathering in front of the church when a worker climbed the rafters to ring the church bells that had been silent since the conflict. In a later interview between my Muslim research assistant and a group of middle-aged men employed by one of the local tourism businesses, they talked about their involvement in the damage the church sustained during the conflict. One of them commented that "if we had known how valuable the site was for Banda's tourism trade, we wouldn't have destroyed it."

Narratives that could be used to address the loss of Christian communities or to commemorate the role of local Christians in the islands' histories at tourist sites like the colonial church are seen as untenable, as they involve the discussion of conflict. In both tourism promotion and regional institutional approaches to reconciliation, sites of memory that invite discussion about conflict are to be avoided. The simplifications and silences that are reproduced in the production and display of culture for tourists are also part of the processes of collective memory that shape evolving understandings of identity and cultural citizenship. As sites and cultural practices are increasingly managed as tourist attractions, they lose their potential to serve as sites of memory and spaces for a plurality of narratives about the past and present relationships of religious communities on the islands.

In Indonesian national ideology of the New Order period, culture was ostensibly a domain separate and distinguishable from religion. The relationship between the categories of religion and culture therefore reflected the application of other modernist binaries through an Indonesian national imaginary. In contemporary Indonesia, culture and the overlapping concept of *adat* are indexical of the local and the particular. The public processes of identifying the local and what can be rightfully labeled culture rely on claims of particularity that might seem to be anathema to religion's aterritorial and universalizing tendencies. Conversely, religion is also a categorical means of national belonging that, while uniting citizens as Indonesians under "one supreme God" (*Tuhan yang Maha Esa*), also delineates their difference in ways that can undermine identities fashioned around the local. Essentially, while the categories of religion and culture are nationally articulated and publicly enacted as conceptually distinct, in practical and historical terms they are not. Communities continually reevaluate their practices, symbols, and rituals to determine which side of the ontological domain they rightfully belong to.

The practices that refashion culture as a tourist object tend to instigate a social frame where religious identity and its relation to culture are simplified. Religion can be either minimized as irrelevant to cultural categories of collective identity or presented as an inseparable part of cultural practices, as in the case of Balinese Hinduism. The way that culture is reconstructed and reimagined for the gaze of the outsider often jettisons the labor and time-intensive ritual practices associated with cultural symbols to make them easy to reproduce, cost-effective, and appealing to an audience. Although the tourism industry in Indonesia promises the allure of authenticity predicated on particularity, it reduces difference to a number of structured, homogenous forms where one ethnic dance-dress-ritual can be easily recognized and just as easily substituted for another. In representations of local identity for tourists, *adat* is presented as a suite of objectified practices that can be inserted into the national context as emblems of ethnicity, unaffected by the passage of time and disambiguated from contemporary religious contexts.

As Acciaioli (2001, 108) observes, one of the main conceptual issues of political promotion of *adat* is that its resurgence "fails to recognize the heterogeneity of local" and makes the assertion that in "each territory a single people's custom is to be sovereign." This effect is magnified in the selection and presentation of regional culture for tourism, where simplified symbols used to represent the local can potentially be aligned with religious identity. Selecting and promoting aspects of regional culture on the international tourist market is one way that groups frame their difference in the terms of national discourse and "seek active participation in their own image building" (Hoskins 2002, 817). As tourism can be used to legitimate ethnicity, it can be a useful strategy for those groups who lack the kind of authenticating markers that can provide the basis of a political community steeped in the discourse of shared traditions. By promoting particularistic practice as part of what the nation has to offer to foreign tourists, it can also help to transform problematic local histories into those more in line with nationalist ones. The reflexivity that tourism practices engender can be utilized not just by the state but by individual groups to create, change, and present their version of self-identity to the world, forcing the nation to respond with greater levels of recognition. The touristic interest in tradition may even spur religious practitioners to reframe their practices as historically significant, a way of attracting a broader audience (Hoskins 2002, 814).

This concept of culture as a contextless display can articulate with the tourist's desire to take cultural performances at face value, "replicas of life in the ethnographic present, static, timeless, without history, without agency, without context," rather than as "contemporary rituals offered in a particular political and touristic context" (Bruner 2004, 4). These kinds of performances are often critiqued precisely because they are divorced from context. However, it is exactly the potential for touristic displays to down-play problems, power differentials, and contentions, allowing participants to renarrate cultural symbols, that can make touristic displays so appeal-ing in Indonesia, especially as a means of minimizing past conflicts or ad-dressing current tensions between diverse groups. This also explains the recent popularity of cultural festivals and tourist events as spaces where the *ideal* of harmony can be presented even if it is a goal that is yet to be fully realized. As anthropologist Edward Bruner (2004, 5) points out in his analysis of the use of culture as a tourist attraction, since all touristic per-formances are novel because they occur in a new context, with a new audi-ence and in a different time, we should see them as essentially constitutive, reflecting and resonating with communities in the process of redefinition.

Normative definitions of identity are created through the confluence of a number of factors, both institutional and situational. In this case, an ethos of avoiding memorialization or discussion of previous conflict, and the tendency for culture to be distilled into singular, simplified narratives for the consumption of tourists overlap and have a pervasive effect on local collective memory and the limits of local frameworks of pluralism. At a time when cultural competency represented in ritual knowledge is one tie that displaced Bandanese Christians can claim to their former homes, those practices are being phased out to better adapt to needs of marketing culture as a tourism object. The unintentional implication of this tendency to represent history and cultural practices as decontextu-alized narrows the potential for Christians to maintain their social and cultural ties to place through their involvement with *adat* practices. An unintentional alignment between religious identity and the cultural au-thority that facilitates claims to belonging is being enacted in the dis-courses surrounding the creation and presentation of "local" culture for tourists. This is a process that also informs the Bandanese people about who they are today.

Although contrasting frames for ascertaining who the original Ban-danese are have long been circulated, the developing sense that the "real" people of Banda had one religious identity challenges alternative modes of belonging that portray the Banda Islands as a microcosm of diversity where belonging is based in adaptation to local cultural systems. Perform-ances and practices related to the tourism industry unintentionally rewrite native concepts of authenticity as dependent on Muslim identity. Along with institutional focuses on safety and reconciliation that are promoted intercommunally and institutionally as a method of avoiding the emergence of new conflict, and as a part of the image-making process that regional elites encourage as a means for economic development through tourism, the discursive possibilities for Christians to assert their claims to being Bandanese are becoming more limited. This has implications for the economic and political possibilities for their resettlement as they may slowly and unwittingly be written out of expressions of history and memory in the islands' tourist trade.

NOTES

1. The *adat* canoes (*belang adat*) belonged to Pulau Ai, Lontor, Kampung Baru, Pulau Hatta, and Waer. Although Ratu (Dwiwarna) is considered a village with *adat*, it historically does not participate in the races because of its female status.

2. The persistence of the identification of the inhabitants of Banda Eli/Elat as the indigenous people of Banda emerged in the form of a protest against a recent film about the Banda Islands' role in the spice trade. In a press interview, Jay Subyakto, director of *Banda: The Dark Forgotten Trail*, stated that all of the original Bandanese were killed in the 1621 genocide. A group representing communities from Banda Eli/Elat protested in front of the Regional House of Representatives Building in Ambon, calling for the film to be banned and legal action taken against the director and producer for falsely stating that the original inhabitants of Banda were destroyed. They pointed out several communities of original Bandanese in Banda Eli/Elat, Ambon, Seram, and Haruku. Screenings of the film in Ambon were canceled because of its potential to ignite local conflict.

3. TNS is an abbreviation for the people from the islands of Teon, Nila, and Serua in Maluku Barat Daya. In 1976, most of the communities on these islands were relocated to Seram and other parts of Central Maluku because of a volcanic eruption.

4. Hatta Island has no cell phone service, so communication with tourists is severely limited. Tourists access information about the island via dive centers and hotels in Banda Neira or through connection with guides in Ambon.

FOUR

Scaling against Pluralism

Hizbut Tahrir Indonesia and Islamist Opposition to Pancasila Citizenship

MOHAMMAD IQBAL AHNAF

Soon after the fall of President Soeharto's New Order regime in 1998, a new Islamist group named Hizbut Tahrir Indonesia (HTI) emerged from the shadows. HTI had been building an underground base for its movement over the course of the previous decade, using a system of secretive, cell-based mobilization. Almost two decades onward, HTI had transformed itself into an important player in the mass-based movement for the establishment in Indonesia of an Islamic state based on shariah. Although over the course of the *Reformasi* period many Islamist movements had tended toward moderation or some measure of accommodation, not least on questions of Indonesian nationhood, HTI was one of the few Islamist groups that remained uncompromising in its opposition to Indonesia's democratic system and its calls for replacing democracy with an ostensibly Islamic political system HTI calls a global "caliphate."[1]

For the first years of the *Reformasi* period HTI continued to make inroads—not just into student circles but even into some government and business circles. Its core constituency was middle and upper-middle class.

HTI's rise to prominence reached its peak in late 2016 and early 2017, when the organization played a central role (with the hard-line but theologically traditionalist Islamic Defenders Front) in the mobilization of hundreds of thousands of demonstrators in rallies held in the capital city of Jakarta. The campaign ultimately led to the trial, ousting, and imprisonment of the Christian Chinese governor of Jakarta, Basuki Tjahaja Purnama (see Hefner, chapter 1, and Bagir, chapter 7). The campaign at first gave rise in HTI circles to hopes for a further consolidation of its influence. But the movement's success and growing prominence also provoked fierce opposition among Indonesian nationalists, patriotic Muslim reformists, and Muslim traditionalists, most forcefully in the country's largest Muslim organization, the forty-million-strong Nahdlatul Ulama; the campaign also raised the ire of some in President Jokowi's government. In the end, the growing public opposition allowed the government to ban the organization on grounds that HTI was opposed to both the Indonesian Constitution and the principles of Pancasila governance. Presidential Decree No. 2 (2017) on mass organizations caused great controversy, with liberal and human rights organizations questioning its compatibility with democratic freedoms. But the legislation was approved by the House of Representatives and passed into law in October 2017. One of Indonesia's most distinguished Muslim intellectuals, Azyumardi Azra, hailed the legislation as a decisive step toward saving Indonesia from ideological turmoil and national disintegration (Metro TV News 2017; *Kompas* 2017).

Brought to Indonesia in 1983, HTI is a part of the international movement called Hizbut Tahrir (HT) founded in Palestine in 1953 by Taqiyuddin al-Nabhani (1909–77). HT started with the revolutionary goal of restoring the global Muslim caliphate; however, officially it claimed to pursue this aim in a nonviolent albeit totalizing manner. The raison d'être for the founding of HT was al-Nabhani's disillusionment with political Islamic movements that failed because of, as he saw it, their participation in "secular systems" of government. Al-Nabhani rejected both the reformism of the Muslim Brotherhood and the militarism of violent Islamists (Taji-Farouki 1996, xi). He offered an alternative strategy, one that aimed to undermine the existing system of government in part by persuading political and military elites to transform the secular state into a caliphate government.

In presenting its program of nonparticipation and noncooperation with "infidel" (*kufr*) institutions like democratic government, HTI emphasizes the need to change the entire society, as opposed to changing the individual, a process it refers to metaphorically as "heating the boiling kettle" (an-Nabhani 2001, 62). HTI believes that a political system (democracy) cannot stand without the consent or trust (*thiqoh*) of the people. It therefore seeks to infuse delegitimating ideas into society so as to bring about popular disenchantment with the existing political system. Unlike Islamist groups like the Muslim Brotherhood, HT Indonesia (HTI) avoids any and all direct participation in democratic institutions such as national elections, instead exploiting the political freedom granted by democratizing Indonesia to build support for its antidemocratic program.

The doctrine of nonparticipation nonetheless does not result in HTI distancing itself from all political processes. For example, HTI has played a central role in campaigns to support implementation of shariah legislation in Indonesia. It has also sought to recruit support from officials in national and regional government. The organization has also worked tirelessly to challenge and delegitimate the principle of Indonesian democracy and Pancasila citizenship, not least with regard to the equality of citizens of different faiths.

This chapter examines HTI's narrative with regard to the necessity of an Islamic political system in the Indonesian context. It explores how this narrative challenges the official normative discourse of Indonesia as a multireligious and Pancasila-based country. The chapter also examines how HTI works to extend or scale up the influence of its alternative, caliphate-based model for state and society—and explains just why in recent years the organization has encountered growing opposition to its programs and appeals.

THE NORMATIVITY OF INDONESIAN MULTICULTURALISM

As Bob Hefner notes in chapter 1 of this book, the term *normativity* is used here to refer to ethical norms or values, themselves the product of complex social and individual processes, that guide individuals or groups on how to live together in religious and ethical differences. This chapter adopts this framework to identify the normativity that currently serves as the raison d'être for democracy and Pancasila in Indonesia, as well as for living together in a multireligious and multiethnic society.

The Pancasila and democracy are the products of a complex social and political negotiation in Indonesian society that resulted in a distinctive—but never universally accepted—answer to the question of whether the nation should be based on just one religion, which is to say Islam. Steering clear of a fully secular formulation, the Pancasila's answer to this question acknowledged the importance and public role of religion in society without making Islam the religion of state. The Pancasila formula for citizenship extends equal rights to all members of society, including all ethnic groups and all officially recognized religions, which currently number six (Islam, Protestant Christianity, Catholicism, Hinduism, Buddhism, and Confucianism).

The key as to why Indonesia opted for this normative framework was the awareness that even though Indonesia is a Muslim-majority country it is also the home of diverse religions, some of whom constitute a majority in their respective territories. Identifying one religion, which is to say Islam, as the religion of state was therefore seen as counterproductive to national integration. This normative ideal did not do away with dissent and demands for a special place of Islam in the state. Since the establishment of Pancasila and democracy in 1945 there have been repeated efforts to make the bases of state and society more explicitly and formally Islamic, ranging from military campaigns to establish an Islamic state to parliamentary campaigns for giving Islam a special place in the constitution. But the fact that these varied efforts have never won broad-based support shows that the existing political system has, at least officially, become the dominant normative framework for Indonesian pluralism.

In my view, this normative work became dominant and legitimate not only because it was seen as a necessary compromise but because it acquired support among major groupings and leaders in society. President Soekarno's idea for the Pancasila was the product of extended discussions with prominent Muslim and secular nationalist leaders in the months leading up to Indonesia's declaration of independence in August 1945. In response to the testimony of Kyai Masykur, a traditionalist Muslim who had led the military struggle against the Dutch, Soekarno convened a meeting attended by Kyai Masykur himself, Mohammad Yamin (a nationalist leader), Wahid Hasyim (a traditionalist Muslim), and Kahar Muzakkir (a modernist Muslim) (Feillard 1999, 32–33). These leaders discussed nationalist, socialist, and Islamic values, and the results of these discussions were then distilled by Soekarno into the political philosophy known as the Pancasila. Although some Islamic groupings continued to oppose it, many Indonesian Muslims regarded the Pancasila as compatible with Islam.

NU's declaration on the relation between Islam and Pancasila issued during its national congress in Situbondo in 1983 states:

> In the Name of God, the Most Gracious and Most Merciful,
> Pancasila as the foundation and philosophy of the Republic of Indonesia is not religion; it does not replace religion and cannot be used to replace the position of religion.
>
> 1. The pillar of Belief in the Oneness of God as the foundation of the Republic of Indonesia as stated in twenty-ninth article of the first verse of the 1945 Constitution inspires other pillars and reflects *tauhid* (Oneness of God) in Islamic belief.
> 2. For Nahdlatul Ulama, Islam is *aqidah* and shariah that includes aspects of human relations with Allah and with fellow human beings.
> 3. Acceptance and implementation of the Pancasila are a reflection of the effort of Muslims in Indonesia to implement shariah.
> 4. As a consequence of this position, Nahdlatul Ulama is committed to promoting its true meaning and pure implementation by all parties. (NU Online 2015b)[2]

Similarly, in a book released during its congress in 2015, Muhammadiyah reasserted the compatibility of the Pancasila and Islam. It uses the Arabic phrase *darul ahdi wa syahadah* (a nation of consensus and testimony) for becoming a blessed peaceful nation to affirm the Islamic nature of the Pancasila state.

> Three prominent leaders of Muhammadiyah, Ki Bagus Hadikusumo, Prof. Kahar Muzzakir, and Mr. Kasman Singodimedjo, with other national leaders, took an active role in formulating the principles and

foundation of the State of Indonesia. . . . With other Muslim leaders, these men formulated and signed the Jakarta Charter, which underlay the preamble to the 1945 Constitution. In a critical moment, one day after the Unitary Republic of Indonesia was declared, Ki Bagus Hadikusumo and Mr. Kasman Singodimedjo saved the unity of Indonesia with their religious and nationalist inspiration. They accepted the removal of the seven words in the Charter. . . . [Accepting] the removal of these seven words was not easy for the Muhammadiyah leaders who represented Muslims at that time. But this position was taken because of their sense of duty to the nation and their commitment to the establishment of the Unitary Republic of Indonesia.

[Muhammadiyah acknowledges] that the concept of the Pancasila is a national consensus [*dar al-'ahdi*] and a testimony [*dar al-syahadah*] [for the purpose of] becoming a peaceful nation [*dar al-salam*] with the aim of creating a progressive, prosperous, and sovereign country under the blessing of Allah. This nationalist view is in line with the Islamic ideal of "*baldatun thayyibatun wa Rabbun ghafur* [a nation that is good, prosperous, and under God's protection]. . . . The Pancasila is the foundation of the Republic of Indonesia, and it serves as an ideology that binds all components of the nation. The Pancasila is not religion, but its substance contains Islamic values that serve as an ideological reference in the plural life of the nation. Therefore, it can be stated that the Pancasila is Islamic because its substance in every pillar is compatible with the teachings of Islam. (Muhammadiyah 2015, 12–13)

These declarations represent and summarize the normative bases, from a Muslim perspective, for Indonesia's legacy of multireligious citizenship. At the same time, however, the Pancasila is relatively unspecific on a host of matters with regard to the precise relation of religion and state. Muslim conservatives have long campaigned for the state to play a greater role in the promotion of Islamic values among that portion of the population that is Islamic. At times, too, they have called for the state to play a more active role in the persecution of those individuals or minority groups seen as deviating from or otherwise "defaming" any of the six recognized religions (see Hefner, chapter 1, and Bagir, chapter 7).

HTI'S CHALLENGE TO INDONESIA'S PLURALIST NORMATIVITY

As the above discussion shows, there has been a long-dominant understanding in Indonesia that the nation is a Muslim-majority country but *not* an Islamic state. It is this principle that HTI has long sought to undermine. As a relatively new organization dedicated to the rather remote goal of establishing the caliphate, however, HTI's influence has long been limited. HTI therefore applies the strategy of "jumping on the bandwagon" of other movements,[3] taking advantage of their campaigns and organizations to boost HTI influence. One way HTI has sought to realize this "bandwagon" goal is by reconstructing narratives on the place of Islam in Indonesia, so as to show that the establishment of caliphate is not just HTI's aspiration but has long had a place in the heart of Indonesian Muslims generally—and even among the founding fathers of the nation. This argument challenges the claim that Indonesia as a multireligious and multiethnic country cannot be based on Islam. In what follows, I focus on HTI's reinterpretation of historical and intellectual legacies of Indonesian Muslim leaders to argue in support of the necessity of Islamic state.

The Islamic Legacy of Nusantara

In all of its commentaries, HTI emphasizes Indonesia's overwhelmingly Islamic character. Ignoring the centuries during which Hindu and Buddhist kingdoms predominated in the region, HTI traces Indonesian history back to the precolonial period when the region called Nusantara was ruled by different Muslim kings. HTI claims that these states pledged allegiance to the Ottoman Empire and governed through the implementation of Islamic law. The implementation of elements of shariah by Muslim kingdoms in precolonial Indonesia is acknowledged by historians. However, HTI's claim that Muslim rulers successfully implemented shariah on a large scale is highly questionable, even though it is true that elements of Islamic law such as cutting off hands for thievery and the death penalty for adultery were enforced by a few rulers during brief periods. Far from being comprehensive, implementation of shariah in these periods was piecemeal (see Hefner 2011a, 283–84).

HTI's campaign to demonstrate the "shariah"-compliant character of early Indonesian polities was made in a series of articles published between 2009 and 2013 on the organization's websites, bulletins, and affiliated blogs. According to these publications, major territories in Indonesia were governed by Islamic rulers from the fourteenth century onward. In Sumatra the rule of Islam began with the kingdom of Perlak, which was then followed by other Muslim kingdoms, including Samudera Pasai and Aceh Darussalam. In Kalimantan, Islamic kingdoms could be found in Sambas, Pontianak, Banjar, Tanjungpura, Mempawah, Sintang, and Kutai. In Sulawesi and Papua, Islamic rule was represented by the wide influence of Muslim rulers in Ternate, Tidore, and Bacan. In the same period, Islamic rulers shaped Javanese social and political affairs through the presence of Muslim kingdoms including Mataram in Yogyakarta, Demak in Central Java, Cirebon in West Java, and Banten at the far western end of the island. Even in areas where today Muslims are not the majority, Muslims were able to rule. In East Nusa Tenggara, for example, Islamic influence is said to have been evident in the existence of the Kingdom of Bima. These kingdoms, HTI claims, not only upheld Islam as a symbolic identity but also effectively replaced *adat* (customary) laws with Islamic law. In Banten, the Islamic kingdom under the rule of Sultan Ageng Tirtayasa enforced laws for cutting off the hands and feet of convicted thieves. Religious authorities had a special place in the sultanate institution as shown by the title of *kiai ali* given to Islamic judges (*qadi*).

According to HTI publications, another important Islamic legacy in Indonesian history has been the use of Islam as the basis of law and of constitutions. The Kingdom of Aceh Darussalam under Sultan Iskandar Muda had an Islam-based constitution called Kitab Adat Mahkota Alam. The replacement of *adat* or customary laws with Islamic laws is said to have taken place in other kingdoms as well. In Mataram, Sultan Agung established an Islamic court called *peradilan surambi* (court on the veranda of the mosque), which ruled according to Islamic criminal laws called Kitab Qisas. In Sulawesi under the rule of Sultan Alauddin, those who failed to perform their religious obligations were subject to punishment by the state.

The dominant role of Islam continued in the struggle for independence in the twentieth century. In HTI's account, the struggle was motivated not only by the desire to gain independence from the colonial powers but by the desire to establish a caliphate. This desire is most evident in the contact between Muslim leaders and Ottoman authorities, who supported Indonesians' struggle for independence. To prove this much-disputed claim, HTI quotes Dutch colonial officers. Here is an example of HTI's narrative.

> It was commonly known among Dutch officers that many sultans in Indonesia pledged allegiance [*bai'at*] to the caliphate in Istanbul. This effectively made Muslims in Indonesia citizens of the caliphate [Islamic State].
>
> Muslims in Aceh were the most informed about their status [as subjects of the caliphate]. The *Sumatra Post* newspaper in 1922 reported that "Muslims in Aceh recognize the caliphate in Istanbul. . . . The caliphate also sent delegations to Indonesia to support Muslims."
>
> In 1912, the same newspaper informed its readers that the [Ottoman] caliphate had sent a delegation to Indonesia to support Muslims in Indonesia. "The Dutch Consulate in Constantinople has reminded the government that the messenger of the Muhammadans has left Turkey for the Dutch-controlled Indonesia with the duty of motivating Muslims in Indonesia [to fight against the Dutch]." (HTI 2012)

In HTI's account, the prominent role of Islam in the struggle for independence is symbolized in the Jihad Resolution issued in 1945 by Hasyim Asy'ari, a renowned Muslim leader and one of the founders of Nahdlatul Ulama. The resolution calling for a military offensive against the Dutch after independence was declared in 1945. According to HTI, this anticolonial fatwa shows the centrality of Islam in the process of Indonesian independence.

On the basis of these and other historical accounts, the HTI argues that the existing Pancasila and the Indonesian system of democracy actually are deviations from the ideals of the nation's founding fathers. Even though not all Indonesian are Muslims, HTI insists that Muslims deserve to have their religion as the foundation of the state because of the dominant role of Muslim leaders in the struggle for independence.

For HTI there is no question that the demand for an Islamic state was a consensus among Muslim leaders, as shown clearly in the discussion within the team that prepared the constitution for Indonesia (BPUPKI) in 1945.

This demand came not only from Islamist leaders who are famous for their aspirations for an Islamic state, such as M. Natsir of Masyumi and Kahar Muzakkar of Darul Islam, but also from major Muslim organizations including Nahdlatul Ulama and Muhammadiyah. HTI claims that NU's support of Islamic state was illustrated in the following view of Kyai Masykur in the debate about the requirement of the head of state. "If in Indonesia implementation of shariah laws by Muslims is an obligation, and yet the Republic is headed by non-Muslims, can this effectively work? And can a Muslim group accept this? Isn't this an evil desire?" (HTI 2012). The demand was reiterated in a famous speech by a representative of Muhammadiyah in the parliament, Ki Bagus Hadikusumo. HTI highlights this passage from Hadikusumo's speech: "I seek protection in Allah from Satan the destroyer. Gentlemen, it has been frequently stated here that Islam is the state ideology. Therefore, the state cannot be separated from Islam. Thus I support the suggestion of Mr. Kahar Muzakkir. If the ideology of Islam is not agreed upon as the basis of the state, [I] cannot accept it! It seems clear that this parliament is instead going to define this state as not standing on Islam and as a neutral state" (HTI 2010e).

For HTI, these historical reports demonstrate that Indonesia's current political system is a betrayal of the goals and aspirations of Muslim leaders at the time of Indonesia's establishment. The nation-state system with its Pancasila philosophy was instituted only as a result of the deception of Soekarno, who hinted that the implementation of Islamic law would be possible at some later date after the establishment of Indonesian independence.

NU against Nationalism

Also central to HTI's argument in support of a caliphate is the claim that the fall of the Ottoman Empire in 1924 was the result of Western colonial propagation of ethno-nationalism against the Ottoman Empire and against the ideals of a global caliphate. By making this claim, HTI seeks to justify its claim that Indonesia should reidentify itself as a Muslim nation that seeks once again to become part of the global caliphate.

Perhaps the biggest challenge to this element in the HTI campaign is the stated position of Indonesia's two largest Muslim organizations, NU and Muhammadiyah, which have together served to affirm the Islamic foundations of Indonesian nationalism. The two organizations function as the backbone of an Indonesian nationalism that acknowledges the important place of religion without calling for the nation to become a theocratic state. Recognizing the two organizations' nationalist commitments, HTI has published a series of articles claiming to show that the founders of both NU and Muhammadiyah were in fact opposed to nationalism and called for Indonesian unity based solely on Islam. The following narrative refers to this series of HTI publications.[4]

HTI highlights a chapter of Hasyim Asy'ari's book *Irshadul mukminin ila Sirati Sayyidil Mursalin* to suggest that the founder of NU was actually opposed to nationalism. According to HTI, Hasyim Asy'ari called for Muslims to eschew all communal sentiments, including patriotism, ethnicity, and nationalism. It quotes this paragraph from his book: "Therefore leave aside differences of kind (*jinsiyah* [sex]), patriotism (*qoumiyah* [ethnicity/tribe]), language (*lughowiyah*), and nationalism (*watahaniyah*). It is these sentiments that caused enmity, hatred, and injustice. They all are brothers because of God's blessing. Arabs, Persians, Romans, Indians, Turks, Europeans, Indonesians are all supporting each other for the love of Allah. They share one goal: that is, MAKE THE WORDS OF ALLAH GLORIOUS, MAKE THE WORDS OF SATAN DEFEATED" (Syabab Indonesia 2015). The publication even includes a photograph of the page to add to its credibility. Interestingly, however, although this quotation seems to reject nationalism, it does not explicitly show Hasyim Asy'ari's support for a caliphate. To lend credence to the latter claim, the book presents other evidence, such as stories about Hasyim Asy'ari's contact with officers of the caliphate government in Turkey in the course of the anticolonial struggle. Asy'ari's anticolonial spirit, HTI claims, was formed during his time in Mecca, when he personally witnessed the fall of the caliphate government in Turkey. HTI cites a 1994 book by Muhammad Asad Syihab that tells a story about Hasyim Asy'ari praying next to the Ka'bah and declaring his determination to raise the banners of Islam and fight against the colonial powers. HTI interprets this as evidence of the commitment of the founder of NU to the establishment of a caliphate.

HTI further uses this narrative to reinterpret a quotation from Hasyim Asy'ari that is popular among traditional Muslims as a basis for associating Islam and nationalism: "Hubbul wathon minal iman" (Love for the nation is part of Islam). For HTI this phrase does not indicate that Hasyim Asy'ari is pronationalist but should be understood as a reflection of his anticolonial spirit. This spirit was further confirmed when he declared the struggle against the Dutch to be a holy war (*jihad*) and called his troops *Laskar Sabilillah* (Armies on the Path of Allah).

This characterization of Hasyim Asy'ari as an antinationalist, however, contradicts the common view within NU circles that in fact he was one of the fathers of Indonesian nationalism. Recently a poster circulated in social media quoted Asy'ari as stating, "Religion and nationalism are two pillars that are not mutually opposed. Nationalism is part of religion, and each strengthens the other." The poster with the picture of Hasyim Asy'ari was circulated in NU circles and was clearly meant to counter HTI's portrayal of Asy'ari as opposed to nationalism and the nation-state (Muslim Media News 2015). By contrast, a different poster released by HTI quotes Asy'ari as saying that those who say that Islamic law is not applicable in the present day are apostates. Even though the words do not explicitly express Asy'ari's support for the establishment of an Islamic state, HTI uses the statement to imply that its campaign for a caliphate is consistent with the views of the revered founder of NU.

The Caliphate and Islam in Indonesia

Even though Indonesia is geographically far from the former center of the Ottoman Empire in Istanbul, HTI claims that Islam in Indonesia had a close relationship with the caliphate in the early twentieth century. The major Muslim organizations in Indonesia, especially NU, were, in HTI's view, founded after the fall of the Ottoman Empire as continuations of Nusantara Muslims' past association with the caliphate authorities in Turkey.

As HTI narrates, in 1924 Muslim leaders in Indonesia were shaken by the declaration of the end of the caliphate government in Turkey. In response, they formed a caliphate committee in Surabaya led by Wondo-sudirdjo and KH A. Wahab Hasbullah, representing modernist and tradi-tionalist Muslims. The committee was tasked with preparing what HTI calls a "caliphate proposal" that was to be delivered in a so-called caliphate confer-ence in Cairo. It is not clear what was meant by this "caliphate proposal," but HTI claims that Indonesian Muslim leaders were concerned by the fall of the caliphate government. The conference was followed by a series of Islamic congresses in Yogyakarta, Bandung, and Surabaya with the main purpose of uniting Muslims after the fall of the caliphate.

For traditionalist Muslims in Indonesia, a central obstacle to uniting Muslims was their concern over the puritanical and antitraditionalist policies of the Saudi Arabian government, including the latter's destruction of Muslim shrines and sites of saint remembrance. Traditionalists consequently sent a delegation as a part of a "Caliphate Committee" to demand that the Saudi government abandon these latter policies. HTI acknowledges that in the beginning this theological schism was central to discussions within the committee. However, it claims that by the later period the main focus of Muslim leaders was unity among Muslims and therefore a search for a way to revive global caliphate governance.

> Historically, the birth of NU is inseparable from the concern for the caliphate. . . . From the beginning NU has never followed secular thought, nor has it ever opposed the formalization of shariah. However, NU does not employ the methods of confrontation or violence and instead chooses a gradual approach toward raising awareness. This is because NU activism has been based on *kaidah fiqhiyah* [principles of Islamic jurisprudence], which say, "Mâ lâ yudraku kulluh lâ yutraku kulluh" (Do not abandon everything if all cannot be achieved) and "Dar' al-mafâsid muqaddamun 'ala jalb al-mashâlih" (Preventing harm is preferable to upholding good conduct). (HTI 2009a)

HTI devotes considerably more of its effort to seek legitimation for the concept of a caliphate from religious authorities within NU than it does from other Muslim organizations. This tactic makes sense because NU is the largest Muslim civil society in Indonesia, and it promotes the idea that Islam and nationalism are compatible. However, because HTI is conscious of the deep cleavages among Muslims in Indonesia, it also makes reference to other Muslim leaders. For example, it cites Ahmad Dahlan, the founder of Muhammadiyah, claiming that he too was a supporter of the formal implementation of shariah and Islam. Even nationalist leaders like the Sarekat Islam's Cokroaminoto, HTI suggests, openly advocated the necessity of shariah implementation for Indonesia. HTI cites this statement of Cokroaminoto: "Even though we have gained our independence, our state and nation will never achieve a just, prosperous way of life and peaceful relations so long as Islamic teachings are not implemented as state laws" (HTI 2012).

By linking these stories and statements to the fall of the caliphate, HTI seeks to demonstrate conclusively that its campaign for the restoration of the caliphate is in line with the deepest aspirations of Indonesia's founding leaders.

SCALING UP: MOBILIZING AMONG ISLAMIC COMMUNITIES

HTI's strategy of "bandwagoning" with mainstream Muslim organizations clearly has helped the movement make progress toward its goal of infiltrating Muslim society and state bureaucracies. In this section, I will discuss conditions and opportunities that have allowed HTI to make progress in these sectors.

Taking Advantage of the "Conservative Turn"

HTI's mobilization has been made possible not only by the political freedom it enjoys but also by developments within Indonesia's Muslim community, events characterized by Martin van Bruinessen (2013b) as the "conservative turn" in Indonesian Islam since the early 2000s (see also Hefner, chapter 1). This conservatism has been expressed primarily by the growing campaign against religious minorities and growing demands for the "Islamization" of public life. Certainly such conservatism is not universal in Muslim circles. Many leaders and communities have countered the conservative campaign by promoting the values of national integration and peaceful coexistence. At the national level, the election of the staunch nationalist Joko Widodo to the presidency in 2014 and 2019 illustrated that, at least politically, there were limits to the conservative turn.

It is nonetheless undeniable that some segments of Muslim society in Indonesia have become more conservative in the *Reformasi* era, and this has provided HTI with an opportunity for mobilization. In the recent period, no issue has united Muslims more across a broad spectrum than the calls beginning in 2007–8 for heightened government action in two spheres:

against pornography and against groups deemed heretical to Islam. In other countries, pornography may be a nonsectarian issue, but in Indonesia it has been primarily problematized by conservative and hard-line Muslim groups. Similarly, the Ahmadiya has been a regular target of attack for HTI, in large part because most mainstream Muslim organizations (including the NU and Muhammadiyah) have called for limits on the group's freedom (HTI 2007d). In lending its support to the anti-Ahmadiya and antipornography campaigns, HTI has been able to present itself as solidly in the Muslim mainstream.

HTI has in fact played a pivotal role in many of these campaigns. This fact was recognized, for example, in a report issued by the International Crisis Group (ICG) that highlighted the role of HTI with regard to the government's ruling against Ahmadiya. HTI worked carefully to coordinate its campaign with the semigovernmental Council of Indonesian Ulama (Majelis Ulama Indonesia, MUI), as well as the Islamic Ummah Forum (Forum Ukhuwah Islamiyah, FUI) and the hard-line militia, the Islamic Defenders' Front (Front Pembela Islam, FPI).[5] While the MUI, a semigovernmental body that represents diverse Muslim groups, worked from within the bureaucracy to pressure the government, HTI took to the streets in collaboration with the FUI, citing the MUI's statements to justify its street protests (ICG 2008, 8–15). HTI's former leader Muhammad Al-Khattah was a key figure in the mobilization of the masses through rallies and ulama gatherings. But Al-Khattah was not the only one from HTI to play a role in providing the MUI with large-scale support. The national spokesperson for HTI, Ismail Yusanto, was also frequently involved in anti-Ahmadiya rallies and ulama gatherings.

It is clear that in campaigning against the Ahmadiya what was important for HTI was not just government action against a small religious organization but HTI's own ability to exercise growing influence in the broader Muslim community. A similar aim underlay HTI participation in the antipornography campaign. In support of the proposed bill on pornography, HTI organized rallies across the nation that demanded measures to "clean Indonesia from pornography and *pornoaksi* [pornographic behaviors] through shariah and the caliphate" (HTI 2008a). The group explained that its position was neither to support nor to challenge the antipornography law but to call for the elimination of pornography and related activities through

128 MOHAMMAD IQBAL AHNAF

the full implementation of shariah and the establishment of a caliphate rather than through the medium of secular legislation (HTI 2008b). The HTI spokesperson Yusanto told an interviewer that the issue of pornography was proof of the relevance of its campaign for shariah: "Here lies the importance of the application of the shariah in society at large. Shariah will provide clear and consistent rules that will apply for all people for all issues, including pornography and pornographic actions. This can be effective only if shariah is implemented comprehensively within the institution of the caliphate. In this way the beneficial aspects of shariah can be realized" (HTI 2008a).

Following the pattern of using popular issues to create sectarian divides, HTI also identified the antipornography campaign as part of a continuing battle between Islam and secularism. The cover of an issue of the HTI magazine *Al-Wa'ie* carried the headline "Draft of Pornographic Law: A Battle between Islam and Secularism" (HTI 2008c).

The MUI's Inclusion Policy

The second post-Soeharto development that has favored HTI's mobilization has been the changing character of the MUI (see Hefner, chapter 1). During the Soeharto administration the MUI was for the most part state oriented, issuing declarations serving the regime's interests and challenging state policies on only a few occasions. Even though it is formally a nongovernmental organization, the MUI has received funding from the government since it was created and has consistently played its part in issuing fatwas to support government development programs. As Nur Ichwan (2005) has explained, after the fall of Soeharto the MUI appeared to shift its allegiances away from the state to the Muslim community (*ummah*) and society. Although it continued to receive funds from the government, the council was given the authority to manage certain Islamic charities and to issue halal certificates, thereby enhancing its financial capabilities and making it increasingly independent from state influence. The MUI still assumes a bridging role between the government and the Muslim community, but it has also moved much closer to socially conservative Muslim groups (Ichwan 2005).

As a part of its effort to reach out to the broader *ummah*, the MUI has become more involved in Muslim politics. In the 1999 election, for example, the Council released a statement of advice (*tausiyah*) supporting Islamic leaders who were opposed to non-Muslim candidates (Ichwan 2005, 56–58). The MUI also became more actively involved in state-promoted Islamization. The most notable indication of this is the widening of the MUI's membership to include activists from new groups, including those with decidedly extreme or radical orientations (Ichwan 2005, 49). With representatives from Islamist groups in its internal structure, the MUI facilitated the formation of Muslim intergroup alliances, such as the FUI and Forum Umat Islam (the Islamic Ummah Forum). Both groups have played a central role in supporting the state-aided Islamization of public affairs, including the campaign for shariah-friendly regulations in certain localities.

The MUI's accommodation with Islamist politics, however, has had certain limits. The MUI's commitment to the state ideology of the Pancasila, democracy, and national integration remains a key point of difference with most Islamist groups, including HTI. Nevertheless, this shift on the part of the MUI leadership has created optimism among Islamists in groups like HTI. In response to these trends, HTI has actively reached out to the MUI to strengthen its own efforts to gain influence in Muslim communities. One example of HTI's engagement with the MUI is its participation in the meetings of the Congress of the Indonesian Muslim Ummah (KUII) organized by the MUI, especially the fifth congress held in May 2010 in Jakarta. This assembly was intended to facilitate the creation of a common strategy for Muslim organizations within diverse sectors of public life, including, most notably, efforts to implement shariah regulations at the regional and national level (Jaringan Islam Liberal 2005). The secretary general of the FUI, Muhammad Al-Khattath, predicted that the congress would lead to a "breakthrough" for the implementation of shariah in all domains of state and society (Suara Islam 2010a).

It was no surprise, therefore, that the HTI saw the congress as a "strategic forum" (HTI 2010e). For this reason, it sought full participation in the congress and expressed its disappointment when the organizers announced that they planned to exclude so-called controversial organizations, including HTI, the Majelis Mujahidin Indonesia / Indonesian Mujahidin Council (MMI), and the FPI (Suara Islam 2010b). This exclusion sparked anger on the part of the MMI and the FPI, both of whom demanded an apology from the congress's organizers. HTI opted for a less confrontational approach by lobbying the congress's organization committee to allow HTI and other militant groups to attend. In the end, the organizing committee reversed its decision and HTI announced its intention to attend (HTI 2010d). In the fifth KUII in 2010, HTI succeeded in getting five of its members into the congress session. Two of them, M. R. Kurnia and Harist Abu Ulya, attended as representatives of HTI, while the other three were representing MUI branches in the provinces of Riau, Bangka Belitung, and Banten. HTI prepared a concept paper on the relevant aspects of shariah to be proposed as a discussion topic at congress sessions. During a session on Muslim leadership, Kurnia proposed four criteria for a political leader. None of them explicitly required a commitment to the caliphate. Instead, he promoted character attributes such as possessing an Islamic personality, defending Islamic teaching from heresies and liberal ideas, being committed to the struggle for the implementation of shariah, and being able to unite the *ummah* (HTI 2010g). HTI accepted the neutral terms of the resolution and put aside its own principles calling for Muslims to challenge or disengage from the existing democratic system.

On another occasion, a local leader of HTI from Riau mentioned the caliphate during a plenary session. He suggested that "any leader integrated into government leadership should be able to enforce shariah." Because a leader has to play a role at the national and international level, he said, "that type of leadership is called caliphate" (HTI 2010g). HTI's leaders from its national board, however, chose a different tone. In a comment made in the aftermath of the congress, Ismail Yusanto admitted that promoting the idea of the caliphate was difficult because of resistance from attendees at the congress. But he claimed that other appeals, including calls for the government to withdraw from the capitalist system and adopt a shariah-based economy, were welcomed (HTI 2010b).

The outcomes of the congress were minimal compared to HTI's goal of steering public opposition to the established political system and the campaign for the caliphate. The congress produced a document called the Jakarta Declaration 2010, consisting of six recommendations that can be read as "integrationist" in nature with regard to the relationship between the government and Islam. Only the resolution that spoke of the importance of "shariah law in all aspects of life" resembled the HTI's earlier proposal. Opposition to capitalism, one of HTI's most frequent rhetorical themes, did not feature in the congress's declaration. The key question of whether the existing political system should be replaced by a shariah-based political system was also not addressed in the resolution. These abstract and "integrationist" recommendations were nonetheless welcomed and used by HTI as evidence of a supposed consensus among the ulama on the failure of the existing political system.

MOBILIZING WITHIN THE BUREAUCRACY

Despite its nonparticipation doctrine, HTI does not always close the door to engaging with those in government. In fact, many members of HTI work as middle-class civil servants—including state university lecturers, government bureaucrats, and experts in the state-funded Indonesian Institute of Sciences. HTI's policy prohibits its members from occupying positions that support (*wasilah*) prohibited conduct (*haram*) such as charging interest or enforcing laws deemed un-Islamic. Included in this category of prohibited activities is being employed in banks and insurance companies as well as serving in the House of Representatives. HTI does allow member participation in professions like law, on the condition that lawyers and judges make only decisions based on shariah—although this is clearly unrealistic because judges in civil courts are bound by national laws. In reality, HTI has used the services of lawyers to defend Muslims' rights within the parameters of existing Indonesian law (HTI 2010a).

An example of HTI's successful collaboration with government was a series of events involving the former governor of South Sumatra, Mahyuddin, a medical doctor and a politician in the ruling Democratic Party. Mahyuddin was notorious for his banning of Islamic groups deemed deviationist. Aside from these actions, he had no record of implementing shariah-friendly policies. Nonetheless, HTI had collaborated with him on a number of occasions, including a seminar involving representatives of Muslim organizations, local companies, and government agencies to discuss the exploitation of natural resources in a shariah-compliant manner, an event held in the governor's office. On another occasion, HTI took advantage of its relationship with the governor's wife to hold a seminar on the political roles of Muslim women, which was sponsored by the government (HTI 2007c).

HTI has not seemed particularly concerned about the backgrounds or reputations of the political leaders it targets for cooperation. Nor have records of corruption bothered HTI in its quest for opportunities to mobilize government officials. An example of HTI's relationships with this type of leader was its interaction with Ali Mazi, the former governor of Southeast Sulawesi who was temporarily removed from office in 2006 because of a graft charge relating to the management of Indonesia's National Stadium in Jakarta. He regained his position in 2007 after the state prosecutor failed to prove the allegation. HTI's engagement with him took place also in 2007, after the international caliphate conference in Jakarta, when it organized a series of promotional programs to spread the results of the conference in many cities across Indonesia. In Southeast Sulawesi, it needed Mazi's support to organize a screening of a video of the caliphate conference in his office with representatives from various Muslim organizations (HTI 2007a). When Mazi was temporarily inactive because of the corruption charge, HTI approached his deputy, Yusron A. Silonde. Knowing that Silonde was preparing to run as a candidate for governor in the next election, HTI paid him a visit and suggested that he implement shariah law once in power (HTI 2007a).

In other locales, HTI joined government campaigns so as to expand its audience. Through this strategy, it appears to have had some success in infiltrating school systems in several cities. In Bogor, for example, HTI cooperated with local offices of the Ministry of Education to hold a series of training sessions for school teachers and principals in the region on teaching Islamic history (HTI 2007a). This provided HTI with an audience to preach its version of Islamic history focusing on the importance of the caliphate. Similar progress was made in Pasuruan, East Java, where HTI was successful in gaining permission from the local office of the Education Ministry to organize Islamic study groups in schools (HTI 2009b). Sometimes the topic offered by the government was unusual or seemed contradictory to official HTI views. In Ngawi, East Java, HTI collaborated with the local office of the Education Ministry to hold a workshop on "healthy reproduction," a campaign it usually portrays as a product of Western propaganda (Syam 2005, 9–14).

Another model of HTI's engagement with the government has centered on involving state officials in its activities. HTI often holds leadership meetings using government facilities and bringing in representatives from the government to deliver opening speeches. Elsewhere, HTI has participated in city parades organized by government and Muslim groups, carrying banners that challenge democracy and promote shariah and the caliphate.

These instances of engagement with the government illustrate HTI's adoption of a strategy of what the Italian Marxist theorist Antonio Gramsci called "a war of position": creating alternative influences in communities without directly confronting their ruling elites. A true revolution, according to Gramsci, is not just about taking over the state but about establishing institutional, intellectual, and moral hegemony. Once a revolutionary movement is successful in gaining a position in the society, it already exercises leadership in opposition to the state, and, with this leadership, revolution may be imminent (Adamson 1980, 222).

GROWING OPPOSITION TO HTI

In July 2016, when I was in Kupang, West Timor, I found that HTI was perceived by both Muslim and Christian communities as a threat to the interreligious harmony that has been the pride of people in Kupang. In this Christian-majority province, the presence of HTI could not be more controversial. HTI was perceived as campaigning against the national ideology, the Pancasila, as well as the related principle of national unity (NKRI), and its presence provoked strong objections from all local communities. In Kupang, a group of Christian youth used force to break up a HTI meeting. The group then continued marching toward the main HTI office in the city and took down the banner from the office (*Timor Express* 2015). Interestingly, Muslim organizations in the city did not come to HTI's defense and instead organized an interfaith gathering to counter religious extremism and antinationalist movements with specific reference to HTI. In this instance, then, the HTI was put in the same box as extremist threats like ISIS and al-Qaeda.

Such measures against HTI do not just take place in Christian-majority areas. A similar reaction has been growing in Java, where concerns over HTI tactics and ideology have been intensifying in the last few years. The former national chairman of NU, Hasyim Muzadi, has expressed concerns about the threat of Islamic extremism by using the term *transnational Islam*, a clear reference to HTI. For Muzadi, the idea of establishing a caliphate is simply not compatible with the values and aspirations of Muslim Indonesians. To protect national integration he has demanded that the campaign for a caliphate be legally proscribed (Muslim Media News 2014). Many NU leaders equate the HTI threat with Middle Eastern–oriented Wahhabism. It was this concern that led the current leaders of Indonesia's largest Muslim organization to promote what they regard as the authentic local practice of Islam, which they call "Islam Nusantara" (NU Online 2015a).

This opposition to HTI has also become a prominent feature of activities among the youth wing of NU, Ansor, which has played a leading role in countering HTI activism. In a number of incidents Ansor attempted to disrupt or close down HTI public events. Opposition to HTI has also led to accusations that the organization is guilty of treason. In Jember, East Java, youth members of NU interrupted an HTI gathering and demanded that the organizers of the event sign a paper that declared loyalty to the national ideology. HTI leaders rejected the demand and opted to disband the gathering. Elsewhere youth organizations from NU have approached local authorities and demanded restrictions on HTI activities (NU Online 2016; Metro TV News 2016; Bangsa Online 2016; Detik 2016). Some Indonesian proponents of human rights and liberal freedom have expressed concerns about actions like these, but in 2016 and 2017 mainstream Muslim opposition to HTI only intensified.

Opposition to HTI is shared by Muhammadiyah, the second-largest Muslim organization, although the sentiment is less pronounced than in NU. A number of Muhammadiyah leaders have raised concern about the use of Muhammadiyah facilities by "outside groups," including those associated with HTI. As early as 2006, a prominent leader of Muhammadiyah, Abdul Munir Mulkhan, triggered a debate within the organization after he expressed concerns about the infiltration of groups like HTI into Muhammadiyah. Mulkhan's views were soon echoed by other actors within the organization and on the pages of Muhammadiyah's official journal, *Suara Muhammadiyah* (Mulkhan 2006). In 2007, the national leadership of Muhammadiyah published several circulars and guides designed to advise its members on how to defend Muhammadiyah institutions from infiltration by outside groups (see Nashir 2007; Setiawan 2006). The opposition of leaders within NU and Muhammadiyah has clearly undercut HTI's strategy of bandwagoning on the influence of larger Muslim organizations.

Anti-HTI sentiment has also risen outside these two mainstream Muslim organizations. In 2016, Bima Arya, the mayor of Bogor, a cosmopolitan city in West Java, provoked public outcry after attending an HTI gathering at city hall. The protest forced the mayor to make a public statement declaring his opposition to HTI's idea of the caliphate (BBC Indonesia 2016). Another setback against HTI's scaling-up efforts was a rally organized by lecturers and students at Indonesia's distinguished national art university (Institute Seni Indonesia) in Yogyakarta to protest growing HTI influence in the university. As a number of the lecturers in the university had joined HTI, they used their teaching authority to prohibit drawing or painting the human body because they believed that it is forbidden in Islam. Promoting such a conservative policy in the university was considered an attack on the university's artistic and pedagogical mission. As a result, the rector of the university joined the rally opposing HTI (*Tempo* 2016).

The anti-HTI sentiment that occurred among mainstream religious organizations and on university campuses was especially significant because these were the two social fields in which HTI previously had made some headway in its mission of recruitment and mobilization. The organization's very success contributed to the realization in other circles that its continuing progress was a serious threat to Indonesian nationhood and religious coexistence.

HTI AND DIFFERENTIATED CITIZENSHIP

Until its dissolution in July 2017, HTI was regarded by its international sponsors as the most successful branch of the global Hizbut Tahrir movement. In most countries, the movement has struggled for followers or been subject to draconian bans. After its official dissolution here in Indonesia, HTI lost its ability to maneuver openly and, no less important, lost all access to the state bureaucracy. It was the latter access, which the HTI had enjoyed for more than ten years, that most helped the organization expand its influence. Notwithstanding the government crackdown, however, no HTI leaders or activists have been prosecuted, and the organization remains active despite its having been banned. As I have written elsewhere (Ahnaf 2017), HTI sustains itself by allying with opposition forces. However, even this strategy faces new challenges today. Because the strategy of bandwagoning with mainstream Muslim organizations such as NU and Muhammadiyah is now impossible, HTI has shifted its attention to those oppositional segments of society that afford it protection without attracting too much attention from security agencies. HTI has taken particular advantage of oppositional grievances emerging in the context of polarizing elections, as occurred in the 2017 gubernatorial campaign in Jakarta. To evade state restrictions, the organization now uses anonymous online accounts, channels its activities through affiliate organizations, and, for its publications, relies on publishers who avoid any mention of the Hizbut Tahrir Indonesia name. These actions are intended to help the organization survive while it awaits a more friendly political climate. In the 2019 elections, HTI urged its membership to vote for Prabowo Subianto, along with (for the national assembly) political parties like the Prosperous Justice Party (PKS), who remain outside the government coalition. The results of the 2019 election did not favor Prabowo or the opposition, and it is likely that HTI will have to endure a period of greatly restricted operation for some time to come.

These developments show that HTI may have reached the limits of its organizational growth. The movement's rejection of democracy, its opposition to Pancasila nationalism, and its emphasis on the *khilafah* have catalyzed significant resistance in growing segments of Indonesian Muslim society. Its members now face the difficult choice of "scaling down" their opposition to Indonesian traditions of multiconfessional citizenship and Pancasila tolerance.

These trends do not mean that the HTI campaign has come to an end. Although they cannot proselytize or organize demonstrations, the HTI membership is not otherwise banned from participating in mosque worship or public life. More significantly, the HTI rank-and-file remain adept in taking advantage of the openings provided by democratic freedoms and circumventing legal restrictions. At the grassroots, for example, distribution of HTI's weekly newsletter during Friday mosque prayers continues in many cities and towns; HTI also continues to hold informal gatherings for its leaders and youth. However, for the moment, one of the organization's main avenues for mobilization and recruitment—public demonstrations—appears closed.

HTI has recently benefited from the growing sectarianism in some segments of Muslim society, especially after Islamist hard-liners in 2016–17 formed an alliance in opposition to the ruling nationalist government of President Jokowi. This made it acceptable for Muslims of various political orientations to ally with HTI, allowing HTI to promote discourses of Muslim political supremacy and differentiated citizenship in Indonesia (see Hefner, chapter 1). HTI penetrated Muslim society, promoting suspicion, fear, and polarization between Muslims and non-Muslims. The resulting climate of antagonism allowed HTI activists to attempt to rewrite the normativities of post-*Reformasi* Indonesian politics, propagating the claim that the Pancasila, the ideals of the Indonesian Republic, and democracy itself were the products of Western political influences—and that they were not final in their national institutional form.

In retrospect, too, it is clear that HTI's emphasis on the establishment of a global caliphate has not only isolated the organization from many in Muslim society but also raised nationalist ire. HTI is rightly seen by many Indonesians as opposed to Indonesian nationhood and Pancasila pluralism, at least as currently understood by most supporters of these traditions. In response to growing opposition in the 2010s, HTI slightly adjusted its rhetoric against the Pancasila and nationalist ideals, but it did so in a way that many Indonesians regarded as unconvincing. The groundswell of opposition to HTI thus grew, ultimately resulting in a successful campaign by Muslim mass organizations and the state to ban the organization from the public sphere entirely. It is not yet clear whether the aspiration for Muslim supremacy and a religiously differentiated citizenship has also declined with HTI's banning.

NOTES

1. Other groups hold strong Islamic-state orientations but either adopt softer terms such as "formalization of shariah" (Majelis Mujahidin Indonesia [MMI]) or call for the creation of an Islamic state but through underground struggles (Jemaah Islamiyah and Negara Islam Indonesia [NII]). For HTI opposition to democracy, see HTI (2007b). On Majelis Mujahidin Indonesia, see Ahnaf (2006); on Jemaah Islamiyah, see ICG (2003, 2007, 2008) and Barton (2005); on the NII,

see ICG (2005) and Ridwan (2008); and on the genealogies of Islamic radicalism in post-Soeharto Indonesia, see Bruinessen (2002).

2. Here and elsewhere in the chapter, translations from Indonesian-language sources are my own.

3. "Bandwagoning" was listed as one of seven techniques of propaganda used by the Nazis. Theoretically, the technique refers to a strategy of communication that intentionally misleads an audience into believing that its own aspirations are those of the movement or group making an appeal (Yourman 1939).

4. These sources include Syabab Indonesia (2015) and HTI (2009a, 2010c, 2010e, 2010f, 2015).

5. The FUI (Islamic Ummah Forum) is an alliance of conservative and Islamist sociopolitical organizations. The group's chairman is a former leader of HTI, Muhammad Al-Khattath.

"Enough Is Enough"

Scaling Up Peace in Postconflict Ambon

MARTHEN TAHUN

During my first weeks in Ambon in late 2015, I received advice from my Christian host to take care when visiting the neighboring Muslim areas of Batu Merah and Kebun Cengkeh. Before the Ambon conflict broke out in 1999, there had been Christians living in both villages, but today all the inhabitants are Muslim. The situation is quite similar in many Christian villages—Christian-majority villages that once had some Muslim residents today have none. Another warning I regularly received was not to eat or drink anything but water when I visited Muslim neighborhoods. "We never know what they put in the food," said my host. Similar stories were told by Muslims—beware of the food cooked by Christians, since it may be contaminated by pork.

During my field research, I violated both recommendations—visiting Muslim areas, including Batu Merah, and passing through an area that once had been a base for the radical Islamist armed militia Laskar Jihad. I also took meals in these areas. Not having experienced the trauma that my host had, and already having many Christian and Muslim friends in these areas, I felt safe. Nonetheless my Christian host was stunned.

This is the face of today's Ambon. Ambon is said to be at peace, but there is also much interreligious prejudice and distrust. Though the large-scale Christian-Muslim violent conflict that started in 1999 subsided by 2004, residential segregation by religion remains widespread. So too does interreligious prejudice; indeed, it is taken for granted. Ambonese society has not fully recovered from the bloody, violent ethnic and religious conflict of 1999–2002 that swept not only Ambon but all of Maluku as well. Dealing with the segregated communities and maintaining peace now have become the postconflict challenge.

This chapter is not so much about causes of the conflict—whether it was a religious, an ethnic, or a political-economic conflict—or about today's problems of prejudice and segregation. The focus in this chapter is on how, despite the past enmity, prejudice, and segregation, people are trying to build and maintain peace. Primarily focusing on the postconflict situation, this chapter begins with a brief historical overview of Ambon, including its colonial legacy, its demography, and the course of the conflict itself. I attempt to explain how these circumstances gave rise to a strong aspiration for peace. While *adat*—tradition and customary law (see Hefner, chapter 1; Larson, chapter 2; and Swazey, chapter 3)—and religion provide some of the normative framework for peace, I argue that the dominant influence today is the almost universal realization that conflict did not bring any good. This sentiment and the norms to which it gives rise are grounded in the collective memory of the conflict. I then discuss a focal incident, an outbreak of new violence in 2011 in Gunung Nona, an incident that tested the postconflict framework for peace. In the next section of this chapter I map the organizations working today for peace and reconciliation, paying particular attention to their efforts to scale up pluralist coexistence through different activities centered on youth and women, through the peace pacts known as *pela*, and through interreligious collaboration. These initiatives demonstrate that, compared to many other postconflict regions in Indonesia, Ambon has seen an exceptional proliferation of organizations and activities working for peace. In the final section of the chapter I discuss the prospects for peace in Ambon by examining the main sites of normative work for peace and reconciliation—involving collective memory of conflict, the revival of *adat*, and religion.[1]

SEGREGATION BEFORE AND AFTER
THE CONFLICT

At the dawn of the sixteenth century, after a long search for the spice-producing islands, Europeans arrived in Maluku. The arrival of Portuguese in 1512 and the Spanish in 1521 turned Maluku into a site of commercial and political competition both with local traders and kingdoms and among European countries. Later, when the Dutch arrived in 1599, the commercial rivalry between Spain and Portugal sparked warfare. In 1605 the Dutch seized and occupied the Portuguese fort in Ambon, changed its name to "Victoria," and made it their base for political, trade, and military activities in eastern Indonesia (Andaya 1993, 114–39; Knaap 2003, 176; Burnet 2013, 162–63). Through the East Indies Company (Vereenigde Oostindische Compagnie, or VOC), the Dutch successfully monopolized the spice trade in the archipelago and maintained a presence in Maluku for nearly three centuries, longer than other European powers.

To establish its power, the VOC designated Ambon as its base for economic, political, and military domination in eastern Indonesia. The city of Ambon, which is located between Ambon Bay and the mountains of the Leitimur Peninsula, grew after the Portuguese built a fortress called Nossa Senhora da Anunciada at the end of the sixteenth century. As power shifted from the Portuguese to the Dutch, Catholic converts renounced their allegiance to Portuguese authorities that had begun when the Jesuit missionary Francis Xavier stopped in Ambon in 1546 and introduced Catholicism. At the same time, people in Leihitu on the northern coast of the island had already embraced Islam, as the result of the influence both of Islamic kingdoms in North Maluku and of the Javanese and Makassarese merchants who had arrived long before the Europeans.

In 1683, the VOC established three regional administrations in Ternate, Ambon, and Banda, which today comprise Maluku Province and North Maluku Province. In 1817, the three districts were brought under a single government, called the Gouvernement der Molukken, with Ambon as its capital. One VOC policy, which dramatically affected local demography, was forced migration. In an effort to control labor and production, whole communities were forcibly relocated from mountain to coastal areas

(Kroeskamp 1974, 49; Knaap 1995, 237; 2003, 182). Food crises caused by colonial policies also resulted in significant internal migration. Widespread food scarcity resulted when the Dutch administration demanded that local residents establish clove plantations on Ambon Island, forcing local people to cut down their sago palms, from which the native staple food was derived. Over time, local residents migrated across the Seram Strait to Seram Island, which was still rich in sago trees (Kroeskamp 1974, 51, 52).

After Indonesian independence, the former Dutch government in Maluku became Maluku Province, with Ambon as its capital. The province stretched from the Halmahera Islands in the north to the Kiser Islands in the southeast. By 1999, because of the challenges of maintaining effective government over a vast area with an increasing population, the central government in Jakarta welcomed a proposal to split the province into two, issuing decree Undang Undang Republik Indonesia No. 46 (1999), which established North Maluku Province as well as two new regencies within the remaining area of Maluku Province. New regencies and subdistricts have continued to be established in Maluku Province since the conflict.

Violence erupted in Ambon on January 19, 1999, the Muslim holiday of Eid al-Fitr, at the bus terminal in Batu Merah. The initial clash was between a handful of Muslim and Christian youth, but it quickly became a mass altercation between Muslims and Christians across Ambon Island and Central Maluku. The violence then spread to Southeast Maluku and North Maluku. In total, the conflict between 1999 and 2002 claimed some fifteen thousand lives and displaced 1.5 million people. It also damaged infrastructure and ruined sociocultural relations in Maluku (Klinken 2001, 2007; ICG 2000a, 2000b; Sidel 2008; Al Qurtuby 2013; Lattu 2014; Bräuchler 2015). As Gerry van Klinken (2007, 115–16) has observed, there were five phases to the conflict. The first phase was between January and May 1999. In mid-1999, the violence diminished in the run-up to the national elections, but by December it escalated to ghastly proportions again. The conflict climaxed in two especially infamous incidents. The first was the destruction of the Silo Church in downtown Ambon. The second was an especially bloody attack by a Christian militia on a group of villagers taking refuge in a mosque in Tobelo, North Maluku, which left some eight hundred Muslim villagers dead (Center for Humanitarian Dialogue 2011). The third phase started in April 2000 with the arrival of an armed Salafi militia from Java, the Laskar Jihad. The fourth phase involved periodic fighting through February 2002, when the Malino Pact II peace agreement was signed. The fifth phase was an attack on Soya Village, but this attack did not involve a large number of people. Since this final outbreak of violence, Ambon has in general been peaceful, with the notable exception of a clash that took place on April 25, 2004, following a parade commemorating the anniversary of the Republic of South Maluku, a largely Christian separatist movement that had been active in the 1950s.

In 2014, the population of Ambon City was 395,423, comprising Muslims (34.59 percent), Protestants (43.06 percent), Catholics (5.50 percent), Hindus (0.09 percent), and Buddhists (0.07 percent). Forty percent of the residents live in Sirimau Subdistrict, at the center of Ambon City (Seksi Integrasi Pengolahan dan Diseminasi Statistik 2015a). Ambon has long been a crossroads for travelers and merchants from different places, including Butonese, Chinese, Arabs, Makassarese, and Bugis, all of whom became integral parts of Ambon City history (Kroeskamp 1974, 50, 53; Chauvel 1990, 4). After independence, Ambon City was still a migration destination, both from within and outside Maluku Province. The 2015 census (section "Data Statistik Migrasi Maluku," in Seksi Integrasi Pengolahan dan Diseminasi Statistik 2015b) showed that 30 percent of the total population of Ambon City were permanent residents born outside Ambon City, the majority of whom came from outside Maluku Province. Judging from the pervasiveness of mixed families (*mata rumah*) in Ambon, the migrants are not only from other islands within Maluku Province, like the Central Maluku Islands, Banda Islands, Kei Islands, Aru Islands, and Ternate, but also from Papua, Java, Madura, and Bali, as well as India, China, and several Arab countries (Bartels 2017, 475–505).

From the perspective of religious demography, each social enclave in Ambon City has its own religious identity. For example, Batu Merah and Waringin Village are Muslim enclaves, while Batu Gajah, Kuda Mati, and Soya are Christian. Religiously based segregation had already begun in the colonial era, but it waned in recent decades as Christians moved into Muslim villages and vice versa. The conflict that started in 1999 has resulted in stronger segregation and was reinforced by a postconflict policy

that required refugees to reside in areas occupied by people of their own religion. This policy was supposed to be temporary, to keep security and
peace, but it has never been revised.

Boundaries of religion and ethnicity were likely factors in the conflict
and surely have solidified since. During the first days of conflict, migrants
from Bugis, Buton, and Makassar (BBM) fled because they were assumed
to control the local economy and were frightened by rumors that the native
Christian Malukans were going to attack them. Exchanges of insults and
vandalism toward religious symbols added greatly to the tensions between
Muslims and Christians.

But were the conflicts really ethno-religious in nature? Were there
other causes? Scholars have long debated this question (Klinken 2001,
2007; Spyer 2002; Bräuchler 2003; Bertrand 2002; Sidel 2006; Al Qurtuby
2013). Using the "communal contenders" network, Klinken (2001, 1) explains the origin of the conflict in terms of competition among local elites
that was the product of long-term social tensions and short-term instrumentalism. From this standpoint, issues of religion and ethnicity clearly
figure among the conflict's catalysts. These tensions were exacerbated during the post-Soeharto democratic transition by electoral campaigns and
disputes over the establishment and boundaries of a new province. Klinken (2007, 104) also argues that Ambon City was prone to conflict because many residents were dependent on the state for employment as civil
servants.

Using a different analytic perspective, Duncan (2005b) argues that focusing on local elites ignores factors that can explain why certain local interests would instigate violence. A holistic approach, he argues, is important for understanding the complexity of the conflict in Ambon. Duncan
offers an approach that includes focusing on the subjectivity and micro-
motivations of both victims and perpetrators to understand the causes and
consequences of the conflict. By means of careful documentation and interviews, Duncan is able to explain why individuals decided to become involved in the violence or refused. He also convincingly demonstrates that,
although religion itself may not have figured among the early causes of the
violence, over time many actors on both sides of the conflict began to think
of it in terms of religious blocs.

MEMORIES OF CONFLICT AND NORMATIVITIES
FOR PEACE

While scholars debate the origin and causes of the conflict, it has rarely been discussed openly by the Ambonese themselves. Klinken (2014, 1–11) identifies three reasons why people are reluctant to speak about what happened. The first is a fear that it will ruin the still-fragile social peace. The second is a fear that prominent institutions and actors in local society will be faulted for their actions and thus be embarrassed. The last is a fear of stirring up psychological trauma. Rizal Panggabean (2014, 389–94) has offered the term *positive avoidance* to describe this attempt to avoid discussing particular issues, especially if it will reopen old wounds and lead to new divisions.

In the course of my own fieldwork during 2015–16, I discovered that, although most people were reluctant to speak openly about the conflict and their own involvement, they were quite willing to claim that the conflict was initiated by "outsiders." This narrative that outsiders were the architects and instigators of the conflict has helped to unite communities, including neighbors and families. People stop blaming each other and instead identify themselves as victims. Regardless of the truth of this belief, it is apparently necessary for peace and has played an important role in the postconflict recovery.

In line with Panggabean's analysis, I see what is happening today as an effort to avoid divisions in society. No matter how important it may be in theory to discuss the conflict, the priority nowadays is to live in peace, move forward with development programs, and recover from conflict and prevent it from recurring. A few activists do feel that it is the government's responsibility to establish an accurate historical record, but in general they do not press the matter. There was indeed a fact-finding committee commissioned by the central government, which worked from January to December 2000, but its report was never made public.

Thus one overriding public ethical norm for peace and recognition in Ambon is grounded in the painful collective memory of the conflict, expressed in the saying "Katong su cape, katong seng mau ba konflik lai" (We are exhausted, we do not want any more fighting). This statement is usually followed by another, "Barenti jua, seng ada yang menang deng konflik ini, katong samua susah" (Enough is enough, no one won, everyone suffers the consequences). These statements affirm the immense agony and destructive impact of the conflict such that no one wishes for it to happen again. This near-universal realization that violent conflicts did not bring any good is at the heart of other public norms and underlies even those otherwise grounded in appeals to religion or *adat*.

In conflicts widely perceived as religious, shared cultural wisdom is often invoked in an effort to overcome boundaries. The Malukan saying "Katong samua basudara" (We are all family) is a widely shared norm grounded on belief in a common origin. This public norm is itself related to a widespread recognition of the key customary practice of *pela*, which is closely related to *patasiwa-patalima, salam-sarani* (Muslim-Christian), and *pela-gendong*.

Patasiwa (literally, "group of nine") and *patalima* (literally, "group of five"), often shortened as *siwalima*, are local cultural practices in Central Maluku that originated from Nusa Ina (the mother island) of Alifuru Chiefdom, located on Seram Island. Thus the invocation of *siwalima* is intended to underscore the interconnectedness of the region's various local polities back to their place of shared origin. In addition, the chiefdoms in *siwalima* are connected culturally in systems of pact relationships known as *pela* (social pact) and *gandong* (genealogical relations). In contrast to the concepts of *patasiwa, patalima,* or *pela gandong,* which have deep roots in Malukan traditions, the idea "Katong samua basudara" as a feature of Malukan identity is new. By way of comparison, a similar saying is also found in Minahasa, "Torang samua basudara," as discussed in Larson's chapter on Manado in this book, and was popularized during the E. E. Mangindaan administration in North Sulawesi Province in 1995–2000 (cf. Swazey 2013, 131).

The meaning of "Katong samua basudara" is also apparent in another saying, "Ale rasa beta rasa, potong di kuku rasa di daging, sagu salempeng dipatah dua." (Whether you feel happy or sad, I feel it too. If you are hurt, so am I. To live together is to share.) The adage highlights the interconnectedness of the *basudara* concept, which manifests itself in depending on and helping each other. The same social logic is also invoked to explain cultural relations of *basudara salam-sarani*.[2]

Some official efforts have been made to uplift traditional values like these as the basis for a shared identity for all the peoples of the Maluku Province. For example, the provincial museum of local culture established in 1973 and located in Air Salobar, close to Ambon City, is named the Siwalima Museum. Another example is the use of *siwalima* in the motto and logo of Maluku Province, which is in the form of a shield (*sawalaku*) painted with images of sago leaf, palm leaf, pearl, clove, nutmeg, spear, mountain, sea, and a *dhow* (traditional sailing vessel). The icons in the logo represent cultural identity, natural resources, and the geographical conditions in Maluku Province.

With regard to religion, it is interesting to note that while within religious communities there have been some attempts to ground calls for peace in religious terms, in general religious phrasings and doctrines are avoided in conversations across Christian and Muslim communities. Even people who work in religious organizations seem keen to avoid associating the conflict with religion. Notwithstanding these efforts, religion is unavoidable in Ambon—in times of war and peace. When the conflicts were going on, some people, both Muslims and Christians, justified killing each other in religious terms. But early on in the conflict, a number of religious leaders started to speak up for peace, obviously not without the risk of being accused as traitors. A case in point is Rev. I. W. J. Hendriks, who was the leader of the Maluku Protestant Church Synod during the time of conflict. From the beginning he took the risk of appealing to Christians to work for peace; he also did not hesitate to criticize Christian theological arguments when these were interpreted exclusively. He observed that it was often especially difficult for Christians to heed his calls to put down their arms when it was clear that the local government was not interested or able to provide for security (Hendriks 2014).

There were similar stories of peace appeals and argument from the Muslim side. For example, Hasbollah Toisuta, now the rector of the State Islamic Institute in Ambon, gave a Friday sermon in Al-Fatah Mosque in November 2000. He was inspired by his reading of the prominent Muslim intellectual Nurcholish Madjid to speak about an inclusive, peaceful Islam. Yet the next Friday, another preacher refuted his message (Toisuta 2014). Some leaders from both Muslim and Christian communities were critically examining the theologies used by belligerents to justify war and were trying to promote an inclusive theology in their place. Hendriks's and Toisuta's stories were recounted in the 2014 book *Carita orang basudara* (published in English as *Basudara: Stories of Peace from Maluku*), which also has stories from other Christian and Muslim leaders about their struggle to interpret norms for peace from their religious traditions.

Today's Ambon shows how the painful memory of conflict has produced a strong motivation for peace. Peace understood primarily as the desire to avoid conflict is now the dominant norm. This norm is scaled up in activities conducted by myriad organizations, including those representing youth, women, schools, universities, the mass media, and government. Before discussing the extent of the impressive scaling work now taking place in Ambon, the following section discusses a focal incident that, in a way, tested the strength of commitment to peace in Ambon and, at the same time, prompts reflection on the prospects for peace today.

GUNUNG NONA INCIDENT, 2011: IS PEACE SUSTAINABLE?

The peace that has prevailed since the 1999–2002 conflict has helped the people of Ambon to recover from their psychological trauma, to organize their lives, and to reinitiate long-stalled development programs. By 2004, the conflict in Ambon had subsided, but no one believed the situation had returned to being in any sense normal. The segregation between Muslim and Christian settlements, for example, was still pervasive, as was the widespread sense of trauma. Yet overt acts of violence had largely stopped. Collaborative initiatives between the government and local communities helped to revive the infrastructure. Muslims and Christians, natives and "migrants" all mingled in marketplaces. Transportation, education, and other public activities had become routine. But the peace was severely tested in September 2011 when, after a bloody incident in Gunung Nona, it seemed large-scale violence might break out again.

On September 11, 2011, clashes between Muslims and Christians erupted in parts of Ambon City. The violence was sparked by an event a day earlier when a Muslim motorbike taxi driver, Darfin Saimin, was found dead in Gunung Nona, a Christian village. According to the police report, the death was a result of a motorbike accident; however, his family felt they had evidence of foul play. Rumors about Saimin's death began to spread, and some said that Saimin had been killed by Christians. Tensions then increased the next day as some of the public began to criticize the police and army for being slow to respond and not preventing angry crowds from forming (ICG 2011). In the clashes that followed, eight people died, hundreds were injured, and thousands were forced to seek refuge away from their homes. More than a hundred buildings were burned down, including part of the Christian university campus in Talake. Text messages received by both Christians and Muslims seemed to have been sent in order to incite hatred and hostilities. Some NGOs suggested that Saimin had been killed by the "security apparatus" with the aim of reigniting conflict in order to increase government funding for peace operations (ICG 2011).

In times of conflict, the borders between Muslim and Christian areas become important lines of defense for protecting communities from infiltration by opponents. In the September 2011 incident, crowds were concentrated along those borders. For Muslims, the border between Muslim Batu Merah and Christian Mardika was the front line for protecting their enclave in Ambon City; for Christians, Batu Gantung was the front line for protecting Kuda Mati, Gunung Nona, and other Christian areas. Yet these clashes between Muslim and Christian youth in Ambon City did not spread to other parts of Ambon Island or to other parts of the Maluku archipelago. In the aftermath of the conflict, there was a sense of hope and relief that conditions in Ambon were actually improving.

Despite all the uncertainty as to who might be the mastermind behind the conflict, an International Crisis Group report (ICG 2011) pointed out that several actors had benefited from the clash. The first set were the police and military, who would receive more income for transportation-security-escort services. The second group included political elites who were trying to utilize the clash to regain the power they had lost. The third group included terrorist networks, determined to use news of the clash for their mobilization efforts elsewhere in Indonesia.

The notion of a mastermind behind the September 2011 incident has never been proven, but many local people believed that someone was trying to provoke hatred between social groups. The incident actually helped bring together local government, religious, and cultural leaders, including leaders of the Indonesian Council of Ulama (MUI), the Protestant Synod, and the Catholic Diocese. The mayhem led the governor of Maluku Province (Karel A. Ralahalu), the military commanding officer of Division XVI Pattimura (Mayjen TNI Suharsono), the head of the provincial police (Brigjen Polisi Syarief Gunawan), the vice-governor (Said Assagaff), and the mayor of Ambon City (Richard Louhenapessy) to meet with Christian and Muslim crowds gathered in several locations and to urge calm. The forum of *raja* (*adat* chiefs) also issued a decree signed by the chairperson, the *raja* of Amahusu in Ambon Island and the *raja* of Sirisori Islam in Saparua Island urging the public in Ambon City to be vigilant and avoid provocation. Leaders from Muslim *negeri* (*adat* villages), the *raja* of Tulehu Negeri in Ambon Island, and the *raja* of Kailolo from Haruku Island also urged the public to exercise vigilance (Media Project 2011).

Since the conflict, many civil society organizations have emerged to support peacebuilding and conflict prevention. The Malino Agreement II signed in 2012 marked a new era of peacebuilding in Ambon. The agreement, however, was criticized because it only partially accommodated Muslim and Christian grassroots groups earlier involved in the conflict. Some groups thought they were left out, and some were unhappy with postconflict development in Ambon. A report by the International Crisis Group (ICG 2011) mentioned that jihadist and terrorist groups had sought to exploit the September 2011 clash to reestablish their power. My research had found similar efforts by hard-line Christian groups. My field observation indicates that there are still many militant groups willing and able to turn to violence if and when violence erupts again.

The result of the September 2011 incident was a renewed determination across Ambonese society to build a more lasting peace. Most significantly, a new peace movement emerged, one promoted by Ambon youth. Called Provokator Damai (Peace Provocateur), the movement was made up of youth who often came together for discussion in the research and development office of the Gereja Protestan Maluku (GPM; Protestant Church) Synod, together with activists from the social movement Ambon Bergerak (Ambon Moves) and the Maluku Interfaith Institute (LAIM; Lembaga Antar-Iman Maluku) forum. A year after the 2011 violence, the city of Ambon hosted a large, national Muslim convention for Qur'an recitation, the Musabaqah Tilawatil Qur'an, which took place peacefully.

These are just some of the initiatives that have taken place in the years since to preserve and deepen the peace.

Since its initial phase, numerous efforts have been made to prevent further conflict. Peacemakers from formerly opposing groups have taken advantage of the peace since 2011 to share information and build personal ties, all in an effort to prevent future violence. One factor that helped their efforts was that the majority of the activists in each group knew each other through their NGO networks long before the conflict, so it was easier for them to remember their shared history as they came together to work for peace (Salampessy 2014, 39–58; Fofid 2014, 15–37).

A decade after the conflict, many of the NGOs established in the immediate aftermath of the conflict have disappeared because of lack of funds and/or ineffective management. But other groups have survived and even thrived. In the following sections I discuss scaling-up initiatives undertaken by different sectors in society, including those of youth, women, religious organizations, mass media, schools and universities, and the local government. Most of these groups are alive and well today, and they are a major force for peace.

SCALING UP PEACE: YOUTH

When Ambon City experienced new clashes, youth in Ambon acted quickly and publicly to prevent messages of hatred from provoking a bigger conflict. New initiatives later known as "Peace Provocations" (Provokasi Damai) showed that, unlike in 1999, today many Ambonese are willing, able, and organized to work for peace. One important figure actively involved in the Provokasi Damai movement is Jacky Manuputty, a pastor from GPM and a peace worker who graduated from Hartford Seminary, in the United States. In 2012, he was named a "Peacemaker in Action" by the Tanenbaum Center for Interreligious Understanding. Earlier, in 2007, he received the Maarif Award from the Maarif Institute in Jakarta for his dedication in supporting social change for peace. Another important figure is Abidin Wakano, director of the Ambon Reconciliation and Mediation Center (ARMC) at the State Islamic Institute (Al Qurtuby 2015) and now the head of Majelis Ulama Indonesia (Indonesian Council of Ulama) of

Maluku. Elsewhere in Indonesia, the MUI is usually associated with conservative Muslim authority and viewpoints (Ichwan 2013; Hefner, chapter 1), yet it is telling that in Maluku the council is led by a peace activist. Yet another important figure is Zairin "Embong" Salampessy, a journalist and human rights activist.

During the 1999–2002 conflict the mass media had spread hatred and violence, but during the Gunung Nona clash of 2011 the media were active in promoting peace and damping tensions (Bräuchler 2003; Manuputty 2012). Media activists challenged the provocative messages and provided clarification by insisting on circulating verified facts about interreligious collaboration to combat rumors and misinformation. Stories about Provokator Damai activities went viral on social media and received support from so-called netizens, successfully helping reduce anxieties for those living far from the border areas of Batu Merah-Mardika and Waiheru-Talake. These activities continued even after the clash in Gunung Nona. Weeks afterward, these interreligious teams went on foot from one security post to another serving coffee to those working at the posts (Manuputty 2012). The message being sent was that the majority of Ambonese did not want any more conflict.

The development of social media has also built ties across communities, through networks like Ambon Bergerak (Ambon Moves). After its successful efforts in the face of the September 2011 violence, Ambon Bergerak enlarged its range of activities to take on environmental issues through #savearu, a movement for environment conservation in the Aru Islands, a chain of islands five hundred kilometers southeast of Ambon but still within Maluku Province. Permits had already been issued by the central government in Jakarta for the Menara Group Company to open a sugarcane plantation, a project seen by many locals as threatening the environment. Online petitions initiated by #savearu garnered more than fourteen thousand signatures from forty-five countries worldwide and forced the government to review the permit (Patty 2013). In January 2015, Ambon Bergerak opened a headquarters, which they called Paparisa Ambon Bergerak. In July 2015, the minister of communication and information, Rudiantara, visited this office while in Ambon Maluku and commented that "Paparisa Ambon Bergerak is an 'ecosystem' of information and communication technology development in Ambon."

A prominent organization connected with Ambon Bergerak is a literary club, Bengkel Sastra Maluku (BSM), established in 2010 to accommodate the hobbies of its members and to rekindle interest in Malukan literature. Its members are also affiliated with an assortment of youth networks. Rudi Fofid, the founder of BSM, received the Maarif Institute Award 2016 in the category for individuals who demonstrate a commitment to diversity, social integration, and peace. BSM had regular literary performances and discussions, and it visited other literary communities in both Muslim and Christian territories. Fofid was well known as a journalist and the head of the Maluku Media Center (MMC), which developed peace journalism in Ambon. He was the vice chief editor of the daily newspaper *Suara Maluku*, and in 2016 he replaced Aziz Tuni, another journalist and a Muslim, who was his close friend, as the chief editor of *Mimbar Rakyat*. One important initiative from BSM, in collaboration with other literary communities, was "Kapata Night" (*kapata* is a Malukan literary form of narrating the past with poems and songs).

Kapata Night is held at the Workshop Coffee café. Established in 2016, the café sits in a strategic location, at the border of the Muslim area of Waringin and Christian Talake. Housed in a former music studio which was burnt down during the Gunung Nona incident in 2011, it has become one of the meeting venues for youth active in Ambon Bergerak. The weekly Kapata Night organized by BSM with other literary communities, both Muslim and Christian, gives opportunities for young poets from all across Maluku to perform and dialogue, building trust and healing prejudices. Literary works at Kapata Night tell of nature, local tradition, and hopes to protect peace and harmony in Maluku. The literary column in *Mimbar Rakyat* every weekend has helped spread the message of Kapata Night to a wider audience.

Another community involved in Ambon Bergerak is the Maluku Hip-Hop Community (MHC), which was established in 2008. According to Morika Tetelepta, one of the founders of the MHC, between 2008 and 2016 the MHC played important roles in developing the music industry in Ambon. Youth from Muslim and Christian villages developed their hip-hop musical skills with very simple facilities. The MHC monitored the hip-hop communities and offered assistance to develop their creativity. Not only interested in hip-hop, the MHC looks forward to catalyzing social change through their works. Creative musical ensembles and powerful song lyrics deliver messages of hope and youthful joy to a wide audience. Ambon Bergerak has made the work of the MHC available online on YouTube.

SCALING UP PEACE: WOMEN'S MOVEMENTS

Women and children were the most vulnerable groups during the 1999–2002 conflict. When men took up weapons to fight, women worked to feed their families and take care of their children and at the same time worried about the safety of their family. Some women took roles working at the public kitchen, and a few even took up arms during the conflict. "When men were fighting, the women had to work to feed the family. During such situations, it was hard to provide nutritious food for children and nursing mothers," said Rev. Margaretha Hendriks, a peace activist.[3] Another activist, Sr. Brigitta Renyaan, similarly explained that "many women became victims of domestic abuse. And children lost hope for a better future because they were exploited to be involved in the armed conflict."[4] Conflict in Ambon thus not only created a perilous situation for women but also threatened the next generation.

During the conflict, Sr. Francesco Moens, PBHK, a Catholic nun from the Netherlands, met with the vice governor, Paula Renyaan, a devout Catholic from Southeast Maluku, to discuss how the peace movement should respond to the violence. The idea received positive feedback from Hendriks and women from the GPM. Supported by Renyaan, the first coordination meeting was held on August 6, 1999, between Catholic nuns and women pastors from Protestant churches at Rinamakana, a Catholic foundation in Ambon. This first meeting also then extended an invitation to Muslim women to join the women's interreligious peace movement. Renyaan and Icha Latuconsina, the wife of the Muslim governor, Saleh Latuconsina, facilitated involvement by other Muslim women, including the governor's sister and wives of other high-ranking officials. The next day the Muslim women, escorted by a security detail, met with Christian women and marched to the office of the governor. Many of the women already knew each other; they were friends, kin, or colleagues, but the conflict had prevented them from meeting in public. In the governor's house, they planned a campaign against violence, cutting pieces of green cloth and writing "Stop the violence" on them. "Philosophically, green, like plants, symbolizes life; therefore the campaign is a prolife campaign," explained Hendriks. From the governor's office, the women took to the streets, distributing the pieces of green cloth to people they met. Reverend Hendriks recalled that during the early days of the Ambon conflict such interfaith actions were regarded as "suicidal."[5]

Support from this network of elite women provided this movement with an opportunity to read their nonviolence declaration, entitled "Suara Hati Perempuan" (The Voice of Women's Hearts) in front of the governor's office. The event was witnessed by the police chief of Maluku, Pangdam XVI/Pattimura, and by the governor of Maluku Province. Muslim and Christian women alternately read the declaration on different days, always accompanied by security escorts. The movement soon attracted many more women, both Christian and Muslim. On the first day of the declaration of "Suara Hati Perempuan," a Protestant representative read the declaration, accompanied by 250 other Christian women. On the second day, it was read by a Muslim representative accompanied by 100 other Muslim women. The women repeated their protests in front of the provincial legislature and at the office of Ambon Municipality. Their voices for peace aired in local and national media and became the first glimpse of hope for peace negotiations. During subsequent meetings, Muslim and Christian women shared their personal stories of suffering and struggle during the conflict. Living in a still-segregated society, they set out to reestablish goodwill among women of different faiths, by, for example, sending each other gifts across community lines by way of security posts.

The women's movement for peace outraged some hard-liners in both religious communities because anyone promoting peace at the height of the violence was considered a traitor. The women thus became targets of violence in their own communities. For safety reasons, some were evacuated to more secure residences.[6] However, the movement continued and progressed notwithstanding sometimes harsh intimidation. The leaders appointed several prominent women to serve as coordinators from all three main communities: Reverend Hendriks from the Protestant church, Sr. Brigitta Renyaan from the Catholic community, and Retty Assagaff from the Muslim community. Retty Assagaff is the wife of Muhammad Said Assagaff, who was vice-governor of Maluku Province in 2008–13 and was elected governor in 2014. The Women's Care Movement (Gerakan Perempuan Peduli, GPP) received formal recognition and expressions of support from President Abdurrahman Wahid (r. 1999–2001) and his wife, as well as from ambassadors of other countries when they visited Ambon. In 2001 they were hosted by the United Church in Australia (UCA) at a two-week peace workshop in Sydney, which led to the launching of Young Ambassadors for Peace (YAP) (Al Qurtuby 2014; Reeson 2015).

The women activists in were also involved in other organizations foregrounding the plight of women in Maluku. A number are still today active in groups like the Yayasan Arikal Mahina, established in October 2002. This foundation's main activities include facilitating the Sirisori Kristen (SSK) and Sirisori Islam (SSI) women's forum on Saparua Island, Central Maluku (Soselisa 2000). Another still-active organization is Yayasan Walang Perempuan, established in 2007, to assist and empower women and children victimized by the violence. An organization associated with Nahdhatul Ulama is Lembaga Kajian and Pengembangan Sumber Daya Manusia (Lakpesdam) of Ambon City, established in 1999, to assist vulnerable groups in society, including women and children. At the national level, the women's movement in Maluku is linked to the government-sponsored National Commission on Violence against Women (Komnas Perempuan).

Another important women's initiative centered on *mama papalele* (the vernacular name for women working in traditional markets). Putting aside their religious sentiments during the conflict, these women continued conducting business in the market and put their lives at risk by passing through conflict areas (Soegijono 2011). One forum where *mama papalele* from Muslim and Christian communities met was in the Mardika Market, which was a neutral area during the conflict (Asyathri, Sukesi, and Yuliati 2014). During the darkest days of the conflict, these market women were among the very few Ambonese free to pass over demarcation lines and into different communities.

Women activists from Maluku were connected through the Malukan Women's Coalition (Koalisi Perempuan Maluku), which was made up of young women activists under the coordination of Mercy Barends. In 2002, among the representatives appointed by Christian communities to join the

Malino Summit II were Sr. Brigitta Renyaan, Rev. Margaretha Hendriks, and the vice-governor, Paula Renyaan. Many of the women activists continued their activities in national and international forums. In 2006, Reverend Hendriks was appointed one of the chairpersons of the Communion of Churches in Indonesia (Persekutuan Gereja-Gereja di Indonesia, PGI); shortly thereafter she became one of the vice-moderators of the World Council of Churches. The efforts of women in Maluku were also highlighted with the appointment of Rev. Lies Mailoa-Marantika to the Komnas Perempuan (Komnas Perempuan 2001).

The GPP later broadened its efforts to include attending to the plight of children who had taken part in the armed conflict. Both the *linggi*s, the Muslim child soldiers, and the *aga*s, the Christian child soldiers, figured among the victims. Many children died in combat, but those who survived were often deeply traumatized. Many had witnessed the killing of family members or relatives. The GPP outreach to former child soldiers included Muslim and Christian women. Legal protections for women and children were later achieved by collaboration across women's organizations, with the passage of the 2004 Law No. 23 on Abolishing Domestic Abuse, the 2007 Law No. 21 on Abolishing Human Trafficking, and the 2002 Law No. 23 on Children Protection.

A few figures of the GPP were later elected to high political positions. Olivia Latuconsina became the vice-mayor of Ambon in 2006–11, and Sitty Suruwaky was vice-regent of East Seram Regency from 2005 to 2015. In the lead-up to the 2009 national elections, Malukan women held the first Malukan Women's Congress, which was opened by the state minister of women's empowerment, Meutia Hatta Swasono. Afterwards, interfaith cooperation among Malukan women led to the election of more female representatives. One by-product of these efforts was the preparation of legislation on women and children's protection against violence in Maluku, which was formalized as a provincial regulation in 2012. When the Election Supervisory Body of Maluku was established in 2012, one of its three appointed members was Lusi Peilouw, a counselor for child refugees during the conflict, subsequently well known for working to secure places for women during elections.

Since its founding, the GPP has worked tirelessly to mobilize women from all faith communities. It has highlighted issues of antiviolence and peace, for women and children and all victims of the conflict. It has scaled up social networks for peace and reconciliation at the local, regional, and national levels; in doing so, it has been one of the major voices for peace and multireligious recognition in postconflict Maluku.

SCALING UP PEACE: INSTITUTIONALIZING *PELA*

The fact that many *negeri* in Maluku are linked by the traditional ties of solidarity and support known as *pela* demonstrates that the tradition remains and in some ways is being revitalized as a mechanism of cultural cohesion (Bartels 1977, 30–31). In the popular traditions of Central Maluku, the term *pela* means "alliance" or social "bond" between two or more villages based on an explicit social pact rather than kinship or genealogy, for the purpose of providing mutual assistance in times of natural or social disaster. The term can be traced to an earlier ritual tradition known as *kakehan*, which was for initiating men into a kind of brotherhood. However, over time and well before the modern period the institution was transformed into a bond of mutual support between two or more villages (Bartels 1977, 57–58; Cooley 1961, 261). The relationship often bridges religious communities as well as villages and draws residents into a fictive kinship for the purposes of mutual cooperation. For example, one Muslim community may help its Christian neighbors build a church, or Christians may help their Muslim *pela* partners build a mosque. In actual practice, the cultural message is not limited to the directly involved communities but establishes a kind of moral culture across regions (Ruhulessin 2005, 277–78; Lattu 2014, 97).

Cooley (1961, 261–66) divides *pela* into two parts based on the intensity of bond and enjoined responsibilities. "Strong pela" or *pela keras* (also known as *pela tulen, pela batu karang,* or *pela darah*) is a social bond affirming kinship within a particular *pela*. Oaths of loyalty among *pela* members require them to help each other during war or in other critical situations, and intermarriage is taboo because their relation is effectively equated with that of siblings. Infringement of the oath is believed to incur punishment from the ancestors. Soft *pela* (*pela tempat sirih*; also known as *pela lunak* or soft *pela*) enjoins cooperation and mutual aid between communities but does not forbid marriage.

Pela are not only commitments to help each other during difficult times. The term also refers to collective interfaith relations between Muslims and Christians, which are symbolically represented in material form and through collaborative activities (Lattu 2014). The symbolic representations function to remind *pela* members of their enduring ties. Externally, the symbolic representations are supposed to illustrate and reinforce relations of trust and cooperation among villages. For example, during the construction of Tuhaha Protestant Church on Saparua Island in 2012, the Muslim village of Rohomoni on nearby Haruku Island contributed one of the four central pillars for the church's structural frame. To this day, the pillar, known as the Rohomoni Pillar, serves as a reminder of how the Tuhaha and Rohomoni *negeri* are connected in one *pela*. In 2016, the chief of Muslim Hitu Lama participated in the groundbreaking ceremony for the renovation of Immanuel Galala Church because Hitu Lama had contributed twelve pillars for the original construction of the church in 1956. The *pela* between Galala and Hitu Lama was renewed in a *panas pela* (warm *pela*) ceremony in 2015.

According to Lattu (2014, 97), the pillars presented to the Tuhaha and Immanuel Galala churches not only symbolize material *pela* but also mark overlapping identities in interfaith relations. The symbolic representation has also meant that each church in fact belongs to both *negeri* within the *pela*, and thus the villages within each *pela* are bound to protect each other. In addition to these material representations, the two *negeri* have conducted *makan patita* ritual feasts that symbolically show their close ties. Preparing, presenting, and eating traditional foods is a way to relive collective memories from the shared past of the two *negeri* and to affirm a bond that unites *negeri* across religions.

Pela are put to the test during times of conflict, but many stories demonstrate that this social pact has proven effective in constraining or diminishing violence. A common practice reported among the *negeri* bound by *pela* or *gandong* during the conflict was the mutual effort to protect each other from attack by other groups and to resist being provoked to attack each other. One example is how Muslim Batu Merah and Protestant Paso allowed each other to pass through on their way downtown (Mujib and Rumahuru 2010, 196). The chiefs (*raja*) of the two *negeri* remained in communication throughout the conflict, offering each other assistance and trying to keep their own people out of the violence. The two leaders were actively involved in briefing their own people about social customs, holding *makan patita* rituals, and visiting each other's *negeri* to protect their relationship. The efforts made by both the *raja* of Batu Merah Negeri and the *raja* of Paso Negeri proved an important contribution to later peace talks process because geographically the two *negeri* lay squarely astride one of the main transport routes on Ambon Island (Bräuchler 2009a, 2015).

After the conflict erupted, many *negeri* in Central Maluku reaffirmed their social relations based on their cultural roots and conducted "warming" of *pela* rituals to renew their commitments as *orang basudara* for a better future. Research by Soumokil (2011) as cited by Lattu (2014, 145–46) has shown that the rekindling of *pela* became an important medium for rebuilding recognition, social relations, and trust in the aftermath of the conflict.

The concept of *pela* is closely connected to Nunusaku mythologies concerning the origin of the islands of Maluku and Nusa Ina, the mother of the Malukan people. *Pela* expresses the idea of brotherhood among all Malukans across religious lines (*kita orang basudara*). The concept of *gandong* is genealogical: Malukans, both Muslim and Christian, come from the same mother. John Ruhulessin, the former general secretary of the GPM Synod, explained that the "hot" or *panas pela* ritual also marked commitment to social unity based on Nunusaku traditions. The warming of *pela* ritual not only served to renew and revitalize the pact between *negeri* but also broadened efforts to achieve recognition, balance, and unity across Christian and Muslim divides (Ruhulessin 2005, 259, 275, 255). Some *negeri* conducted this ritual in the immediate aftermath of the violence. However, the process continues even today. For example, *panas pela* rituals were conducted by Christian Galala and Muslim Hitu Lama from Ambon Island in 2015 and Christian Amahai from Seram Island and Christian Ihamahu from Saparua Island in 2016.

One other striking example of *pela* revival and reinterpretation is its application in modern institutions like interschool relations or interuniversity relations. Migration during the conflict changed the religious and demographic composition of many schools, making them more religiously homogenous. In 2013, the Ambon Reconciliation and Media Center (ARMC) at the State Islamic Institute (IAIN) of Ambon initiated a new *pela* relationship between two public high schools in Ambon that are now religiously homogenous: one Christian (SMA 9 in Ambon) and one Muslim (SMA 4 Salahutu). In 2016, the two schools conducted a warming *pela* ritual. At the university level, it is interesting to note a recent *pela* pact between the two institutions that cooperated to organize the 2016 international conference supported by the Consortium for Netherlands-Indonesia Christian-Muslim Relations: UKIM Ambon (Christian) and IAIN. This was especially poignant because the UKIM campus had been burnt down several times during the conflict, including during the 2011 Gunung Nona incident. Their *pela* relationship thus provided a symbol and an impetus to rebuild their relation for the future. Both sides hope that the reciprocal recognition and relationship expressed in the *pela* pact can contribute to initiating cooperation for creative, innovative, and inclusive education in the future.

There are also stories of *pela-gandong* relations showing that at times the institution has proved ineffective at maintaining peace (Mujib and Rumahuru 2010, 194; Bräuchler 2009b, 106–8; 2015). Nonetheless the institution survived and has been revived; it can even be said to have helped lessen casualties and rebuild relations between conflicting local polities (*negeri*). From this point of view, *pela* remains an important cultural value and practice for social trust and peacebuilding. Using Ruhulessin's concept (2005, 277–78), *pela* can also be regarded as a source of public ethics or normative work for interreligious recognition and relationships in Maluku, not only between *negeri* but across all of Malukan society.

The regional government has also used elements of "local wisdom" (*kearifan local*), including *pela-gandong*, in its effort to create and scale up a new public ethics and sustainable peace. In 2013, the Malukan provincial government issued a decree establishing the Institute of Malukan Local Culture (Lembaga Kebudayaan Daerah Maluku). Its function is to collaborate with government in protecting, empowering, and developing traditional customs and practices as a united *siwalima* to support a national development plan in Maluku. The following year, the First Cultural Congress in Maluku took place on November 6, 2014. The congress issued the

Maluku Cultural Declaration, which stated that all elements that make up Malukan culture originated from local ethnic groups in the Malukan Islands and were an integral part of Indonesian cultural diversity. The message conveyed was that Maluku and Malukan culture are not "problems" but vital parts of the unity and diversity that is Indonesia.

In 2015, the then-vice president, Jusuf Kalla, inaugurated the People's Congress of Maluku (Musyawarah Besar Masyarakat Maluku) in Ambon. The congress urged the central government to focus on building equality in the province, in particular regarding the cultural and geographical diversity of its population, and to include people from Maluku in the national government. The declaration rejected any and all efforts at provocation and affirmed the unity of *orang basudara* under the umbrella of the Republic of Indonesia. Although both congresses affirmed the importance of national identity and citizenship in Maluku and Indonesia, civic and national themes like these have figured less in local Malukan approaches to peacebuilding and civic coexistence than have local public normativities and the simple desire to prevent any further outbreak of violence.

SCALING UP PEACE: INTERRELIGIOUS ACTIVITIES

Another avenue of public-ethical and organization scaling in postconflict Maluku has involved societal and semigovernmental religious organizations. Three especially crucial religious organizations in Maluku are the MUI, the GPM, and the Catholic Diocese of Amboina. All three groups have come together to work as strategic partners with the government. In 2004, the three institutions established the Maluku Interfaith Institute (LAIM). LAIM conducts interfaith discussions, networks between Muslims and Christians, and organizes peacebuilding workshops, typically in association with other civic organizations. Since 2011, LAIM has not been as active, though its two most prominent figures, Jacky Manuputty, a GPM pastor, and Abidin Wakano, a Muslim lecturer at IAIN who is now the head of the Provincial MUI Maluku, are still quite active in peacebuilding initiatives through other organizations.

Another interfaith organization important in postconflict peacebuilding is the Forum for Interreligious Harmony (Forum Kerukunan

Umat Beragama, FKUB). Partly supported by the government, FKUB Ambon is in most respects similar to the FKUBs that have been established in all provinces, cities, and regencies of Indonesia since 2006 (see Erica Larson, chapter 2 in this book). The process of establishing an FKUB in Maluku was not without a challenge, because it overlapped with LAIM's work. Having an FKUB in Maluku, however, has helped with opening up lines of communication and cooperation between government and religious leaders.

More significant government initiatives for scaling up interreligious harmony have centered on the idea of declaring Maluku a "Laboratory of Interreligious Tolerance," a phrase invented by the governor Muhammad Said Assagaff, and to hold two large national religious events in Ambon in 2012, which took place just one year after the Gunung Nona incident. The two events, sponsored by the Islam and Christian Directorates General of the Ministry of Religious Affairs, were a national Qur'anic recitation competition (Musabaqah Tilawatil Qur'an or MTQ) and a church choir festival (Pesta Paduan Suara Gerejawi or Pesparawi). Against the backdrop of fresh memories of conflicts between Muslims and Christians, these two events became important symbols and celebrations of interreligious cooperation and came to be described with the tagline of "Maluku as a Laboratory of Interreligious Harmony." This idea of Maluku as a laboratory of harmony has been invoked by government and religious leaders as well as carried by mass media, which turned it into a tagline for Maluku Province.[7]

One part of the laboratory idea was the construction of three new public buildings: an Islamic Center, a Protestant Center, and a Catholic Center. The local government also announced plans to build "multicultural villages [kampungs]"; the latter was an idea originally promoted by some activists, although criticized by others.[8] Critics of these initiatives suggested that the idea of Ambon as a "laboratory" was too top-down in its connotations. These same critics have suggested that it might be more effective for the government to support integration processes in more natural settings, as in local communities, rather than experimenting with new organizations or community structures. Another objection has been that constructing separate religious centers (Islamic, Christian, Catholic) will not help to overcome segregation.

The two events of the MTQ and Pesparawi were greeted enthusiasti-
cally by many local people. The MTQ is an annual national event sponsored by the Directorate General for Islam in the Ministry of Religion. Each
province in Indonesia usually sends one delegate to compete in several
competitions in the MTQ. The first MTQ was held in 1968. The twenty-
fourth national MTQ took place in Ambon on June 8–15, 2012, less than a
year after the Gunung Nona clash, and in the immediate aftermath of several smaller incidents. Despite these troubling events, thousands of Muslims from across Indonesia attended the MTQ conference. The event's organizing committee also included Christians, like Rev. John C. Ruhulessin,
the head of the GPM Synod, who worked tirelessly with local pastors to
urge Christian residents to guard the peace. During the conference itself,
Christians offered their houses to visiting Muslim participants from other
provinces. The UKIM library, which had been destroyed during the Gunung Nona incident, also became one of the venues for the competition. In
addition, thousands of Christians in Ambon supported the event through
public prayer in the Cathedral of Diocese Amboina.

Three years later, the eleventh national Pesparawi choir festival took
place in Ambon and was attended by thousands of Christians from all
provinces in Indonesia. In his opening speech, Governor Said Assagaff reminded the audience that Pesparawi was not only a Christian event but
significant for all religions in Indonesia, including Islam. This event became an impetus to show the world that Maluku "was no longer a conflict
area or conflict laboratory, but rather the best laboratory for interreligious relations Indonesia." Just like the MTQ, in which Christians took part,
the Muslims in Ambon took part in this church-sponsored event. The
Muslim community in Batu Merah, where the 1999 conflict had first bro-
ken out, welcomed Pesparawi participants who passed by their area. The
elders greeted the guests by bringing *kain gandong*, a long white fabric used
in the traditional ritual welcoming of guests. As Lattu writes (2014, 124–
25), *kain gandong* is a symbol of the purity and honesty of the host. In
panas pela tradition, or in other rituals in Maluku, welcoming guests who
are *pela* partners with *kain gandong* also symbolizes a shared, common
ancestry.

These two events were clear expressions of effective collaboration between government, religious leaders, *adat* leaders, and the population of

Maluku as a whole. Both events were a source of great pride for local officials and ordinary Ambonese. They were seen as evidence of the ability of
Muslims and Christians to unite under the banner of Indonesia's national
motto of Unity in Diversity (*Bhinneka tunggal ika*).

HOW TO SUSTAIN PEACE

In the course of this study of public normativities and scalings for peace in
postconflict Ambon, I came to realize that the sayings "Katong su cape, katong seng mau ba konflik lai" (We are exhausted. We don't want any more
fighting) and "Katong samua basudara" (We are all family) vividly express
the most influential normative ideals for pluralist coexistence in this region. Together they convey a sense of exhaustion and moral fatigue but also
a hopeful appeal for recognition, cooperation, and coexistence.

Women and youth were especially prominent in efforts to move from
the exhaustion of war to the rebuilding of peace. The women's movement
succeeded at reimagining and revitalizing Ambon's legacy of religious diversity. The inclusive character of the women's movement could be seen
from its very beginning, involving women from different backgrounds,
both religious and professional, and utilizing different relationships and
networks, both formal and nonformal. The women's movement has also
thoroughly internalized the ideals of "Katong su cape, katong seng mau ba
konflik lai." It has invoked the saying as a public norm for scaling up trust
and peace both during and after the conflict, and with special attention
to the plight of women and children. As part of civil society, its goals are
attempted through, as Hefner (2001, 10) has put it, a cultural quality of
"democratic civility," emphasizing equality, recognition, and respect while
putting aside ethno-religious differences.

Through the activities of the Ambon Bergerak forum, youth in Ambon
have also played a role in bridging divides in society and overcoming postconflict prejudices and tensions. The main challenge Ambon Bergerak
faces as an urban youth movement is to maintain a range of diverse activities and to embrace the many youth still outside the forum, who
often feel marginalized from interfaith relations as a whole. Religious institutions have also played a central role in postconflict peacebuilding and

reconciliation and have done so in a way that involves extensive cooperation with local, regional, and national government.

Adat is another potent cultural resource for peace. *Pela* pacts may have
failed to prevent the 1999–2003 conflict, but they have played a salient role
in peacebuilding efforts and social reconstruction. In the postconflict period, many *negeri* started to revive *pela* institutions, convinced that they
could serve as a unifying institution in society. A challenge remains, however. Not all communities have *pela* relations; and among those that do,
they extend to only a few communities. The challenge then is how to scale
up *pela*-like structures to be both extensive and inclusive, without losing
their moral force.

As the normativity based on collective memory of conflicts, "Katong
su cape, katong seng mau ba konflik lai" will remain central to peacebuilding initiatives for many years to come. In this regard, the MTQ and Pesparawi festivals can be seen as an attempt to create an alternative memory
of peace between diverse communities. The challenge is that Ambon today
has a new generation with vague and sometimes distorted memories of the
conflict.

In general, the saying "Katong su cape" offers an appeal and a motive
for a new beginning of peaceful coexistence. But the challenge remains as
to how the motivation, commitment, and activities for peace can be made
real and institutionally effective in everyday life. Ambon society still faces
many challenges. "Katong su cape" tends to emphasize the forgetting of the
conflict rather than its direct engagement and normative resolution. This
approach may be necessary and may work well enough for the time being,
but it is important that other groups continue to nurture their own narratives and normativities of the conflict, not all of which are consistent with
peacebuilding appeals.

The real test for Ambon's many vibrant peace movements will come if
and when another communal clash takes place. The Gunung Nona incident in 2011 was one such test. But rather than destroying the peacebuilding edifice, this incident actually worked to strengthen it. The question is
what might happen in the future. The possibility of conflict is still quite
real; new tensions are emerging in today's free and democratizing Indonesia—for example, during election campaigns, when some are tempted to
use exclusive appeals. In this regard, the women's movement in Ambon

again offers useful and general lessons. The movement started with the simple, unideological realization that the conflict brought no good for women, children, or families. From this simple ethical conviction the movement was progressively enlarged to address wider issues of protection and civil rights for women and children. The women involved further contributed to the discourse and policy of women's rights at the national level. With all its experiences of conflicts and tensions, and at the same time as it remains actively involved in peacebuilding, Ambon, while struggling to hold its own, may at the same time contribute to a national discourse and policy on peaceful coexistence and multireligious recognition.

NOTES

1. This chapter is based on seven months of field research in Ambon. The author is deeply indebted to the many people and organizations that made it possible to conduct interviews; only a few of them featured in this chapter, but more are not mentioned yet are equally invaluable. I wish to thank in particular Abidin Wakano, Brigitta Renyaan, Hasbollah Toisuta, Helena Rijoly, Jacky Manuputty, John Ruhulessin, Khalik Latuconsina, Lusi Peilouw, Margaretha Hendriks, Morika Tetelepta, Rudi Fofid, Rusda Leikawa, Wesly Johannes, and Yance Rumahuru, as well as colleagues at the State Christian Institute (IAKN) Ambon, the State Islamic Institute (IAIN) Ambon, Indonesian Christian University in Maluku (UKIM), Paparisa Ambon Bergerak, and Rumphius Library-Ambon.

2. Abidin Wakano, interview by author, April 7, 2016.

3. Rev. Margaretha Hendriks, interview by author, January 9, 2016.

4. Sr. Brigitta Renyaan, interview by author, May 28, 2016.

5. Rev. Margaretha Hendriks, interview by author, January 9, 2016.

6. Helena Rijoly, interview by author, January 19, 2016; Sr. Brigitta Renyaan, interview by author, May 28, 2016.

7. Website for Makulu Province, n.d., accessed September 5, 2015, www.antaramaluku.com.

8. Discussion with Jacky Manuputty, November 21, 2015.

Gender Contention and Social Recognition in Muslim Women's Organizations in Yogyakarta

ALIMATUL QIBTIYAH

The "City of Tolerance" branding of Yogyakarta has long been an at least partial reality for residents and visitors. In the neighborhood where I live—Wonocatur, Banguntapan, in Bantul—and in other areas as well, the *halal bi halal* expression of greeting and respect that marks the Idul Fitri celebrations at the end of holy month of Ramadan involves people of all religions, asking and giving forgiveness. Tolerance is also reflected in the 2012 Law on the Special Status of Yogyakarta, of which Article 5 starts with an assertion that the province's government will uphold the Republic's unity in diversity.

Yogyakarta's normativity with regard to gender issues derives at least in part from long-held traditions of Javanese culture and ethics. The term *garwo,* meaning the husband or the wife, which is an abbreviation of *sigaraning nyowo* (half of the soul), implies that women and men have more or less the same importance in the family. Of course, the division of roles between men and women in Javanese tradition is also a technical, kinship matter. Kinship in Java (as in much but not all of Indonesia) is bilateral, traced equally through paternal and maternal relatives. In Java a child receives his or her own name with no maternal or paternal "family" name. The presence of several queens in Java and the Indonesian archipelago's history is often cited as another example of relative gender tolerance (Errington 1990; Goody 1976): some examples are Queen Sima in Central Java; Tri Buana Tungga Dewi in East Java; the female sultana of Aceh, who ruled consecutively between 1641 and 1699; Queen Siti Aisyah We Tenriolle in the nineteenth-century Ternate; and Bundo Kandung in Minangkabau (It 2005; Vreede-de Stuers 1960).

Yogyakarta was also an important center for the early women's movement in Indonesia. During the First Women's Congress, which was held in the city in 1928, half of the participants wore hijabs (KOWANI 1978, 33–55; Blackburn 2007). 'Aisyiyah representatives Siti Moendjijah and Siti Hajinah were later chosen as the congress's deputy head and delegate. In the years since the congress, many progressive female leaders have hailed from Yogyakarta.

Of course, gender inequality is also present in Javanese culture. It is reflected in popular expressions such as "Surgo nunut neroko katut" (A wife will go wherever her husband goes, to heaven or hell, whichever is his destination) or the sometimes-heard identification of women with *kasur, dapur, pupur* (mattress, kitchen, face powder), or *manak, masak, macak* (giving birth, cooking, dressing up). When a woman gets married, she often becomes known, no longer by her own name, but by her husband's. Gender inequalities in Java are also intertwined with class. Noble women (*priyayi* or *ningrat*) follow more rigid and hierarchical gender patterns than do commoners (Dzuhayatin 2001, 257). In rural communities, men and women work together in the fields, albeit with a gendered division of labor. In petty market trade as opposed to large-scale and long-distance enterprise, women are typically more numerous and active than are men.

Although there are cultural grounds for some variety of gender equality in Java, the ideal has recently come to be rejected by a number of social movements claiming to speak in the name of Islam. With its numerous college campuses, Yogyakarta today hosts Islamist organizations that oppose equality, such as Hizbut Tahrir Indonesia (HTI), whose presence has grown in recent years (see Ahnaf, chapter 4). It appears that gender-related discourse in Yogyakarta is not normatively homogeneous but contentious. Debates over the values of gender equality are expressed through counternarratives published both in print and online.

In this chapter, I explore and map out views for and against gender equality among several prominent Muslim women's organizations active in the Yogyakarta region. I highlight the rationales and normativities the movements highlight to justify their viewpoints, and the activities in which they engage to disseminate and scale up their views. The three groups on which I focus in this chapter are 'Aisyiyah, Muslimat Nahdatul Ulama (MNU), and Muslimat Hizbut Tahrir Indonesia (MHTI). Data from their respective parent organizations (Muhammadiyah, NU, HTI), as well as from the nongovernmental organization Rifka Annisa and from the Sunan Kalijaga State Islamic University's Center for Women's Studies, will be presented here to extend and compare the findings. The organizations' influence is not limited to Yogyakarta. Hence, although the research for this chapter was conducted in the Yogyakarta region, it reflects broader, national dynamics with regard to debates over gender equality in Muslim Indonesian circles.

'AISYIYAH, MULIMAT, AND MHTI

The three Muslim women's groups were not formed independently but were founded in part by their parent organizations, all of which are led by men. Muhammadiyah created 'Aisyiyah, Nahdatul Ulama established Muslimat NU, and Hizbut Tahrir established Muslimah HTI (MHTI). Muhammadiyah is a centenarian organization (founded in 1912), while NU is more than ninety years old (founded in 1926). Hizbut Tahrir is quite young (see Anhaf, chapter 4), as it only entered Indonesia in the 1980s; in 2017 it was officially dissolved by the government of President Joko Widodo and Vice President Jusuf Kala.

'Aisyiyah

'Aisyiyah is the women's arm of Muhammadiyah, an Islamic reform movement dedicated to the principles of religious purification through a return to the Qur'an and Sunnah, and *amar ma'ruf nahi munkar* (enjoining good and forbidding wrong). 'Aisyiyah was established on May 19, 1917, on the anniversary of Prophet Muhammad's Night Journey (the Isra and Mir'aj). This organization's existence cannot be separated from Muhammadiyah, which had been founded just five years earlier. Siti Bariyah was chosen to lead the new women's organization, assisted by eight other women on the executive board. (Contrary to a widespread belief, the female leader of the new organization was *not* the wife of the founder of Muhammadiyah, KH Ahmad Dahlan). The organization was named after Prophet Muhammad's wife, who was known as an intelligent and pious woman, with the hope that 'Aisyiyah members would follow her example (Pimpinan Pusat 'Aisyiyah 2004). 'Aisyiyah was the only formal Muslim women's organization that participated in the 1928 Women's Congress, which had both Muslim and secular participants. The organization today has an estimated four million members, and branches are found in all regions of Indonesia (Putra 2017, 9).

The Muhammadiyah-'Aisyiyah interpretation of the Qur'an emphasizes that there is no difference in *da'wah* or "outreach"/proselytization activities with regard to gender, and this progressive principle has long shaped the character of the movement as a whole (Qibtiyah 2015a). The four pillars on which 'Aisyiyah stands are education, health care, social welfare, and economic affairs. As affirmed in the forty-seventh conference of 'Aisyiyah in Makassar in August 2015, the organization is officially committed to progressive Islam, cultural enlightenment, and women's empowerment. As an autonomous organization under the Muhammadiyah canopy, 'Aisyiyah is active in all Indonesian provinces, from Sabang to Merauke. It operates some 19,181 kindergartens. On March 10, 2016, the organization also founded the Universitas 'Aisyiyah in Yogyakarta—the first university in the country managed by a women's organization.[1] The organization also seeks to advance women's participation in the economy. 'Aisyiyah has established no fewer than 568 cooperatives, 1,029 household enterprises (Bina Usaha Ekonomi Keluarga, BUEKA), and dozens of Baitul Maal wa Tamwil microfinance services. In the field of health care, the organization runs eighty-seven general hospitals, 105 maternity hospitals, sixteen pediatric hospitals, twenty community health care centers, 106 clinics, seventy-six mother and child clinics, and many other health consultation centers (Pimpinan Pusat 'Aisyiyah n.d.). It makes additional contributions to social welfare by running orphanages, nursing homes, and training centers, as well as organizing aid for poor children and the elderly.

The organization's advocacy for policies to empower the poor, women, and children is conducted locally as well as at the national level. 'Aisyiyah cooperates with the Indonesian government as well as a long list of local, national, and international organizations. Its international partners in recent years include the Asia Foundation (TAF), the Netherlands Embassy, the Global Fund for Children (GFC), the United Nations Development Program (UNDP), the United Nations Children's Fund (UNICEF), the United States Agency for International Development (USAID), John Hopkins University (JHU), and AusAID (Pimpinan Pusat 'Aisyiyah n.d.). Through these and other activities, 'Aisyiyah underscores the vital religious *and* public role of women in Indonesian and Muslim public life.

Muslimat NU

Nahdlatul Ulama's women's associations consists of three age-differentiated entities: Muslimat (for adult women), Fatayat NU (for young adult women), and the NU Female Students' Association. The founding of Muslimat NU, the first of these organizations to come into existence, was spurred by the colonial conditions in the 1930s and by Muslim women's calls to organize to support the nationalist cause. The first appeals for the establishment of an autonomous women's organization were heard at the Thirteenth NU Congress in Menes, Banten, in 1938. Calls were again heard at the Fourteenth NU Congress in Magelang, in 1939, and again at the Fifteenth NU Congress in Surabaya, in 1940. Muslimat was actually established only several years later, at the Sixteenth NU Congress on March 29, 1946. Its establishment was triggered not only by the desire to improve opportunities for girls' and women's education but by the Dutch colonial crackdown on the nationalist movement's male leadership. Indonesian Muslims and the NU leadership had become keenly aware of the need to include women in the struggle (Pimpinan Pusat Muslimat NU n.d.). That it took twenty years (since the founding of NU in 1926) to establish Muslimat reflected the strong patriarchal culture within NU ranks more than it did any inconsistency on the part of female activists. The conviction that it was enough for women to stay at home, without active involvement in the organization, prevailed among NU's male membership. However, under the circumstances of the independence struggle, opinions changed, and the founding of the organization was supported by many prominent senior male leaders, including most notably KH Wahab Chasbullah.

The Muslimat's mission statement also reflected the social, educational, and political circumstances of the times: "To achieve a prosperous society, inspired by the teachings of Sunni Islam, so that the Indonesian Republic enjoys prosperity and justice, and is blessed by God." The organization's mission statement went on to list four core goals: first, to have members of Indonesian society, particularly women, become religiously, socially, and civically conscious; second, to have members of Indonesian society, particularly women, become qualified, independent, and devoted to God; third, to have members of Indonesian society, particularly women, become aware of their obligations and rights as individuals and members of the public, in accordance with Islamic teachings; and fourth, to build a society blessed by God in which justice and prosperity are evenly distributed (Pimpinan Pusat Muslimat NU n.d.).[2]

Muslimah Hizbut Tahrir (MHTI)

The establishment of MHTI was also linked to the mission and history of its parent organization, Hizbut Tahrir Indonesia (HTI). As Anhaf makes clear in his chapter in this book, the latter organization arrived in Indonesia in the 1980s and utilized *da'wah* proselytization on large university campuses across the country to build a following. From the 1990s onward, the organization's outreach extended into state bureaucracies, mosque networks, and private businesses and homes.

Hizbut Tahrir was brought to Indonesia by Abdurrahman al Baghdadi. The organization had previously been banned in several Middle Eastern countries, including Jordan, Syria, and Egypt (Mubarok 2008, 129). Officially HTI is dedicated to nonviolent mobilization. However, its rallies and media statements often carry an element of verbal violence (Qibtiyah 2016, 175–76). In Indonesia, the organization has seen its ranks swell since the early *Reformasi* period, largely as a result of its campaigns on large university campuses, including the Agricultural University in Bogor, Padjajaran University in Bandung, Airlangga University in Surabaya, Hasanudin University in Makassar, and several campuses in the Yogyakarta area (Mubarok 2008, 131). One of its most public campaigns in the early 2000s centered on its appeal for legislation mandating state enforcement of Islamic law, which it promoted with the theme "Save Indonesia with Shariah." HTI organized rallies in cities across Indonesia (Mubarok 2008, 130). It was also active in the 2016–17 campaign against the Chinese Christian governor of Jakarta, Basuki Purnama Tjahaja (see Hefner, chapter 1; Bagir, chapter 7). However, in the aftermath of the latter campaign, the government in July 2017 took measures to dissolve the organization, on the basis of a revision to the 2013 Law on Mass Organizations. Wiranto, the coordinating minister for political, legal, and security affairs, cited three reasons for the government's actions: that HTI provided no substantial benefit for the nation's development, that HTI opposed the national ideology of the Pancasila, and that the organization's actions were raising tensions in Indonesian society (Movanita 2017). With the dissolution of its parent organization by the government, MHTI was also formally dissolved, although some of its chapters continue to meet privately.

On matters of gender and women's rights, HTI and MHTI are uncompromisingly antiliberal. Both organizations regard the concept of gender equality as a Western ideology and cultural product designed to undermine Islamic values and religion. According to Arum Harjati (2013), a Muslimah HTI leader, the work-life balance of Indonesian women distorts the natural law outlined in Islam. Women's employment outside the home destroys family bonds. The concept of gender equality also goes against the "Islamic" idea that, by their very nature, men are the heads of the household and income earners while women are homemakers. MHTI brochures also make clear, however, that Muslim women have a role to play in HTI mobilization, inasmuch as they are "shariah-obedient, smart, conceptual, political, nonviolent mothers of the generation and pearls of civilization" (MHTI, n.d.).

On a day-to-day basis, MHTI activities revolve around intensive sessions of individual and group religious study and guidance by female

Muslim teachers. The women's organization also sends delegations to campuses and establishes alliances with other conservative or Islamist groups to challenge government policies regarded as contrary to Islam. As with HTI as a whole, the ultimate goal of MHTI is to contribute to the implementation of shariah and the establishment of a caliphate in Indonesia.

In December 2016, MHTI organized the Fourth "Mothers of the Archipelago" Congress (Kongres Ibu Nusantara) at the Yogyakarta Expo Center. The event's theme was "The State as the Supporting Pillar of Family Prosperity" (Negara Soko Guru Ketahanan Keluarga). According to MHTI data, six hundred women from various professions attended the event. It was resolved at the congress that the continuing and systematic deterioration of family bonds was the result of the country's preoccupation with capitalist profit-seeking. This course of action, it was said, was causing a great assortment of social ills, including drug abuse, motorcycle gangs, LGBT activism, and promiscuity. The MHTI resolution made clear that only the establishment of a caliphate could resolve these problems; in so doing it would also sustain and protect the family and women. "Because of this, the solution to the problem of family destruction is to engage in a common struggle for the establishment of a caliphate, through which the state will indeed become the supporting pillar of family prosperity," said MHTI spokeswoman Iffah A. Rochmah (2016).

CONTENTIOUS GENDER ISSUES IN INDONESIA

Muslim debates on gender focus not only on social relations in ordinary life but also on matters of worship (Qibtiyah 2012). To see the dynamics of thought and policies among 'Aisyiyah, Muslimat, and MHTI and their parent organizations Muhammadiyah, NU, and HTI on the issue of female leadership, my research focused on three issues: (1) the possibility of women leading prayers (i.e., serving as an *imam*) for adult men; (2) the acceptance of women in the highest leadership of their parent organizations; (3) the response to a polemic regarding the leadership in the Royal Court (*kraton*) of Yogyakarta, after Sultan Hamengkobuwono X announced the possibility of a woman becoming the ruler of the sultanate.

Women Leading Prayers for Adult Men

Female leadership in prayers under certain circumstances is more easily and widely accepted in 'Asyiyah than it is in either Muslimat or MHTI. The disposition in 'Aisyiyah is related in part to rulings of Muhammadiyah's National Tarjih Congress in Malang, East Java, in 2010, according to which in certain settings a woman can become a president or lead prayers for adult men (Dzuhaytin 2015, 200). Diah Siti Nuraini, secretary-general of 'Asiyiyah, said female leadership is possible, for example, when the husband is a convert and cannot say prayers fluently, while the wife can.[3] The scholar-delegates at the congress explained that the general condition for a prayer leader is that the role should be from "the best of all of you," without stipulating that such a person must be a man or a woman (Muhyidin 2013).

However, some 'Aisyiyah activists disagree with this ruling and insist a female imam cannot be accepted under any circumstance. One woman interviewed for this chapter explained that prayer requires concentration and that men may be unable to concentrate if they hear a female voice. Therefore, female leadership in prayer may be allowed but only for the Zuhr and Asr prayers, which are not read aloud.[4] Muhammadiyah public intellectual Ahmad Muhsin Kamaludiningrat also disagreed, but on different grounds. He said women serving as imams was prohibited because the Prophet Muhammad never sent his wife Aisha to lead prayers for adult men.[5] Muhammadiyah Yogyakarta Province head Gita Danupranata said he leaves the matter of women imams to the organization's jurisprudence division and added: "I am not very familiar with the results of the discussions. The *fiqh* aspects are clear, we follow what we had agreed upon, based on a fatwa from the *tarjih* session, which discusses the issue. [This means that] if an adult male is present, he will be the imam."[6]

While the question of female prayer leadership has been extensively discussed in 'Aisyiyah and Muhammadiyah, neither Muslimat nor NU has discussed the issue.[7] This does not mean, however, that the matter is of no importance to those NU members who are concerned about gender matters. For example, for Mochamad Sodik, a young NU intellectual and the director of the Center for Women's Studies at Sunan Kalijaga State Islamic

University in Yogyakarta, whether a woman can or cannot become an imam is a cultural matter, and Indonesian society is just not ready to give the matter serious attention: "There is no problem with contemporary interpretations, the problem is within our culture, which is just not ready yet [for female imams]. In this case, we have to consider local wisdom. For those who wish to see change, there needs to be educational effort. The change shouldn't be implemented without such educational outreach, because the effort won't be productive."[8]

Other women in Muslimat NU adopt an even stricter line. For example, according to Fathiyah, a member of Muslimat NU, prayers for men should always be led by men because this is a basic principle of Islamic worship and there should be no human interference with it:

> A woman should not be an imam for adult males; prayer is a religious duty, enjoined by God. It is made absolutely clear in the hadith that the first rows in congregational prayers are for men, then children, then women. Woman cannot be an imam. . . . If there is a hadith that allows women to lead prayers for men, we should question its validity. . . . I'm firm when it comes to shariah, and prayer is a matter of shariah. In private cases, when the wife knows the prayers better than her husband, she should teach him. If he cannot [learn], then just use a cassette, or do whatever you must to support him, and follow him, because the imam should be male. There are many references in Islamic tradition on this matter. If a person questions them, I urge that person to learn about the schools of Islamic law [madhhab] and their history. Prayer is sacred, people should not interfere with it.[9]

MHTI rejects any suggestion that women should be able to lead prayers for men. The principle they invoke is the same one that they invoke in all spheres of social life: it is men who must lead women—at home, in mosque, and in all social organizations.[10] MHTI activists, like those of HTI, identify the call for female imams with feminism. And they perceive feminism as a Western product contrary to Islamic teachings, the aim of which is to destroy the family order as sanctified in Islam (Kurniawan 2012).

Female Leadership in Social Organizations

The matter of women's leadership in their parent organizations, which is to say in Islamic organizations that include men, is also subject to debates in each of the organizations under discussion in this chapter. Much as was the case with female leadership of men in prayer, the formal involvement of women in the leadership of NU is considerably less welcome than it is in Muhammadiyah and 'Aisyiyah.

According to the organization's bylaws, members of Muhammadiyah are "men and women aged seventeen and above" (Pimpinan Pusat Muhammadiyah 2005, 31). Since 2010, the chairwoman of 'Aisyiyah has also been recognized as a member of the Muhammadiyah organization's central executive board at the national level. Although many Muhammadiyah and 'Aisyiyah activists assumed that the same policy of women's representation would be implemented at the regional and local level, few chapters have followed suit. Even Muhammadiyah's Yogyakarta city chapter ignores the regulation. According to the chapter head, Pranata, it was never clear whether the policy was intended to apply to levels other than the central board. However, Pranata also explained that he was not opposed to implementing the regulation at the local level, if it was indeed recommended.[11] Notwithstanding the efforts of women at 'Aisiyiyah congresses in 2015, as of November 2016 only two provincial branches of Muhammadiyah have implemented the policy of including women in regional executives.

According to NU guidelines, to become a member one needs to be "any Indonesian citizen who professes Islam, has reached puberty, and agrees to obey the organization's rules" (Pengurus Besar NU 2015, 22). According to one local Muslimat activist, Amelia, although so far no woman has been involved in NU's central executive leadership, female representation is in principle not a problem.[12] Others say that the absence of women in the highest leadership is not an issue in the first place because women have their own organization, Muslimat, and that women have been represented from time to time on various advisory councils—if not yet on the NU's national executive.[13]

As these and other comments indicate, the participation of women in lower-lying assemblies, institutions, divisions of their parent organizations has for some time now not been a problem for Muhammadiyah or NU. In

2015–20, 'Aisyiyah even had a policy that its main leadership should be involved in those lower-ranking divisions so that the programs sponsored by those divisions run smoothly and effectively. A similar pattern is seen in NU. In MHTI, according to Basyariah, the situation resembles that of Muslimat NU. This is to say, at the main HTI office in the United Kingdom, there is a women's section director; the same structure is applied in Indonesia.[14]

Leadership in Yogyakarta Kraton

In recent years, the matter of leadership in the Yogyakarta royal court (*kraton*) has been in the media and academic spotlight, triggered by the fact that all five children of the current sultan are daughters. In legal terms the controversy began in the aftermath of the issuance of the 2012 Law on the Special Status of Yogyakarta. Article 18 of this legislation requires a candidate for the governor of Yogyakarta to present a résumé that includes a profile of his wife (not a husband). Several parties signaled that this regulation discriminates against women (Qibtiyah 2015c, 1).

The controversy surrounding the Yogya court and female leadership escalated in 2015, in the aftermath of several formal declarations by the sultan that have come to be known as the *Sabdatama, Sabda Raja,* and *Dawuh Raja.* Not only groups within the *kraton,* but also outsiders, including mainstream Muslim organizations, objected to various aspects of the sultan's announcements. One of the more controversial stipulations in the sultan's decision was that henceforth the sultan's royal titles would not include his identity as "God's vice-regent on earth," or *khalifatullah.* This declaration caused great consternation in local Muslim circles. The head of Muhammadiyah branch in the city of Yogyakarta, Heni Astiyanto, said the following in an interview for the national newsweekly *Tempo* on May 7, 2015: "The abolition of the religious leader title practically changed the Yogyakarta Kraton's identification with the sultanate of Mataram. The sultan did not have to abolish the *khalifatullah* title if his aim was to modernize the *kraton.* The *khalifatullah* office does not indicate that the sultan is a solely Muslim leader. The *khalifatullah* means governance over the earth, not only over a particular religion. If the title is removed, it means there is a new king. But of which kingdom? The *kraton* of Yogyakarta is the Sultanate of Mataram" (*Tempo* 2015).

Another controversial aspect of the sultan's 2015 declarations had to do with his announcement that his eldest daughter would succeed him as Yogyakarta's ruler. On this matter, Heni, like most mainstream Muslim leaders, was adamant in his opposition: "The sultan's decision has raised his eldest daughter, G. K. R. Pembayun, to the rank of crown princess. We disagree, not because of [our opposition to gender] equality, but because of the tradition [that says] that the ruler should be a male." A similar sentiment was expressed by the deputy head of the executive board of NU in Yogyakarta, Jadul Maulana, a well-known progressive activist. Maulana told *Tempo* on May 7, 2015, that he was committed to gender equality but felt that the question of a female ruler was a matter of tradition. A strong supporter of democracy, he also objected to the abolition of the khalifatullah: "Khalifatullah is part of the teachings of the Qur'an. Not for discriminatory purposes, but to guide leaders in carrying out their duties in line with God's teachings. It's universal. If Sultan Hamengkubuwono X abolishes the khalifatullah, it will be tantamount to cultural suicide" (Tempo 2015).

The sultan's decisions were rejected not only by groups and individuals from outside the court but also by his eleven siblings (Anshori 2016, 1). The decision was also rejected by large segments of the Yogyakarta public. A group that named itself Warga Kauman (Residents of the Kauman) displayed two hundred banners around the central city bearing the words "Reject the Sultan's Decision: Supporters of the *Khalifatullah*" (Tolak sabda raja: pejuang khalifatullah) and "Restore the Order: Yogya Forever Special" (Kembalikan paugeran: Jogja tetap istimeawa) (Hudzaifah 2015, 1).

Not all groups rejected the sultan's decision. Some supported it or some of its provisions related to female leadership. One of 'Aisyiyah's leaders said the following: "Look at *Adabul maraah fil islam,* which speaks about women's leadership and the *fiqh* of women; generally there is no problem about female leaders in all sectors and levels. The foundation is in Surah An-Nahl of the Qur'an, verse 97, and in At-Taubah, verse 71, where the word *auliya* is understood as a leader, not only a helper. 'Aisyiyah has not issued a statement regarding this. It seems to be an internal affair of the *kraton*."[15]

An NU official, who asked not to have his name disclosed, said it was not a problem if the sultan wanted his daughter to become queen, but he disagreed with the abolition of the *khalifatullah* title inherited from the Sultanate of Mataram. That decision would have dire consequences—implying that the religion of the Yogyakarta Sultanate could be changed to be some religion other than Islam.[16] A similarly critical viewpoint was published on the website of the provincial board of NU in Yogyakarta. The statement explained that the key issue was not whether a woman could become a leader or king; rather, it pertained to the religious and traditional heritage of the Sultanate of Mataram in Yogyakarta. This is in line with Bray Sri Paweling's argument in a book titled *Islam Jowo bertutur sabdaraja: Pertarungan kebudayaan, Khasebul Katholik dan kerja misi* (2016). He and others have argued that the *sabdaraja* has been part of "fundamentalist Catholic" efforts to remove Islam as the ethical and religious foundation of the Yogyakarta court.

When asked about Muhammadiyah's or 'Aisyiyah's official viewpoint on the matter, 'Aisyiyah chairwoman Noordjannah Djohantini said that both organizations are aware that their members have divergent opinions on the sultan's declarations and that there was no need for the organizations to take an official stance on court matters. Noordjannah stated that personally she felt the *kraton* could be led by a queen as long as the court's historical and cultural legacy was not compromised.[17]

As these and other examples show, the 'Aisyiyah leadership is far from unitary, but it tends to be more progressive on gender issues than NU Muslimat. But there is a range of opinion from conservative to progressive feminist in both organizations. In this regard, both organizations stand in striking contrast to MHTI, whose understanding of scriptural prescriptions on matters of gender tends to be inflexible and antiliberal, consistent with its conviction that feminism in any form is a Western creation designed to destroy Islam.

Polygamy

Since the First Women's Congress in 1928, the issue of polygamy has been fiercely debated both across and within Muslim women's organizations. Some women activists and scholars forbid the practice, while others say it should be allowed under certain circumstances. Those women activists today who allow polygamy tend to do so more for the sake of preventing adultery than because they think it is an ideal form of marriage. In a book published by 'Aisyiyah's central board on family matters in Islam, entitled *Tuntunan menuju keluarga sakinah* (Guidance toward a safe and happy family), it is clearly stated that marriage in Islam is based on the principle of monogamy (Pimpinan Pusat 'Aisyiyah 2015, 71). Nuraini, the organization's secretary-general, made this same point in an interview: "Muhammadiyah does not advocate polygamy. It is necessary to rethink the harm it causes to women and children. Ahmad Dahlan's [the founder of Muhammadiyah] practicing of polygamy was a proselytization strategy, just like that of the Prophet Muhammad. But today, even if the reason is the same, any instance of polygamy must be made subject to negative social sanctions."[18]

Another 'Aisyiyah member, Nurhidayani, said that it is almost always impossible for polygamy to be fair, so it is better that such a marriage not be formalized at all. Under certain emergency circumstances, for example when there is no son, and when all concerned parties agree, polygamy may be allowed. But women have equal rights in *mu'asharah* (the mutual relation of husband and wife), to enjoy their relationship, and to have heirs and an inheritance. For example, if a man is infertile, he must accept his fate or divorce his wife or let her divorce him.[19]

A different perspective on the topic of polygamy was offered by Amelia of Muslimat NU. In her view, polygamy is an emergency measure, but some NU members still see it as a "blessing" to become the second and otherwise additional wife of, in particular, a traditionalist religious scholar (*kyai*):

> Islam does make room for men to have more than one wife. However, polygamy is permissible only in emergency situations; it is not something that one can do as one pleases. Even in NU some groups argue that what Islam really promotes is monogamy. The view, however, is not popular in the broader NU community. Some NU members still see it as a blessing, so sometimes women are willing to become the second, third, or even fourth wife of a religious leader. I think the practice of *sirri* [temporary] marriage is also one of the causes of

widespread polygamy. Not only within NU. We see it [*sirri* marriage] as more harmful than beneficial—the legal status of the children is unclear, the wife is often neglected and even abandoned, and so on.[20]

A very different perspective on the question of polygamy is adopted by members of Rifka Annisa, a progressive Muslim women's organization. This organization firmly opposes polygamy, owing to what members regard as violence against women intrinsic to all polygamous marriages. An activist in Rifka Annisa, Saeroni, made the following observation:

> Rifka Annisa does not agree with allowing polygamy. In reality, polygamy causes great damage. The Qur'anic verse [that allows it] was more about justice . . . in terms of the social situation of those times. In 2002, of all 1,062 requests to register polygamous marriages, around 600 were followed up, and only about 50 were granted by the court. Applications for divorce caused by polygamy number more than two thousand a year, and the trend is upward. The highest number was in 2013–14. . . . In Islamic law, polygamy is complicated, a consideration of justice must be there. How do men enter a polygamous marriage? [In reality] there are several ways: first, by forging their identity documents; second, by forging divorce certificates; third, by forging the first wife's letter of consent.[21]

The uncompromising stance of Rifka Annisa is shared by NU intellectual Mochamad Sodik of Sunan Kalijaga University; however, his view is not shared by all in Muslimat NU: "In Islam monogamy is a priority, and a happy family is one that is monogamous, not polygamous. Polygamy opens a door that is better closed so as to avoid household conflict. Polygamy as such is a construct that potentially engenders unhappiness."[22]

For MHTI polygamy is *mubah*, permitted, because it is mentioned in the Qur'an. God has made it halal in an absolute sense (Komara 2009). However, MHTI activists explain, a polygamous marriage must also be just and responsible. Justice in a polygamous marriage means fairness beyond love—and must include fairness in the division of income and time among wives, spending for children, and other matters. The husband should discuss these and other issues with the wife—but in the end, MHTI activists explain, it is the husband's decision, since he is the leader of the household. Interestingly, however, although HTI has a "favorable" view of polygamy, the incidence of the practice among members is low, with only 1 percent of HTI men actually living in polygamous marriages.[23]

'Aisyiyah is progressive when it comes to the issue of polygamy. This quality is seen in its official views published in *Tuntunan menuju keluarga sakinah*, which states that monogamy is the principle on which marriage is based. Muslimat NU is not as forward-looking, and in some NU circles polygamy is seen as normatively acceptable. To MHTI, for the sake of what its leadership regards as fidelity to the Qur'an, polygamy is permissible, and justice is defined primarily not in terms of love or emotions but in terms of economic fairness for the wives and children.

LGBT Issues

The LGBT issue is not a new phenomenon, as there are historical records of it in the religious texts and art of all cultures. One prominent example of LGBT-related issues is the story of Lot in the Qur'an and the Old Testament; but there are also examples closer to Indonesia, such as the Warok Reog Ponorogo (a transgender dance role) or the *bissu* (transgender ritual specialists) among the Muslim Bugis in Sulawesi. However, the US Supreme Court's decision in 2015 to legalize same-sex marriage had the unexpected effect of triggering acts of intolerance against gay men and lesbians and trans people all around the world; here in Yogyakarta, the famous Islamic boarding school for trans people in Kota Gede, Yogyakarta, became the focus of antigay violence and eventually had to close (Aziz 2016, 33). Another sign of the growing controversy surrounding LGBT issues involved a well-known Canadian Muslim activist and writer who is openly lesbian, Irsyad Manji. During a visit to Yogyakarta in May 2012, Manji was attacked by Islamist activists while preparing to give a lecture at the Institute for Islamic and Social Studies (LKiS) (Parwito 2012). Earlier, Manji's talk at the Center for Religious and Cross-Cultural Studies (CRCS) at Gadjah Mada University had been canceled by the rector in the aftermath of demonstrations by Muslim student activists from the Islamist student group KAMMI (Simanjuntak 2012).

In Muslim society today there are two currents of opinion on LGBT issues: a minority support LGBT rights and a larger majority reject them (Qibtiyah 2015b, 205–7). Members of the first group include some Muslims who themselves belong to the LBGT community. Their approach to scriptural reasoning tends to be contextual and hermeneutic, taking exception to received scriptural and legal commentaries. The proponents of this view thus argue that same-sex love is a gift of God, not a crime or act of violence against others. Some people say that in accordance with nature, love should occur between man and woman. But who in this case can determine whether something is natural or not? If God has decreed that love between man and woman is alone natural, why do so many people fall in love with people of the same sex?

A second argument in support of LGBT rights is that Islam does not forbid homosexuality, but only anal sodomy (Aliansyah 2015, 1; Salvatore 2016). In many passages in the Qur'an the Prophet Muhammad is quoted as condemning those who follow the lifestyle of "Lot's people," but not once does the Prophet reproach what today we would call those with LGBT identities. A third argument cited in support of LGBT rights is that Lot's people (as described in the Qur'an) are not synonymous with gay men and lesbians. In the verses of the Qur'an it is clearly stated that many in Lot's community were actually married and heterosexual. In other words, the fact that God cursed Lot's community does not necessarily mean he was condemning gay men and lesbians.

Critics of the pro-LGBT position claim that a Qur'anic verse explicitly condemns homosexuality. However, the well-known Muslim scholars and gender rights activists Musdah Mulia and Husein Muhammad (Mulia 2011; Husein 2011; 'Aini 2013) insist that the sexual conduct in question is not homosexuality as such but actions that exceed certain "limits" and include violence (represented by the term *al-fahisyah*, for example, in Surah Al-A'raf, verse 80). A fourth and final argument made in support of LGBT rights is that, contrary to the claims of antihomosexual activists, allowing LGBT rights will not result in a population imbalance. Since time immemorial only 4 percent of people have been homosexual; moreover, overpopulation is more of a problem nowadays than is a shortage of offspring.

Those who reject LGBT rights and see nonheterosexual relationships as un-Islamic make the following arguments. First, they say to be gay or

LGBT is a choice, not a matter of nature. Second, they say that homosexuality is an evil social disease clearly condemned by God. If homosexuality were something innate or natural, it would have emerged earlier in human history and not only in Lot's time. Third, they view homosexuality as morally repugnant (*fahishah*). And fourth, they claim that same-sex marriages will threaten the stability and continuity of the human population because they do not produce offspring.

Between the two positions is a moderate view. Muslims who adopt this position do not support the legalization of same-sex marriage but do reject discrimination, marginalization, and violence against LGBT people. Muslims who support this middle position tend to argue that marriage must take place on the basis of a heterosexual relationship. However, this group does not condemn LGBT people. As citizens, the latter are seen as having rights to live in a safe environment and to be treated equally to non-LGBT people.

Where do 'Aisyiyah, Muslimat, and MHTI position themselves on these questions? 'Aisyiyah's official position, as regularly stated in the organization's journal, *Suara 'Aisyiyah*, is that marriage is and must be heterosexual. However, the organization is quick to add that it "does not approve of violence and discrimination against any citizens, regardless of their sexual preferences, as religious organizations are responsible to guide and proselytize in humanistic ways" (*Suara 'Aisyiyah* 2016, 39). However, there are other points of view in 'Aisyiyah and Muhammadiyah. The official journal of Muhammadiyah, *Suara Muhammadiyah*, has in recent years featured headlines that promote an unqualified rejection of homosexuality and LGBT rights; in 2015 headlines included such phrases as "Reject LGBT," "Protect Children from LGBT," "A Disease, Not a Human Right," "This Threat Is Real," and "LGBT Must Be Opposed." Kamaludiningrat agrees with *Suara Muhammadiyah* that the issue of LGBT is a kind of "proxy war" or "cold war" between the West and the Muslim world and needs to be addressed carefully.[24]

The NU leadership also tends to officially oppose LGBT rights. NU deputy supreme leader KH Miftahul Akhyar delivered the NU's central board's position on the matter in Jakarta on February 25, 2016. The board urged the government to stop all liberal propaganda aimed at normalizing homosexuality and to refuse all foreign aid in support of LGBT rights. It also urged that representatives from NU in the National Assembly to draft a law to ban all LGBT-related activities. To prevent homosexuality, NU officials emphasize, family bonds need to be strengthened with premarital education and religious consultation (Fathoni 2016, 1). Notwithstanding these uncompromising statements, NU officials also emphasize that LGBT persons should not be isolated or attacked but should be given moral guidance. Muslimat NU in Subang demanded that the government enlighten and rehabilitate LGBT people to return them to "God's path" and heal their "illness" (*Pasundan Ekspres* 2016).

This view is similar to Muslimat NU activist Fathiyah's stance; she argues that LGBT people should be encouraged to return to their "original" or "true" sexuality, because humans are by nature heterosexual. If a trans woman wanted to work at her business, it would be better not to accept that person, as their presence could affect other workers.[25] Nurhidayani from 'Aisyiyah has a different point of view. She would accept an LGBT person for employment but would at the same time try to heal him or her. Muhammadiyah's Yogyakarta city head, Pranata, agrees with 'Aisyiyah that there should be guidance and counseling to help LGBT people and that they should not be subject to acts of violence or social discrimination.[26]

MHTI, on the other hand, completely rejects the existence and civic legitimacy of the LGBT community. Representatives from this organization state unequivocally that homosexuality or transsexuality in any form is incompatible with human nature and God's commands. MHTI emphasizes that strong family bonds are important in preventing children from becoming lesbian, gay, bisexual, or transgender.[27] MHTI leader Ahmad Jaelani, a member of the HTI central board, wrote on HTI's website that LGBT conduct is *haram* (forbidden) and that those who engage in it should be subject to death by stoning (Jaelani 2016).

On the issue of LGBT, then, 'Aisyiyah and Muslimat-NU tend to take a middle ground. They reject efforts at legalizing same-sex marriage. They do not see same-sex marriage through the normative prism of civic rights or equal social recognition but regard it as a matter of religious ethics. At the same time, however, they oppose discrimination or violence against LGBT individuals. Their rejection does not require or recommend physical punishment but instead advocates *da'wah* (religious appeal or education) to make LGBT individuals "normal," which is to say, heterosexual. As is the case with so many other issues, MHTI is more rigid and condemnatory, basing its argument mainly on (its understanding of) scriptural sources and medieval jurisprudence (*fiqh*). MHTI rejects the idea that LGBT matters have anything to do with social recognition or civil rights, insisting that homosexuality is against God's law—and that those who think otherwise do so with the express intent of undermining Islam.

TYPOLOGY OF GENDER NORMATIVITY

Differences between 'Aisyiyah, Muslimat, and MHTI at first sight seem conspicuous and large, but there are also certain similarities. To illustrate these differences we can identify three general approaches to gender issues: textual, moderate, and progressive. Like all typologies, this one is something of a simplification. It is important to note that each organization can move from one approach to another, depending on the issue under discussion. The use of this typology can, however, help in understanding the sources of the organizations' normativity in their interpretation of Islam. One of the first interesting observations is that a moderate-progressive tendency is more common among the old groups, Muhammadiyah and NU, while HTI, which is relatively new, tends to be quite conservative (Qodir 2009).

Textualist approaches to religious knowledge tend to be literal, ahistorical, and piecemeal rather than holistic and contextual. According to the great Pakistani thinker Fazlur Rahman (1982, 2), textualists display a common failure to appreciate the underlying unity of the Qur'an. They fail to understand the difference between the general principles and specific responses to particular historical events. Because of their literalism, they are convinced that the understanding of revelation centuries ago in a patriarchal society remains universally relevant today. With regard to gender issues, their interpretation tends to be unabashedly patriarchal in representing women's roles, status, and rights as subordinate to those of men. Literalists generally oppose the notion of reform, especially with regard to gender issues and feminism, which they consider Western ideologies that are incompatible with Muslim tradition. Some literalists argue that people who endorse non-Islamic norms, no matter how innocently, violate Islamic law and thus oppose God (Burhanudin and Fathurahman 2004).

People who are recognized as moderates accept elements of feminism, as long as these elements do not stand in contradiction with what they perceive as the fundamental values of Islam. They argue that not all feminist ideas come from the West. Since Islam provides a foundation to solve the problem of gender inequality, this aspect of feminism is in line with Islamic values. Moderates also believe that Islam is the perfect religion. The Qur'an and hadith provide guidance that encompasses gender relations. However, unlike the literalist group, moderates use contextual methodologies to understand scripture, insisting that, even if scripture does not change, its understanding often does (Burhanudin and Fathurahman 2004).

The majority of NU and Muhammadiyah scholars belong to this middle category. Munawar Chalil, one of the most prominent Muhammadiyah intellectuals of the 1930s, in his books *Kesopanan perempuan Islam* (Modesty for Muslim women; 1936) and *Nilai wanita* (Women's values; 1954), shows just such a moderate perspective on matters of gender. Islam does not regard women as of lesser worth, he writes, but neither does it deify them, as they are human beings. It also does not see them as identical with men. They are different, but as human beings they are "on the same level." What differs are their roles and responsibilities in accordance with their natures, which are different but complementary (Chalil 1954).

Members of 'Aisyiyah and Muslimat generally belong to the moderate group, although the former also adopt more progressive perspectives on some gender matters, including polygamy. The progressive approach treats the Qur'an and hadith as sources of divine guidance and law but applies *ijitihad* to take into account the context of revelation and interpretation (Abdullah 1996; Amal and Panggabean 2005; Rahman 1982; Saeed 2005). Progressives active in academic settings also make use of philosophy, psychology, sociology, and anthropology to produce a richer understanding of the scriptures' historic and contextual meanings. They believe that texts should be open to discussion and, if necessary, reinterpretation. Using these approaches to scripture and interpretation, moderates, including many here in Yogyakarta, promote what some have called a "postdogmatic religiosity" (Abdullah 2002; Qibtiyah 2007).

Most in the progressive or contextualist group accept some feminist notions of equality in matters of the economy, society, and politics. Although they recognize that there are biological differences between men and women, they insist that both sexes have equal status, rights, and roles in their families, communities, and nation. Musdah Mulia, a prolific feminist scholar from NU and professor at Syarif Hidayatullah State Islamic University in Jakarta, argues that the only hierarchy given by God is between the *Kholiq* (God /Creator) and *makhluq* (God's creation) (Mulia 2005). Invoking Islam's most elementary creedal doctrine, *tauhid* (God's oneness), Mulia argues that mankind must submit completely only to God. Equally important, so as to be true to the principle of God's oneness, believers must not discriminate or oppress fellow human beings. Mulia further observes that in the eyes of God the most dignified of humans are those who are pious, and this includes both men and women.

According to progressive writers, women's status in the early years of Islam was higher than it became in subsequent centuries. In the tenth century, male jurists systematized Islamic law and did so in a way that restricted the public activity of women far more than had been the case at the time of the Prophet Muhammad (Afsaruddin 1999; Mulia 2005). Mulia argues that the closer one gets to the era of Prophet Muhammad, the less gender bias one sees.

In contemporary Yogyakarta and Indonesia as a whole, most progressive thinkers come from neomodernist circles such as the younger generation of NU and Muhammadiyah (Saeed 2005), as well as groups like Rahima, YKF (Yayasan Kesejahteraan Fatayat), Amal Hayati-Rifka Annisa, FK3 (Forum Kajian Kitab Kuning), and Yasanti. Their most prominent representatives include such authors and activists as Musdah Mulia, Ruhaini Dzuhayatin, Cicik Farha, Nasaruddin Umar, Hamim Ilyas, and Muhammad Husein. To be progressive on gender or other matters does not at all mean abandoning scripture; rather, it means interpreting God's commands in different and contextual ways. For example, with regard to leadership and polygamy, 'Aisyiyah and Muslimat offer similar textual interpretations, but the interpretive and sociological arguments they present make 'Aisyiyah appear more feminism-friendly. All three organizations have reservations about LGBT rights and same-sex marriage, opposing proposals to legalize same-sex marriages. However, 'Aisyiyah and Muslimat clearly and unequivocally condemn violence and discrimination against members of the LGBT community, whereas MHTI demands their criminalization and, in certain circumstances, death.

The dynamics seen in discussions of and contentions over gender issues in Yogyakarta Muslim women's organizations should not obscure the fact that certain ideals of gender equality enjoy broad support in 'Asyiyah and Muhammadiyah and a somewhat less pervasive but still notable level of support in Muslimat and NU. 'Aisyiyah's opposition to polygamy, its support for women's representation in the executive leadership of Muhammadiyah, its acceptance of women leading prayers for adult men in certain circumstances—all these bear witness to a significant level of support for the ideals of women's equality. The situation with Muslimat and NU is more complex—but the organization's internal diversity and somewhat greater conservatism with regard to gender ideals is perhaps not surprising in light of Muslimat and NU's rural roots and their membership's less "middle-class" social background. Nonetheless even in these two organizations, the past generation has seen significant changes in gender matters, not least with regard to women's participation in religious organization and outreach, as well as in higher education and employment. Compared to these two mainstream Muslim organizations, MHTI and its parent organization, HTI, are the real outliers. Their perspective on gender matters is uncompromisingly antiprogressive. It is important to remember too, however, that, as Robert Hefner makes clear in chapter 1 of this book, HTI is among the more transnational of Islamist organizations in Indonesia. And a key feature of this transnationalism has been a rejection of Indonesian values and traditions in favor of those claimed by HTI activists to be more authentically Islamic.

As the Yogyakarta example shows, the struggle for gender equality is not easy, not least in the face of staunchly conservative groups like MHTI. Groups like MHTI who oppose gender equality continue to argue that the ideal is a Western concept that threatens to destroy key Islamic institutions and values. Moreover, debates over questions like these occur not only within organizations but in communities and families. Gender issues thus remain at the heart of contentions over plurality and recognition in contemporary Indonesia. However, the examples of the women's associations discussed in this chapter, especially 'Aisyiyah and Muslimat, suggest that great changes have already taken place and that the accommodation and recognition of diverse views are, in a very real sense, a key feature of the new gender reality.

APPENDIX: INTERVIEWS

Abidah M.—Nasiatul 'Aisyiyah chairwoman in 2008–12—May 19, 2016.

Aisyah, Siti—'Aisyiyah leader—March 23, 2016.

Amelia, Fatma—Muslimat NU Yogyakarta secretary general—December 10, 2015.

Ansori—Rifka Annisa research and training manager—December 22, 2015.

Basyariah, Nuhbahtul—MHTI leader in Yogyakarta—December 19, 2016, and February 5, 2017.

Danupranata, Gita—head of Muhammadiyah in Yogyakarta Province—July 25, 2016.

Djohantini, Noordjannah—'Aisyiyah Yogyakarta chairwoman—March 29, 2016.

Fathiyah—member of Muslimat NU—August 9, 2016.

Kamaludiningrat, Ahmad Muhsin— Muhammadiyah member—August 8, 2016.

Nuraini, Diah Siti—'Asiyiyah secretary general—December 27, 2015.

Nurhidayani—'Asiyiyah member—August 10, 2016.

Pranata, interview by author, July 25, 2016.

Saeroni—Rifka Annisa research and training manager and activist—December 22, 2015.

Sodik, Mochamad—NU member and director of the Center for Women's Studies at Sunan Kalijaga State Islamic University in Yogyakarta —March 29, 2016.

NOTES

1. Noordjannah Djohantini, interview by author, April 29, 2016.
2. All translations from Indonesian-language sources are my own.

3. Diah Siti Nuraini, interview by author, December 27, 2015.

4. Interview by author, August 10, 2016.

5. Ahmad Muhsin Kamaludiningrat, interview by author, August 8, 2016.

6. Gita Danupranata, interview by author, July 25, 2016.

7. Fatma Amelia, interview by author, August 17, 2016.

8. Mochamad Sodik, interview by author, March 29, 2016.

9. Fathiyah, interview by author, August 9, 2016.

10. Nuhbahtul Basyariah, interview by author, December 13, 2017.

11. Pranata, interview by author, July 25, 2016.

12. Fatma Amelia, interview by author, December 10, 2015.

13. Interview by author, August 9, 2016.

14. Interview by author, February 5, 2017.

15. Siti Aisyah, interview by author, March 23, 2016.

16. Interview by author, March 24, 2016.

17. Noordjannah Djohantini, interview by author, March 29, 2016.

18. Nuraini, interview by author, December 27, 2016.

19. Nurhidayani, interview by author, August 10, 2016.

20. Amelia, interview by author, December 10, 2015.

21. Saeroni, interview by author, December 22, 2015.

22. Mochamad Sodik, interview by author, March 29, 2016.

23. Nuhbahtul Basyariah, interview by author, December 13, 2017.

24. Kamaludiningrat, interview by author, August 8, 2016.

25. Fathiyah, interview by author, August 10, 2016.

26. Pranata, interview by author, July 25, 2016.

27. Nuhbahtul Basyarlah, interview by author, December 13, 2016.

SEVEN

Religion, Democracy, and Citizenship, Twenty Years after *Reformasi*

ZAINAL ABIDIN BAGIR

For many scholars it has become clear that, even if Indonesia continues in a pathway of democratic consolidation, it will nonetheless also continue to display features different from anything that may be labeled "liberal democracy" (Stepan 2011; Menchik 2016). The nonliberal character of Indonesian democracy stems in part from the way the state has been conceived since the beginning of its history, especially with regard to state-religion relations. The difference is undoubtedly due to the makeup of Indonesian society, a Muslim-majority population with significant religious and ethnic diversity. As shown in recent research, in Indonesia citizenship may be called "nonliberal" in the sense of being differentiated and informal (Berenschot and Klinken 2018; Klinken and Berenschot 2018; Kloos and Berenschot 2016). As an affirmation of citizenship is considered a necessary path to the consolidation of democracy, the form of citizenship will affect the very meaning and practice of democracy in Indonesia.

The chapters in this book portray the contestation to define and enact recognition and citizenship in an arena that has been shaped by many forces in the past and by the ongoing struggle today between different groups in society as well as the state. The contests unfold in different local, cultural, and historical contexts and, in many cases, show how processes of recognition and citizenship are religiously differentiated in different ways and to differing degrees. Arguments for and against a particular form of recognition and citizenship reflect the struggles to shape normativities for coexistence, raising questions about whether all have equal rights, regardless of their belonging to particular religious or cultural communities, or sexual orientation for that matter. In this regard Indonesia is in general far from a Rawlsian "well-ordered society" but reflects something closer to Mouffe's (2013) "agonistic pluralism" (see also Hefner 2018a). This may be seen more clearly in the three important clusters of events in 2016–17, which are the subject of this chapter and—as this book was in press—the 2019 presidential election, which accentuated some of the trends seen over the past five years. While the events are clearly unfinished, they are nevertheless instructive, showing important elements in the ongoing contestation and providing a fitting conclusion to the essays in this book.

The first cluster of events took place around the dramatic gubernatorial election in the capital city of Jakarta, which saw unprecedented mobilization of Muslims outside any formal political groups, and the defeat of a popular governor, Basuki Tjahaja Purnama (Ahok), a Christian of Chinese descent, for, at least partly, religious reasons (see Ahnaf, chapter 4). Second, a few months later, the government's banning of Hizbut Tahrir Indonesia (HTI), which campaigned for shariah law and a caliphate (*khilafa*) form of state and participated significantly in the demonstrations against Ahok, *and* the government's deployment of Pancasila-based argument, sent a strong message that the government led by the President Joko Widodo would tolerate Islamist aspirations only to a certain extent and was willing to use its power to draw boundaries in the name of the Pancasila as the nation-state ideology. Third, and later in 2017, in developments that were not related but were played out by many of the same actors in the same political and social atmosphere of heightened polarization, the Constitutional Court reached decisions on two important issues. One rejected the expansion of adultery law; the other gave further recognition to indigenous religions, which had not previously been acknowledged as "religions" proper (see Hefner, chapter 1). The protest against both decisions by conservative Muslim groups, many of which were involved in the anti-Ahok mobilization, signaled yet another aspect of the complexity of forces at play in contemporary Indonesia's contention. These involved *both* resistance to a further legal "Islamization" and new efforts to uphold and extend equal citizenship.

The events took place mostly in the capital city of Jakarta, which is one of many locales in Indonesia but which at the same time and even in a de-centralized Indonesia still occupies a central place on the national stage. As will be shown in this chapter, the events also reverberated to—and were amplified or resisted by—other parts of Indonesia that exhibit more vari-eties of religious and ethnic composition and different local and historical contexts.

Focusing on the three sets of events in 2017, this chapter portrays the dynamics of pluralism and citizenship in contemporary Indonesia and the vigorous competitions played out in this arena. At the same time, it is also intended to provide the national-level background of and conclusion to the other chapters in this book, which focus on particular regions or organi-zations. The contexts of those chapters are quite different, but to a great ex-tent they are affected by similar dynamics and forces: religious diversity in the midst of religio-demographic imbalance; political ruptures in the capi-tal, which immediately affect the regions; and assertion of the authority to dominate and redefine public identities, but also resistance to those efforts at domination.

Different stories have been told around those events. The Jakarta elec-tion has been represented by many national and international mass media as the rise of conservatism, intolerance, "Islamization," the failure of "Mus-lim democracy," and a victory for prejudice over pluralism (see Kingsbury 2017; Arifianto 2017). But stories that assume a particular characteristic of Indonesia (moderate, tolerant, "Muslim democracy") always seem to over-simplify a more complex picture. This chapter looks at these events as part of a long and unfinished story about competition between groups that stand for and promote different norms for recognition and coexistence, and thus different definitions of citizenship in Muslim-majority Indonesia. The ideals upheld by the groups opposing Ahok, as will be shown in this chapter, imply a religiously differentiated citizenship that would maintain the dominance of Islam in the Muslim-majority capital. As other chapters in this book indicate, a similar norm was also prevalent in other places, including in the Christian-majority Manado, where the Christian population coexists with Muslims but aspires to maintain Christian dominance.

The issue is not simply the existence of diverse norms, then, but how they compete and whether they are successfully scaled up beyond their place of origins and initial practice. The Jakarta election was a story of the successful scaling up of Islamist norms—successful in having Ahok imprisoned and also in disseminating its appeals beyond Jakarta. A popular *salafi* preacher expressed the feeling of many others when he said that without the case of Ahok it would have taken many years to remind Indonesian Muslims about the necessity of Muslim leadership—Ahok's recklessness was, as it were, God's effective way to remind Muslims about this ostensibly Qur'anic principle. Nevertheless, soon civil society organizations (CSOs) and the government responded and tried to resist any further advance of this exclusivist idea, in the name of an equal rather than a religiously differentiated citizenship.

No less important in exploring these contentions is to observe efforts to *normalize* their animating ideals. Especially since 1998, when political power was decentralized and citizen participation increased greatly, norms of coexistence forged between citizens or groups of citizens as well as the processes by which they are subsequently scaled up and institutionalized have become deeply consequential. The events in Jakarta show not only how certain (religious) groups compete to define the norms of how they recognize and relate to others but also how the dynamics taking place in society cross the state-society divide. The process of judicial review at the Constitutional Court, initiated by petitions from a group of "nonreligious" minorities and supported by CSOs that promote pluralism, equality, and religious freedom, was another facet of the struggle for citizenship that reflects a significant and successful process of scaling. In all these examples we see that the competition over citizenship and coexistence has been intense and has involved varied scaling initiatives, from street politics to the formal review process at the Constitutional Court.

In an attempt to understand these dynamics, the remainder of this chapter situates recent developments in their historical context, focusing on the trends in the last few years, and then discusses the three crucial clusters of events in 2017. This chapter is not intended to forecast the future of Indonesian democracy. Indeed, forecasting would be very difficult, as the

2019 presidential election, which took place as this book was in the publication process, illustrated the volatility of the contestation among actors and how quickly changes occur. My aim in this chapter is instead to understand the "agonistic pluralism" of normativities and the forces at play in today's Indonesia.

THE NEW ARENA, 2014–19: POLARIZATION HEIGHTENED

Some twenty years ago, the *Reformasi* movement started a far-reaching process of democratization in the aftermath of two major periods of post-independence Indonesia: twenty years of the first president Soekarno and thirty-two years of President Soeharto's "New Order." In the twenty years since 1998, Indonesia has had five more presidents, three of whom were elected through direct presidential elections.

The first five years after 1998 were tumultuous. A few months after the dawn of *Reformasi* in May 1998, the country experienced a period of large-scale ethno-religious communal conflicts, which left thousands dead. To the surprise of many observers, however, these conflicts finally subsided (Barron, Jaffrey, and Varshney 2014). A new wave of terrorist violence started with the Bali bombings in 2002. However, with the exception of the bombings of churches in Surabaya in mid-2018, in general Indonesia has been regarded as successful in dealing with terrorism. The first five years were also marked by four amendments to the 1945 Constitution, by the formal separation of the military and the police, and by the start of decentralization. The first direct presidential elections were held in 2004 and went peacefully. The same was true of the 2009 presidential elections, which were won by Susilo Bambang Yudhoyono (SBY). Thus, despite the violent conflicts, Indonesia slowly but steadily seemed to be moving toward a consolidated democracy (Liddle and Mujani 2013).

In 2012 a new figure, Joko Widodo, rose to national prominence. The former mayor of Solo, Central Java, Jokowi (as he is widely known) had become popular for his democratic populist appearance; he won national and international awards for his achievements in Solo and won his second term with 90 percent of the vote. Just two years into his second term, in 2012 he was nominated to become the governor of Jakarta. His running mate was an unlikely candidate—Basuki Tjahaja Purnama, who had previously been the district head of Belitung, an island off the east coast of Sumatra. This unlikely pair won the election, despite predictions that their opponent, the incumbent governor at that time, would beat them easily in the first round. Only two years after taking his role as Jakarta governor, in 2014 Joko Widodo competed in national presidential elections against the ex-general Prabowo Subianto, the son-in-law of former president Soeharto, and won.

Much as he had done on the eve of the downfall of the New Order, Prabowo recruited the support of conservative Muslim groups—and, as in his late New Order escapades, he was aided by his adviser Fadli Zon (Hefner 2000, 201–17). Jokowi was smeared as *abangan* or nominal Muslim and even as a non-Muslim and procommunist. This challenge to Jokowi was so serious that he had to produce a kind of manifesto stating explicitly, "I, Jokowi, am part of Islam *Rahmatan lil Alamin*"—that is, not only affirming that he was a Muslim but distinguishing his Islam from that of his opponents in describing Islam as a "Blessing for the World" in contrast to the exclusive and violence-prone religious politics of his opponent (*Kompas* 2014). Supported by prodemocracy activists, Jokowi's election was seen as the victory of democracy against an attempt to return to the pre-1998 political order. The 2014 presidential election was also fiercely competitive and colored by unprecedented "black" campaigns, which left society further polarized. But it also enlivened Indonesian politics and was marked by the rise of a new political force: volunteers. *Tempo* magazine chose volunteers, a number of whom were activists supporting Jokowi, as its 2014 "People of the Year."

After his victory, Jokowi faced great challenges from the parliament, which was dominated by a coalition of parties supporting Prabowo (Hamayotsu and Nataatmadja 2016). By 2016, however, Jokowi had managed to neutralize the coalition of parties in the parliament opposing him (Mietzner 2017; Tomsa 2017). But the next challenge came in the form of extraparliamentary street politics that achieved momentum in opposition to Ahok's candidacy as governor of Jakarta. By and large Jokowi has managed to contain this challenge and has weakened the opposition, ending the year with the highest approval rating for his governance (Sulistiyanto 2018).

The series of protest against the Chinese Christian governor were led by conservative Islamic groups, including most importantly the Islamic Defenders Front (Front Pembela Islam, FPI), a hard-line group established in 1998, notorious for its vigilantism, and, second and less directly, the conservative Indonesian Council of Ulama (Majelis Ulama Indonesia, MUI), which is partly funded by the government. Protests were also supported by Prabowo's party, Gerindra, in coalition with the right-of-center Islamist political party, the Justice and Welfare Party (PKS). It was ironic that in 2012 Ahok ran for the vice-governor position on Gerindra's ticket, but two years later he left the party, citing conflict of interest as one of the reasons. Although the Jakarta gubernatorial election was only one among more than five hundred local elections, it had great national significance. It was regarded as a prelude to the expected fierce campaign for the presidency in 2019, which, as it turned out, again pitted the sitting president Joko Widodo against Prabowo. The campaign also reflected an unprecedented, explicit polarization among and between Muslims and others in society beyond Jakarta.

In the 2017 Jakarta gubernatorial election, Ahok's main election rival was Anies Baswedan. Ironically enough, Baswedan had been Jokowi's spokesperson during the 2014 presidential election campaign and was later appointed as Jokowi's minister of education; he was subsequently ousted from his cabinet post only weeks before the parties that would challenge Ahok for the governorship nominated Baswedan as their candidate. Anies was backed by Prabowo and his party, Gerindra, together with the moderate Islamist political party PKS and the more ethno-religiously inclusive PAN. In addition, a group of conservative Muslim organizations, including the FPI, had earlier announced that they were looking to support a "Muslim governor." As a result of these and other initiatives, Anies quickly became *the* Muslim candidate for the governor's office. Rizieq Shihab, the self-declared "Grand Imam" of FPI, had organized demonstrations since 2014, in explicit opposition to the fact that, after Jokowi became president, Ahok automatically ascended to the governor's post. The demonstrations against Ahok continued over the entire course of his tenure. However, they also did not succeed in stopping his aggressive and controversial programs, including the eviction of poor people living along the city's riverbanks, programs that were heavy-handed but were intended to address

Jakarta's chronic flooding. A half year prior to the 2017 gubernatorial elections, Ahok appeared to be still the most popular candidate for the upcoming election, with polls revealing support among some 70 percent of the public.

Against this backdrop, the alleged blasphemous remark by Ahok in September 2016 was too good to be overlooked by his opponents. Ahok claimed that a Qur'anic verse on the obligation to "elect a Muslim leader" had been politicized by his opponents—"They lied using the Qur'anic verse" became "The Qur'anic verse is a lie." The blasphemy allegation brought the anti-Ahok campaign to a totally different level. The electoral campaign became stormy. It was marked by waves of large demonstrations, the most significant of which was the third Aksi Bela Islam (Defend Islam Action) or Action 212, as it was known, on December 2, 2016. It called not just for Ahok's defeat in the April 2017 election but for his imprisonment on charges of blasphemy.

The mobilization was greatly helped by the MUI, which issued a statement declaring that Ahok's pronouncement *was* blasphemous. While the MUI was not involved officially in the Aksi mobilizations, several prominent figures in its leadership joined forces to create the National Movement to Guard the Fatwa (GNPF-MUI). With a number of other Muslim leaders and organizations, Rizieq Shihab campaigned fiercely in support of the idea that Muslims voters were religiously obliged to choose a Muslim candidate in elections. The anti-Ahok campaign was projected into the streets, social media, and in mosque sermons in Jakarta and across Indonesia. "Campaign" is an understatement—anti-Ahok efforts included intimidation of Ahok supporters in urban neighborhoods, as when, for example, Muslim supporters of Ahok were told that they would not receive a proper Islamic burial ritual if they persisted in their support for the Chinese Christian.

Despite the mobilization of hundreds of thousands of people and the attacks against him, Ahok got the most votes (42 percent) in the first round of the gubernatorial election, leaving behind two other candidates significantly. If the election had been held anywhere other than Jakarta, Ahok would have become governor. Only in Jakarta is there a requirement that a candidate has to get more than 50 percent of votes to win. In the second round, when he was head to head with Anies, Ahok lost, with his overall share of the vote remaining at 42 percent.

While many media present the loss of Ahok as evidence of rising intolerance or a victory for radical Islamists, a number of prominent moderate Muslims took strong exception to this view. (See, for example, Imam Shamsi Ali's statement [Ali 2017] and Yenni Wahid's [Huda and Hazliansyah 2017].) Despite the explicit religious language used to mobilize against Ahok, there were debates among scholars about what factors most contributed to his electoral defeat. Some scholars argue that the issue was not mainly religious identity politics but also reflected resentment against Ahok among the poor in Jakarta, who had become the victims of his aggressive urban-renewal evictions (I. Wilson 2017). While accepting that religious sentiment did play a role, Vedi Hadiz and Inaya Rakhmani (2017) has argued that a more complex articulation is in play: "Issues of inequality and injustice in Indonesia are likely to be increasingly framed on the basis of racial as well as religious identities" (see also Warburton and Gammon 2017; cf. Bagir 2018).

In their recent analysis of extensive survey data, Mietzner and Muhtadi (2018) have offered an even more nuanced explanation. They show that Islamic conservatism has not actually risen but has declined over the past few years; at the same time, the core constituency of conservative Muslims has grown more educated and more affluent. How then are we to explain the sudden and massive mobilization against Ahok? The first answer is that in reality the campaign was not sudden. The antipluralist groups had been active for some time. Their numbers grew during the ten years of the presidency of SBY, as they displayed acts of intolerance toward nonmainstream religious groups and Christians and were never sanctioned for their actions. The difference was that most of these acts of intolerance were relatively confined, taking place here and there, and were regarded as exceptions to the general pattern of harmonious relationships between diverse groups (Bush 2015). But 2016 was the year when the antipluralist activists reaped what they had sown. As shown by Mietzner and Muhtadi (2018), Jokowi, unlike SBY, did not accommodate these forces; they opposed his campaign in 2014, and by 2016 there were indications that Jokowi had succeeded in containing the opposition and had a good prospect to win a second term. After opposition in the parliament was neutralized, the only outlet remaining was extraparliamentary protest. The political parties such as SBY's Partai Demokrat and Gerindra saw the power in hard-line Islamist street protests and turned to them for support.

It is telling that on April 19, 2017, soon after initial vote tallies from the second and final gubernatorial election showed that Anies was leading, Prabowo celebrated the hard-won victory, conveying his thanks to the people who had played roles in the victory; he mentioned Rizieq, the FPI leader, by name. When Rizieq himself entered Istiqlal Mosque to celebrate the victory, among the chants heard was "Islam won." The victory was almost complete when a month later Ahok's blasphemy trial finished. He was found guilty and immediately imprisoned—and was not even able to finish the remaining five months of his term as governor. For the Islamist proponents of Action 212, the event was a symbol of Muslim political awakening. The campaign against the Christian Chinese Ahok was for them not at all discriminatory. It was instead the affirmation of the principle of a religiously differentiated and stratified citizenship, a Muslim supremacism that they regarded as appropriate and necessary for a Muslim-majority country.

During the 2019 presidential election, the divide between Jokowi's and Prabowo's camps was less explicitly articulated in political-religious terms. In fact, having selected the senior cleric Ma'ruf Amin as his vice president and with quite substantial support from NU, Jokowi could have been seen as more "religious" than his rival. Yet Prabowo was backed up by the Islamist hard-liners Rizieq Shihab, Bachtiar Nasir, and the "212 alumni," and these supporters did not hesitate to use more explicit and exclusive, thus (in some people's eyes) more ostensibly "Islamic," appeals. So although not as clearly as in the earlier Jakarta gubernatorial election, the Islamic card was still played. In the aftermath of these electoral contests, the principle of a religiously differentiated citizenship is now regularly brought up and defended unashamedly in national elections. While the notion may be seen as an obstacle to a pluralist democracy, it is important to remember that expressions of these ideas and their scaling up were made possible only in the free space opened by post-1998 democratization. Indeed, as events in 2018–19 showed, the elections themselves were an important instrument for this exclusivist scaling.

How did non-Muslims respond to these developments? It was not surprising that the political turbulence in the capital created serious ripples in other places, especially in non-Muslim-majority areas in eastern Indonesia. Merry Kolimon (2017), the head of the Christian Evangelical Church in Timor Synod, released a letter voicing her deep disappointment over the imprisonment of Ahok. She encouraged people to voice their protest against the injustice and warned that, if action was not taken, intolerance and radicalism would destroy the nation. In Christian-majority Manado, Christian Minahasan *adat* paramilitaries rose up, demanding that the FPI be disbanded (Pinontoan 2017; see also Larson, chapter 2). The prominent Catholic priest Father Franz Magnis Suseno, reacting to the imprisonment of Ahok and the hateful vitriol accompanying the election campaign, asked, "Is Indonesia going to be Pakistan?" While accepting the results of the election, he expressed deep concern, noting that, despite all promises of equal citizenship in pluralist Indonesia, non-Muslims apparently do not yet have a truly equal status (Suseno 2017). Both Kolimon and Suseno urged Indonesians to return to the national consensus of the Pancasila as the country's uniting consensus. This appeal for a return to Pancasila values was soon be acted upon by the Jokowi government.

ACTION 212: VARIETIES OF "ISLAMIZATION"

The idea of Muslim leadership has long been a key element in the Islamist social imaginary. In this regard, as discussed earlier, the issue is not at all new.[1] But in late 2016 and 2017, in the midst of election campaigns, this message had an unprecedented reach and carried stronger persuasive force. What also made it different this time was the dominance of Islamist organizations involved in the mobilization, groups that otherwise did not occupy central positions in Indonesian politics. They included the FPI, the MUI, Wahdah Islamiyah, the Indonesian Council of Young Intellectuals and Ulama (Majelis Intelektual dan Ulama Muda Indonesia, MIUMI), and Hizbut Tahrir Indonesia (HTI). Together these groups organized the series of demonstrations called the Defend Islam Action (Aksi Bela Islam).

Before looking at those organizations, it is important to take note of just who did not join the anti-Ahok campaign. Conspicuously absent were leaders of the largest and oldest Muslim organizations, Nahdlatul Ulama (NU) and Muhammadiyah, the main voices of civil Islam. They discouraged their members from joining the demonstrations, although, according to many in the two organizations, in the end their membership was actually present in significant numbers (Qodir 2017). The two organizations are not committed to a secular state but do oppose the idea of an Islamic state; in their view one of the duties of the state is to accommodate religious values and facilitate religious piety. They are undoubtedly in favor of democracy, though they may hold the idea of, to use Menchik's term, "communal tolerance"—a general tolerance and acceptance of non-Muslims, though still with a preference for Muslim leadership in areas where Muslims make up the majority of the local population (Menchik 2016; cf. Bush and Munawar-Rachman 2014).

With the exception of HTI (discussed in more detail in Ahnaf, chapter 4), which explicitly calls for a transnational caliphate, most of the 212 organizations do not advocate the establishment of a full-fledged "Islamic state" but instead aspire to some variety of "statist Islam" (Hefner 2000). Nevertheless, while on some issues they may unite, each grouping is distinct. The FPI, through its notion of "NKRI Bersyari'ah" (a unitary Indonesia that implements shariah), demands greater recognition of Islam by the state through constitutional means. It accepts Indonesia as a nation-state, but one that is not secular. In his many speeches, Rizieq has said that all Muslims are "naturally" for shariah and as such would prefer a state that enforces it. The Indonesian state has already recognized shariah in many forms. National laws on marriage, divorce, and inheritance are already significantly based on shariah, and for these there are already Islamic courts. There is also a national law on pornography, which the FPI supported. In some areas of Indonesia, there are local bylaws that uphold shariah on issues related to morality, education, and "protecting *aqida* [binding beliefs, creed]." Further, there are laws on shariah banking, on *zakat* alms, and on halal products. "We do not have criminal laws based on shariah yet. But it does not mean that the parliament and the government may not accept this in the future" (Shihab 2017).

After the police's questioning of him for hours in 2017 on charges that he had insulted the Pancasila, Shihab gave a speech to his supporters arguing that his organization was not at all opposed to the Pancasila as the basis of Indonesian state or to the constitution. He spoke confidently about the Pancasila, noting that he had written his graduate thesis on the subject and arguing that a Pancasila state did not preempt implementation of shariah. For him the pinnacle of the Pancasila was the first principle, "belief in one and only God," and it was in turn supposed to be the foundation for the Pancasila's other principles. In addition, he argued that this first principle should always be understood as acknowledging the idea written in the earlier version of the preamble to the constitution, the Jakarta Charter. In that document the principle of belief in God is followed by the clause "with the obligation to carry out shariah for Muslims." In the Indonesian Constitution this clause was deleted a day before it was officially pronounced in August 1945.

How does Shihab propose to achieve this goal? He has stated categorically that the implementation of shariah should be achieved through constitutional means. With this, what he has in mind is electing Muslim politicians to the parliament who share a commitment to the idea of statist shariah, or forming a coalition among such politicians. They may be affiliated with any political party, but as long as they agree on the idea, they may form something like a "transparty caucus" for shariah. While the FPI is not known for advocating so-called local shariah bylaws, Shihab's idea amounts to doing something similar at the national level. The campaign may take the form of advocating a new law, such as the antipornography law, or defending old laws it sees as needed by Muslims, such as the religious defamation law during its review at the Constitutional Court in 2010.

This formal political and judicial aspiration is often expressed in street politics, such as those displayed in Action 212. Indeed, in the past the FPI was known not mainly for its political campaigning but for vigilantism carried out in the name of *amar ma'ruf nahi munkar* (enjoining good, forbidding evil). Rizieq's earlier vigilante acts did win support from some in the Muslim community, but not nearly as significantly as his role in the Action 212 campaign. For the time being, at least, the movement is trying to erase the collective memory of the violence it carried out in the past and to set out on a road to mainstream politics (Woodward and Nurish 2017).

Bachtiar Nasir and Muhammad Zaitun Rasmin, two other prominent leaders in the GNPF-MUI, represent a different type of Islamism. Before (and probably as well as after) the Action 212 campaign, neither leader was inclined to go along with Rizieq Shihab, partly for reasons having to do with their different Islamic theologies and practices. Nasir and Rasmin were educated in Saudi Arabia, and their Islamic orientation is *salafi* or (as it is sometimes known) neo-*salafi*; Shihab too was Saudi educated, but his theology and practice are closer to those of the traditionalist Nahdlatul Ulama. What unites them is the agenda to Islamize the Indonesian nation-state in an exclusivist and religiously differentiated way (Woodward and Nurish 2017), although their strategies for achieving this end are otherwise different.

Bachtiar Nasir's Ar-Rahman Qur'anic Learning Center (the original name was in English; shortened to AQL, an Arabic word meaning "intellect") was established in 2008 in Jakarta. In addition to the learning groups (*pengajian*) in the capital, it operates several Islamic schools with hundreds of students, specializing in memorization of the Qur'an. Nasir is also well known owing to his frequent appearances on television and his conspicuous presence in social media. Beyond these educational programs, his national standing has grown since Action 2012 after he helped establish the Indonesian Council of Young Intellectuals and Ulama (MIUMI) and then served as its general secretary. The MIUMI has a strong base in the well-known Pesantren Gontor, Nasir's alma mater. It now has branches in Java, Sulawesi, and Sumatra; its executive director is Hamid Fahmi Zarkasyi, who was also one of the sons of the founder of Gontor. Other than these educational enterprises, the AQL was also active in international humanitarian charity, sending aid to Palestine and Syria and in this way winning support among the Muslim public, including from entertainment celebrities. Nasir's anti-Shi'a position is clearly displayed in his comments on the Syria issue as well as in the MIUMI's agenda—this position at the same time distinguishes him from Rizieq Shihab. Nasir was the chairman of the GNPF-MUI until 2018.

Zaitun Rasmin's Wahdah Islamiyah (Islamic Unity) was established in 2002 in Makassar and now has more than 120 branches and more than two hundred schools in different parts of Indonesia. It combines conservative *salafi* piety with a variety of nationalism (Chaplin 2018). Similar to Shihab and Nasir's ideological orientation, Wahdah Islamiyah is premised on the conviction that as the majority Indonesian Muslims have particular rights, which means that Islamic morality has to be protected and respected. In particular, Muslims have to be allowed to practice shariah—even if what shariah is varies among its different proponents. In addition, and as seen in Rasmin's involvement in Action 212, the Muslim majority must have a Muslim as their state leader. The state has to be "Islamized," not in the sense of creating a full-fledged "Islamic state," but in "Islamizing" state actors and influencing their policy making. A modern, democratic nation-state is thus not contrary to Islam or, more particularly, to Wahdah Islamiyah's *salafi* brand of Islam. But what such a democracy does involve is a religiously differentiated citizenship: Muslims should have particular rights and privileges in virtue of their particular religious demands, even while insisting that this does not mean discrimination against non-Muslims and that it does not betray Indonesian national principles of the Pancasila or the Constitution. The organization works *with*, rather than *against*, the state. Chaplin (2018) observes that the members of Wahdah Islamiyah are active citizens and at the same time agents of Islamization in their everyday lives. This mixture of salafism and nationalism and the *salafi* reinterpretation of citizenship is not simply a pragmatic tactic to make the movement more socially and politically acceptable but its leaders "have increasingly come to see themselves as an inseparable part of the nation's social fabric" (Chaplin 2018, 214).

Left to themselves, Nasir and Rasmin might not enjoy sufficient support to command a mobilization of hundreds of thousands of Muslims in Jakarta. Their standing has been elevated since they joined the central organization of the MUI. On the other hand, their presence after the 2015 National Congress of the MUI marked the "honeymoon" period between the MUI and the Islamists (Ichwan 2017). In the 2015–20 structure of the MUI, besides Nasir and Rasmin, two other leaders from the MIUMI assumed leadership positions.

The three organizations at the core of Action 212, then, share ideas and strategies but also have clear differences.[2] Rizieq was always in the center of the demonstrations with his fiery speeches. Nasir and Rasmin are from quite different types of movements and theological orientations. They were all nonetheless united in their aspiration to elect a Muslim governor in Jakarta.

In retrospect, we may observe two outcomes of the anti-Ahok campaign. First, despite their success at bringing down a strong non-Muslim governor, politically speaking the Islamist groups' idea of "Islamization" did not go as far or have as long-lasting an impact as the organizers had hoped. Many commercial products as well as institutions, from grocery stores, to restaurants, to cooperatives, were created, carrying the brand of "212," but they were not as successful in their operations as expected. Several organizations dedicated to maintaining the unity and mission of "212 alumni" emerged but were unable to unite, instead making contradictory claims about just who was an authentic 212 representative. A few months after Action 212, Rizieq Shihab was in self-exile in Saudi Arabia, evading criminal charges, including one related to a sex scandal. Meanwhile, Nasir and Rasmin had become more famous but began to tone down their ideas; they even met Jokowi in the presidential palace, to the dismay of hard-core elements in their movement. The Reunion of 212 in December 2017 could not manage to repeat what happened a year earlier. Influential religious leaders such as Ma'ruf Amin and Din Syamsuddin, who a year earlier had appeared favorable to Action 212, now opposed the effort, saying the Reunion was unnecessary since the anti-Ahok campaign had achieved its goal of punishing the blasphemer.

The dream that the "unity of Muslim *ummah*" exemplified in Action 212 would be carried over into and affect hundreds of local elections in 2018 was also not realized. In two of the most important provinces, West Java and East Java, no similarly based Islamist coalition materialized, primarily because the political parties that had earlier united in Jakarta (Gerindra, PKS, and PAN) decided to support different candidates, and the candidates did not align neatly into a stark contrast between Muslim and non-Muslim. The case with the West Kalimantan election seems to be different, because there the two strongest candidates are clearly differentiated on religion and ethnic lines: Malay-Muslim versus Christian-Dayak (IPAC 2018b).

These examples show the limits of politics based on religious sentiments or, from the standpoint of electoral politics, of garnering the support of religious pressure groups: when the election is not as competitive, there is less incentive to accentuate religious or ethnic divisions (Jaffrey and Ali-Fauzi 2016). However, in anticipation of and to preempt the growing polarization, Jokowi had taken actions to strengthen his support among Muslims, especially NU and the MUI, and had sought to "tame" several public figures who in the past had opposed him. By late 2017 Jokowi's popularity was higher than ever. Since he had consolidated his support among many Muslim organizations, the religious card worked less effectively against him. As a matter of fact, Jokowi himself opted to play the card and outbid his opponents by choosing Ma'ruf Amin as his running mate for the 2019 elections. Amin was the head of the conservative MUI and two years earlier had played a pivotal role in consolidating a diverse assortment of Islamist and conservative Muslim groups in Action 212.

The collateral damage from the electoral campaign in the form of heightened social polarization may be more lasting. The success achieved in the Jakarta election, grounded in a discriminatory idea toward citizens from minority backgrounds, constitutes a serious challenge to pluralist ideas; the same strategy may be deployed again to pursue a particular agenda whenever there is a need and the conditions are ripe for it, as was attempted in the 2019 presidential elections. The growing polarization influenced public debates around Jokowi's performance and, more deeply, around wedge issues such as attitudes toward nonmainstream groups (especially Ahmadiyah and Shi'a), LGBT activism, and communism. These and other antiliberal positions are increasingly associated with Action 212.

More generally, a conservative understanding of Islam on all these issues seems to have become mainstreamed and made normative. In the heat of the election campaign, with the machinery of political parties running full speed and in the midst of information overflow in social media, different Islamic voices were heard but were delegitimized as less authentically Islamic. The end result has been, at least for now, that the "moderate" position appears to have shifted to the right, as represented by figures such as Nasir and Rasmin (IPAC 2018a, 4). A "conservative turn" (Bruinessen 2013a, 2013b) may be an apt term for this phenomenon. Yet even here this trend is neither final nor absolute, as pluralists at the same time have made some progress, and the government has resisted pressures to shift toward a "mainstream" more conservative than a few years earlier.

PANCASILA REVIVAL: OVERLAPPING
CONSENSUS OR TOOL OF EXCLUSION

The movements that arose toward the end of 2016 and continued through mid-2017, when Ahok was finally defeated and imprisoned, did indeed constitute a serious threat to Jokowi's government. He might have underestimated the religious-political opposition left over from the campaign for the 2014 presidential election, but now he had no choice but to face it. His strategy had two prongs: first, to weaken his opponents, by banning the Islamist HTI and letting the police press different criminal charges against other Islamist leaders (Rizieq, Nasir, Munarman, and al-Khattath, though later many of their charges were dropped); and second, to broaden and strengthen his base of support, especially among Muslims, including not only organizations such as NU and various CSOs but even some supporters of the 212 campaign.

When the November 4, 2016, demonstration (Action 411) took place, it ended in a riot outside the presidential palace. However, Jokowi was conspicuously absent from the residence at the time. By contrast, at the peak of the Action 212 demonstration, the president decided to walk across the street from his presidential palace and join the Friday prayers taking place there, becoming part of the Muslim *ummah* and sharing the stage with such 212 stalwarts as Shihab, Nasir, and Rasmin. He even shouted the *takbir* (*Allahu Akbar*, God is great), which was FPI's "trademark," in front of hundreds of thousands of people. In the weeks that followed, Jokowi busied himself with visiting Muslim leaders, mostly from Nahdlatul Ulama, Muhammadiyah, and the MUI, while at the same time ramping up the rhetoric of Indonesian unity, the Pancasila, and the state motto of *bhinneka tunggal ika* (unity in diversity).

The Jokowi government's full response, which was broadly supported by many pluralist CSOs, including Muslim organizations, was equally farreaching. A report published early in 2018 (Fachrudin 2018) called 2017 one of the most important years in the history of the Pancasila. Already in mid-2016 Jokowi had signed a presidential decree declaring June 1 as the national day commemorating the birth of the Pancasila; he then sponsored a Pancasila Week for the first time (May 29–June 4). Later in the same year, and in the aftermath of the campaigns against Ahok, the president created a presidential working unit to develop (*pembinaan*) the Pancasila ideology; in February 2018 the unit was transformed into a formal and permanent institution called the Bureau for the Development of Pancasila Ideology (Badan Pembinaan Ideologi Pancasila).

More consequentially, in July 2017 the president signed a regulation in lieu of law that revised the 2013 law on mass organizations; in October 2017 the regulation was presented to the parliament to become part of the revised law. This new legislation simplifies the procedure for banning mass organizations that promote ideas in opposition to the Pancasila; specifically, such organizations can now be disbanded without prior court process. The first and most important target of the legislation was clear: Hizbut Tahrir Indonesia, which was disbanded in October 2017. The Pancasila was no longer just a "state ideology" but had been transformed into a more powerful legal instrument. This series of measures reminded many human rights–minded Indonesian observers of the way in which the Pancasila was used during the New Order. While many prodemocracy and human rights organizations criticized this decision, quite a number of CSOs concerned with the rise of intolerance supported it. So did many Islamic organizations, including, and most prominently, Nahdlatul Ulama (Yuliawati 2017). Universities took part in the Pancasila revival as well, declaring their commitment to revive the Pancasila and fight radicalism on campus—a move that sometimes veered toward what Hadiz (2017) has called "hyper-nationalism." Well-known state universities such as Gadjah Mada University (Yogyakarta), Diponegoro University (Semarang), and Surabaya Institute of Technology sanctioned a few lecturers known to be affiliated with HTI (Sholih 2018; Mamduh 2018; Kresna 2017); UIN Yogyakarta banned the full-face veil (*niqab*), though the regulation was soon revoked after widespread protests (Putsanra 2018).

Regardless of the fact that NU and other Muslim groups supported the government's Pancasila campaign, it was unfortunate that it now appeared to push conservative Muslim groups to the opposite side of the issue. Several days after the first Pancasila Day on June 1, 2017, Yusril Ihza Mahendra, the chairman of the Islamist party Partai Bulan Bintang (Crescent and Star Party), and a former government minister as well as the leading defense lawyer for HTI, said that Jokowi had mistakenly identified the birth of the Pancasila as June 1, 1945, which was the first time Soekarno proposed the five principles named the Pancasila. But the version announced on that day put the principle of belief in God in final position, not initial position as was the case in the version of the Pancasila now recognized. Mahendra said that in making this mistake President Jokowi had denied the "complete" Pancasila as set forth in the Jakarta Charter, which has a clause mentioning "the obligation of Muslims to follow shariah." He also stated that during the era of Jokowi, the Pancasila has frequently been placed in opposition to Islam (Mahendra 2017). His criticisms were echoed by many others, including Rizieq Shihab, who was charged at the end of 2016 with defaming the Pancasila (although the charge was dropped in 2018) (Shihab 2015). Rizieq told the story of how the demonstration to reject the pornography draft law in 2006 had manipulated the Pancasila and the national slogan, *Bhinneka Tunggal Ika* (Unity in Diversity), thereby implying that Muslim supporters of the legislation were anti-Pancasila.

Rizieq also warned his followers to be careful of attempts to discredit Islamist aspirations in the name of the Pancasila. Having written his master's thesis at the International Islamic University-Malaysia on the Pancasila, he had long argued that the national doctrine did not preclude shariah. Indeed, many of the conservative groups discussed in the earlier section do not formulate their norms in opposition to the Pancasila or the constitution; they profess their loyalty to the Indonesian ideal of a unitary nation-state (NKRI) while also advocating greater rights for Muslims. What they offer is a reinterpretation of these tenets that does not run contrary to Islam and that gives preference to Muslims in matters of leadership and implementation of shariah.

Banning HTI may also be seen as politically more expedient than targeting the FPI, which has stronger ties to certain officials within the government and political parties. The FPI itself is not less hostile to democracy than HTI is and may even be more hostile. Rizieq's rhetoric has branded democracy as *haram* and Muslims supporting it as apostates (cf. I. Wilson 2015). Rizieq holds this view despite the FPI's support of certain candidates in local as well as presidential elections. But he claims that such participation is allowed because the situation is one of "emergency" (*darurat*, an Islamic jusriprudential principle), thereby for the time being allowing participation in democracy. While HTI was targeted through legal means, the

FPI's power was significantly weakened when its leaders, especially Shihab, were indicted on criminal charges.

The resistance toward the Islamist mobilization came not only from the government but also from many CSOs working for democracy, pluralism, and human rights, many of which had supported Jokowi in 2014. They were, however, caught on the horns of a dilemma, which ultimately led to serious disagreements. The controversy was actually broader and had started during the Jakarta election campaign. A report by the Jakarta-based Legal Aid Foundation (Lembaga Bantuan Hukum, LBH) took note of this dilemma (LBH Jakarta 2017). CSOs with the agenda of pluralism were worried about what they perceived as rising intolerance, shown in the anti-Ahok mobilization as well as in the fact that Ahok's rivals (Anies Baswedan and Sandiaga Uno) seemed to court the support of organizations like the FPI. On the other hand, Ahok's policy was indeed seen as having marginalized Jakarta's urban poor, so many activists working on issues of social justice made electoral alliances with Anies to advance their agenda of defending the poor and opposing urban renewal evictions (Savirani and Aspinall 2017). This situation is further complicated by Jokowi's move to ban HTI and other policies to restrict the Islamists, which prompted human rights advocacy groups to make clear their objections. The breach was quite serious and has not fully healed to this day; as a matter of fact, during the 2019 election, it even worsened.

THE CONSTITUTIONAL COURT: DEFINING CITIZENSHIP FORMALLY

The tumultuous course of events in 2017 did not end there. An equally significant episode, not related to the Jakarta election but involving many of the same actors, concerned two decisions of the Constitutional Court. One case concerned an attempt to expand an article in the Penal Code on adultery and sexual violence to also include fornication and same-sex sexual relations; the other was the deceptively simple issue of administrative procedures for filling out citizens' identity cards. Both became issues of contention between conservative Muslim organizations and CSOs that work for human rights; the decisions in both cases favored the latter. The significance of these examples is that they point to other forms of normative scaling, ones in which pluralist ideals have at least for the moment prevailed.

Established in 2003, the Constitutional Court has been among the most important institutions of the new democratic era, because it carries a mandate to review national laws in light of constitutional principles. With regard to religion, the Court has become the most important state institution to interpret religious freedom, especially in terms of how far the state may interfere in matters of religion and the extent of how Islam in particular may influence national law. Up to this point the Court has taken up eleven cases related to religion.[3] Where minority religious groups have been involved in petitioning the Court, the demands usually concern equal (nondiscriminatory) treatment. Where Muslims as individuals or part of mainstream organizations have gone to the Court, the petitions, in many though not all cases, demand more recognition of (particular interpretations of) Islamic teachings or removal of what the petitioners claim are unconstitutional limitations on Muslims' religious freedom. For example, in 2007, a Muslim's petition to remove restrictions on polygamy in the 1974 law on marriage was rejected (Indonesian Constitutional Court 2007). In 2008 a petitioner's request to remove what he saw as a limitation on the jurisdiction of Islamic religious courts, that is, excluding criminal matters, was also rejected, with the judges arguing that Islamic law is one but not the only source of law in a multireligious Indonesia (Indonesian Constitutional Court 2008).

The Court's decisions on religion-related issues refer to the constitution as the basis of its arguments, but they are equally colored by a view on state-religion relationships and, in some cases, even by particular religious, especially Islamic, teachings. This pattern reflects a politics of religion that originated in the historical context of the first three decades after Indonesia's independence in 1945. The contention has been shaped by fierce debates between proponents of a more "Islamic" Indonesian state and their more "secular nationalist" opponents, as well as by practices with respect to policy making and implementation. These currents in the country's policies and politics recognized religious diversity in Indonesia and expanded the policy of accommodation of Islam that had started during colonial times. In general it privileged six world religions while marginalizing the so-called indigenous religions, which were regarded as "culture" or "beliefs" (*kepercayaan*; see Hefner, chapter 1). In practice, especially with regard to lower-level regulations, this policy privileges the majority religion (which is different across different areas) and mainstream expressions of that religion (Bagir 2018).

An examination of the Constitutional Court provides a window into how, at the highest state level, norms concerning state-religion relations and citizenship are established. In addition, in the absence of explicit pronouncements on the politics of religion in the constitution, the Court has played the role of normalizing a particular state-religion view. The 2017 decision by the Constitutional Court on the Civil Administration Law was surprising and may be regarded as historic precisely because it disrupts some of these trends in the politics and state management of religion.

The ID Card Case

Because of the political legacy that distinguished between world religions and indigenous belief systems, and the use of the term *religion* only for the former, followers of the latter had long been marginalized (see Hefner, chapter 1). In the first years of the New Order era (1966–98), they were forced to choose one of the five world religions acknowledged by the state at that time (today six are recognized). They were also vulnerable to accusations of having no religion or being communists. For much of Indonesian history many of their basic human rights were also denied, including rights to education, health, and employment (Maarif 2017). It was not just the state that discriminated against these groups; they were also marginalized by the majority, normative Muslim groups (Hefner 2011b). Since 1998 many CSOs have worked on the issue of *adat*, emphasizing the rights of the indigenous people with regard to their lands or forests, and, more recently, their indigenous beliefs/religions. Among the most important of these CSOs is the Alliance of the Indigenous (*Adat*) Peoples of the Archipelago (Aliansi Masyarakat Adat Nusantara or AMAN; Hauser-Schäublin 2013), the National Commission for Violence against Woman (Komnas Perempuan), and the National Alliance of Bhinneka Tunggal Ika (ANBTI), as well as an array of more locally based organizations. Two organizations that

merit special attention because of their role in advocating for the petition-
ing of the Constitutional Court are the Yogyakarta-based Satunama and
Lakpesdam NU, the research and policy-oriented bureau in the Nahdlatul
Ulama.

The petition in this latter case was initiated by a group of followers of
indigenous religions and *aliran kepercayaan* (mystical associations), supported by Satunama. These groups petitioned the Court to allow the followers of indigenous religions and *kepercayaan* to fill in the name of their
belief sytem in the "religion" column of the ID card. The prior regulation,
reinforced in a 2006 law, stipulated that the followers of such "unrecog-
nized" religious or belief traditions had to fill in the religion column with
the name of one of Indonesia's six "recognized religions" (Islam, Prot-
estantism, Catholicism, Hinduism, Buddhism, and Confucianism)—or
leave the column blank. The latter option was actually an improvement on
the previous law, in that it provides a seventh option of leaving the religion
box blank, but it was seen by the petitioners as still leaving room for state
discrimination and social stigmatization. The Court's acceptance of the petition disrupts the long-accepted definition and boundaries of religion in
Indonesia by implying that the category of "religion" should be understood
to also include spiritual beliefs or *kepercayaan*.

A number of Muslim groups, especially the MUI, were startled by the
Court's ruling and felt that the decision, which did not refer to any MUI
statements, was against what they regarded as the "national consensus."
Din Syamsuddin, the former head of Muhammadiyah and a member of
the MUI's board of advisers, stated categorically that *kepercayaan* or indigenous religions are different from (true) religion. The "consensus" mentioned by the MUI apparently refers to several regulations from the 1970s
that formalized the distinction between the six recognized religions
(*agama*) and the *aliran kepercayaan* or spiritual belief systems by identifying the latter as "culture" rather than "religion." This distinction has been
preserved to this day, with "religions" being under the jurisdiction of the
Ministry of Religious Affairs and *aliran kepercayaan* (as well as indigenous
religions) being under the Ministry of Education and Culture. It was on
these grounds and against this historical background, then, that mainline
and conservative Muslim groups objected to the Constitutional Court decision. Although the national Communion of Churches in Indonesia (PGI)

welcomed the decision, a good number of Protestant churches, especially in Christian-majority regions, voiced similar objections to the Court decision (Sutanto 2018).

Nothing can be done to change or revise the decision, since the Constitutional Court's decisions are not subject to appeal. However, the MUI stated bluntly that it was determined to oppose any efforts to implement the decision in policy practice. Thus, six months after the decision, the government has yet to provide an operational regulation to guide officials at the local level on how to implement the Court's decision. Nevertheless, in practice the decision has already made a difference. Among other things, it has raised the confidence of indigenous religion groups. In Kalimantan, for example, only a few weeks after the decision, an indigenous group known as Kaharingan has openly and officially declared that they are not Hindus but have their own religion; in keeping with this declaration, they have seceded from the Directorate General for Hinduism of the Ministry of Religious Affairs (Sutanto 2018). In some places, the local civil registry offices have loosened the restrictions against the indigenous groups to obtain ID cards that mention *kepercayaan* instead of any of the six religions.[4]

The Sexual Relations Case

On December 2017, a few weeks after the decision on the ID card case, a second ruling by the Constitutional Court dealt another blow to Islamist groups and caused heated public debate. It centered on the Court's rejection of a petition to criminalize sex outside marriage as well as within same-sex relationships. This case is especially interesting in light of the fact that advocacy for LGBT rights has experienced serious setbacks in recent years, especially since 2016, as a result of the actions of both conservative religious groups and state-based agencies. In general, issues related to sexuality, adultery, and prostitution have been one of the major targets of the morality regulation in local bylaws passed since the early 2000s, many of which were inspired by a particular understanding of shariah. This issue has been very politicized, especially during local elections (Buehler 2016). The petition to expand the articles in the Penal Code related to adultery to also include fornication and LGBT sexualities was an attempt to influence *national* law, in line with conservative Muslim understandings of sexual morality.

The petition was filed in 2016, and the decision was handed down in December 2017. The petitioner was a group called AILA (Aliansi Cinta Keluarga or Family Love Alliance), chaired by Bachtiar Nasir, one of the most prominent leaders of Action 212; the petition was also officially supported by the MUI. AILA was also meant to refer to *a'ila*, an Arabic word meaning family. The alliance sought to build a network to strengthen the institution of the traditional family through training, publications, counseling, and research. The membership included preachers and academics working in universities or research centers such as the MIUMI. One of its first programs was training to counter "the propaganda for feminism and gender equality," with LGBT issues high on its list of targets (Salimah 2004).

Unlike the KTP case, in which there was no dissenting opinion, it was significant that the judges of the Constitutional Court were seriously divided on the sexual relations case, with four of the nine judges expressing a dissenting opinion. All the dissenters were Muslims, while three out of the five judges who supported the rejection of the petitions were non-Muslims. The fact that the four judges would have accepted the petition is significant. This means that AILA's struggle through the Constitutional Court was almost successful, and had it been so, it would have significantly changed the law without any way to appeal it. Furthermore, some of the arguments of the dissenting opinion are extraconstitutional, embellished by references to religious sources (mostly Islam, but with additional claims that all religions are against adultery, fornication, and same-sex relations).

The two Constitutional Court decisions issued at the end of 2017 are instructive. They show that the contestation of normativities related to coexistence is being played out in street politics as well as in higher-level state circles. The Constitutional Court has become a formal but important avenue for scaling up of civic normativities, in a way that may well have enduring impact. The issue partly touches on inclusion of citizens: those not belonging to six world religions and those with different sexual moralities or orientations. In the first case, the impact of partial exclusion is denial of fulfillment of their basic rights; in the second case, it may amount to (over) criminalization (A'yun 2017). And in those two cases the groups that may be characterized loosely as conservative were on the losing side.

The ID card ruling is the more far-reaching, since the petition was accepted by the Court, meaning that the law has to be changed. It is true that, as Klinken and Berenschot (2018) argue, citizenship in Indonesia is "highly informal," and as a result legal victory even at the highest level does not automatically translate into better recognition of rights in the lives of citizens. Indeed, representatives of the MUI have stated that they are committed to opposing the full implementation of the decision and that the Ministry of Internal Affairs does not need to implement the decision of the ID card (KTP) case. If the ministry gives in to this pressure, the Constitutional Court does not have any power of enforcement. Since the decision in November 2017, the ministry has attempted to implement its decision, while accommodating the MUI's objection through alternative wordings of the KTP.[5] Realizing that the Court does not have enforcement powers, many CSOs and the National Women's Commission (Komnas Perempuan) are trying to safeguard implementation of the decision through consultations with the ministry as well as outreach to promote a broader social acceptance of the decision. The informality of citizenship, as shown in these examples, does not mean that rule of law does not have any effect but rather means that its fulfillment requires additional mediators. This is a conclusion in accord with cases of citizenship discussed by Berenschot and Klinken (2018).

On the other hand, the MUI's increasing awareness of the importance of the Constitutional Court may in the future become more decisive. While the Court may still be regarded as independent, the judges may also not be immune from influence coming from public pressure or their own religious commitment. In this regard, Nadirsyah Hosen's study (2016) of the religiosity of the judges is interesting. In his assessment of the personalities of thirteen past Muslim judges, he came to the optimistic conclusion that they are committed to an inclusive and "nationalistic" understanding of their religion, emphasizing the compatibility of Islamic law and the constitution in Indonesia. But support for this view of the judges is harder to confirm when, as in the ruling on sexual relations, the Muslim judges reach contrasting conclusions. Even if Hosen's claim is true, we may anticipate that religious groups, including conservative ones, may in the future see that they have a vital stake in the recruitment of new judges.

In the end, difficulties in enforcing the Court's decisions should not tempt us to dismiss their importance. If the outcomes of the two petitions had been different, the result would have been further "Islamization" of a narrow and exclusivist sort. More importantly, legal victory, such as in the ID card case, constitutes a very significant starting point, without which further progress to fulfill the rights of particular groups of citizens would be considerably more difficult. Moreover, even at this early stage these decisions have brought significant improvements to the lives of some Indonesians, such as the practitioners of long-excluded indigenous religious communities.

SCALING UP PLURALISM: AN UNFINISHED STORY

The theme of "rising intolerance" initially associated with the anti-Ahok movement may not be the best way to summarize what has happened in Indonesia in the years since 2016–17 (Mietzner and Muhtadi 2018). Nonetheless, these years may be seen as a critical juncture in Indonesian democratization. The presidential election of 2018–19 showed that the polarization that had grown since the 2014 presidential election and then during the 2017 Jakarta gubernatorial election became even more pronounced during the 2019 presidential election. Elections have been important moments when ongoing changes often accelerate and deepen. Their impact may or may not be lasting. There is reason to believe that, while the 2019 election was officially over by May 2019, the tension and the polarization to which it gave rise may be deliberately maintained by other means, probably until the next election, and at times by groups with varied agendas. Whatever the outcome, it is clear that the contestation between different normativities and scalings for recognition and citizenship has become more, not less, pronounced over the past several years. Events during this same period show clearly that the contestation is not simply an issue of discursive debates but is linked to contests for power and collaboration across the state-society divide. The less centralized distribution of power after

1998 means that the result is not easily predictable, and in some cases the collaboration may not advance democratic goals (Hefner 2009).

Among the most difficult questions is the issue of how to deal with antipluralist groupings in a pluralist democracy. On one hand, the expression of the exclusivist idea of Muslim leadership was made possible by democratization. Thus the government's resistance in the form of a repressive policy that bans an organization regarded as anti-Pancasila is inevitably controversial. Does defending pluralism or countering intolerance allow for repression of antipluralist ideas? While some CSOs work with the state to defend pluralism, there is also the worry that in doing so they are actually facilitating undemocratic policies. This difficulty is reflected in the division among CSOs, between those who see pluralism as threatened and those who are concerned with protecting social freedoms.

The question becomes even more difficult when issues of injustice (or perceptions of it) are brought forward, sometimes by the same conservative religious groups. Are the groups promoting intolerance or fighting injustice? In the case of the Jakarta election, scholars debated this extensively. Although it is difficult to deny the strength of religious/racial exclusivism involved in the campaigns against Ahok, social justice issues also figured in the entire episode. Pluralism is not an isolated value: it has to be seen in relation to social justice issues, including, as in the Jakarta electoral campaign, the marginalization of Muslim poor (Alvian 2017; Hadiz 2017).

In this regard, another event in 2017, the struggle of the indigenous religious groups to secure state recognition through a judicial review at the Constitutional Court, shows a different entanglement of recognition and social justice or redistributional issues. The main issue in this case had to do with the fact that lack of recognition hinders access to distributional resources. The complexity of these issues—pluralism and freedom, recognition and redistribution, injustice and intolerance—makes it only natural that even within CSOs working for pluralism and human rights there can be serious differences and debates.

While this story is clearly unfinished, the episodes of the past two years have helped to clarify many things. Democratization opened up a free arena not only for "good guys" but for a competition of normativities, a fierce one. Voices that were denied during the pre-1998 authoritarian era have found their place in this new arena and demand to be heard and accommodated.

The episodes during 2016–17 underscore another point: many factors determine the success of scaling initiatives, and even small differences in circumstances may result in deeply consequential outcomes. The second Defend Islam Action (in November 2016) showed the unpredictable success of mobilization, when some two hundred thousand people showed up for the demonstration, which ended with a riot right in front of the presidential palace. A slight mishandling of the situation could have resulted in a very different outcome. So did the events that led to an even larger show of force a month later. Similarly, the Constitutional Court's decision on the petition to expand the article on adultery was rejected by four out of nine judges. If one judge had taken a different position, the result would have had very different moral and legal consequences for Indonesia and would have marked a huge step forward in a narrowly understood version of "Islamization."

There may yet be more narrow and twisting paths like these in the future. The future of Indonesian pluralism is contingent on the play of many social, political, and economic factors—and the victory of antipluralist forces is by no means guaranteed. Yet, while one can debate whether recent changes in the Indonesian political landscape are permanent—and, in particular, whether the "moderate center" has indeed shifted to the right—we may say that the pluralist undercurrent in Indonesia remains strong but will be continuously tested. Despite their many achievements, Indonesia and Indonesian democracy are still unfinished projects.

For one thing, the post-1998 amended constitution—though it continues to be interpreted and though the interpretations range from the very conservative to the progressive—provides a firm ground for a pluralist Indonesia sustained by a robust recognition of universal human rights. For another, CSOs remain vibrant and experienced in responding to new challenges. These organizations include not only long-established religious organizations, such as Muhammadiyah and Nahdlatul Ulama, but also other non-Islamic organizations, as well as those grounded in more universal conceptions of pluralism and human rights.

In a country in which religion plays so important a role in public life, and religious piety is promoted even by the state, resistance toward moral liberalization is to be expected and is not necessarily undemocratic. Competition between diverse groups representing different political, economic, and moral standpoints will remain a central feature of Indonesian public life for many years to come. As long as the competition between groups—and we may say that in this era this mostly means between different varieties of *Muslim* groups—does not descend into physical violence, this contestation may be a sign of a healthy democracy.

NOTES

1. For a comprehensive history of Islamization, see Merle C. Ricklefs's (2006, 2007, 2012) three volumes on the subject; see also Hefner's (2013) critical review of Ricklefs's third volume. Buehler (2016) looks at the politics of "shariahization" in recent times, post-1998. Menchik (2016) studies the views of leaders of the moderate organizations Muhammadiyah and Nahdlatul Ulama on tolerance, more specifically on Muslim leadership, and has found that there is a tendency to prefer Muslim leaders, especially in majority-Muslim areas.

2. For detailed information about the formation of the GNPF-MUI, see IPAC (2018a).

3. In addition to six cases that I discuss in Bagir (2015), there have been a number of other cases, including those dealing with interreligious marriage in the marriage law, the adultery issue, the ID card case in the civil administration law, another case on halal product law, and a third review of defamation-of-religion law. For more discussion on the Constitutional Court's decisions related to religion, see Butt (2016).

4. This is shown in a study done by Satunama in six locations. The results of the research have not been officially released as of this chapter's writing.

5. At the time of the writing of this chapter, the ministry provides four alternative wordings on the ID card.

WORKS CITED

Abdillah, Masykuri. 1997. *Responses of Indonesian Muslim Intellectuals to the Concept of Democracy (1966–1993)*. Hamburg: Abera Verlag Meyer.

Abdullah, Amin. 1996. *Studi agama: Normatifitas atau historisitas?* Yogyakarta: Pustaka Pelajar.

———. 2002. "Hermeneutic Method." Paper presented at the Short Course Southeast Asia: Islam, Gender and Reproductive Rights conference, Sunan Kalijaga State Islamic University, Yogyakarta.

Acciaioli, Greg. 2001. "Grounds of Conflict, Idioms of Harmony: Custom, Religion and Nationalism in Violence Avoidance at the Lindu Plain, Central Sulawesi." *Indonesia* 72 (1): 81–114.

Adam, Jeroen. 2008. "Forced Migration, Adat, and a Purified Present in Ambon, Indonesia." *Ethnology* 47 (4): 227–38.

Adams, Kathleen. 2006. *Art as Politics: Re-crafting Identities, Tourism, and Power in Tana Toraja, Indonesia*. Honolulu: University of Hawai'i Press.

Adamson, Walter L. 1980. *Hegemony and Revolution: A Study of Antonio Gramsci's Political and Cultural Theory*. Berkeley: University of California Press.

Afsaruddin, Asma. 1999. *Hermeneutic and Honor: Negotiating Female "Public" Space in Islamic Societies*. Cambridge, MA: Center for Middle Eastern Studies, Harvard University.

Ahmed, Shahab. 2016. *What Is Islam? The Importance of Being Islamic*. Princeton, NJ: Princeton University Press.

Ahnaf, Mohammad Iqbal. 2006. *The Image of the Other as Enemy: Radical Discourse in Indonesia*. Bangkok: Silkworm Press.

———. 2011. "From Revolution to 'Refolution': A Study of Hizb al-Tahrir, Its Changes and Trajectories in the Democratic Context of Indonesia (2000–2009)." PhD diss., Victoria University of Wellington, Wellington, New Zealand.

———. 2017. "Where Does Hizbut Tahrir Go from Here?" *New Mandala*, June 2017, www.newmandala.org/hizbut-tahrir-indonesia-go/.

227

'Aini, Inayatul. 2013. "Kisah homoseksual kaum nabi Luth dalam Al-Qur'an menurut penafsiran Musdah Mulia dan Husen Muhammad." BA thesis, Sunan Kalijaga State Islamic University, Yogyakarta.

Ali, Imam Shamsi. 2017. "Pilkada DKI yang membanggakan." *Republika,* April 23, 2017. www.republika.co.id/berita/jurnalisme-warga/wacana/17/04/23/oou5b 1396-pilkada-dki-yang-membanggakan.

Aliansyah, Muhammad Agil. 2015. "Rasanya yang diharamkan Islam bukanlah homosesksualitas." Merdeka.com, April 14. https://www.merdeka.com/peris tiwa/dosen-ui-rasanya-yang-diharamkan-islam-bukanlah-homoseksualitas .html.

Ali-Fauzi, Ihsan, Samsu Rizal Panggabean, Nathanael Gratias Sumaktoyo, H. T. Anick, Husni Mubarak, Testriono, and Siti Nurhayati. 2011. *Kontroversi gereja di Jakarta.* Yogyakarta: CRCS.

Al Qurtuby, Sumanto. 2013. "Interreligious Violence, Civic Peace, and Citizenship: Christians and Muslims in Maluku, Eastern Indonesia." PhD diss., Boston University.

———. 2014. "Religious Women for Peace and Reconciliation in Contemporary Indonesia." *International Journal on World Peace* 31 (1): 27–58.

———. 2015. "Ambonese Muslim Jihadists, Islamic Identity, and the History of Christian–Muslim Rivalry in the Moluccas, Eastern Indonesia." *International Journal of Asian Studies* 12 (1): 1–29.

———. 2016. *Religious Violence and Conciliation in Indonesia: Christians and Muslims in the Moluccas.* London: Routledge.

Alvian, Rizky Alif. 2017. "Ekonomi-politik Aksi Bela Islam: Pluralisme dalam krisis?" *Maarif* 11 (2): 53–70.

Alwi, Des. 2010. *A Boy from Banda: A Spice Island Childhood.* Jakarta: Banda Naira Culture and Heritage Foundation.

Amal, T. A., and S. R. Panggabean. 2005. "A Contextual Approach to the Qur'an." In *Approaches to the Qur'an in Contemporary Indonesia,* edited by A. Saeed, 107–34. Oxford: Oxford University Press.

Amnesty International. 2016. *Amnesty International Report 2015/2016: The State of the World's Human Rights.* New York: Amnesty International.

Andaya, Leonard Y. 1993. *The World of Maluku: Eastern Indonesia in the Early Modern Period.* Honolulu: University of Hawai'i Press.

An-Nabhani, Taqiuddin. 2001. *Concepts of Hizb ut-Tahrir.* London: Caliphate Publications. Originally published as *Mafahim Hizb ut-Tahrir* (n.p.: HTI Press, 2001).

Anshori, Ridwan. 2016. "11 Adik Sultan HB X tetap tolak sabda raja." *Sindonews,* May 9, 2015. http://daerah.sindonews.com.

Arifianto, Alexander R. 2017. "Jakarta Governor Election Results in a Victory for Prejudice over Pluralism." *Conversation,* April 20, 2017. https://theconversa tion.com/jakarta-governor-election-results-in-a-victory-for-prejudice-over -pluralism-76388.

Asad, Talal. 1986. *The Idea of an Anthropology of Islam.* Occasional Paper Series. Washington, DC: Center for Contemporary Arab Studies, Georgetown University.

———. 2003. *Formations of the Secular: Christianity, Islam, Modernity.* Stanford, CA: Stanford University Press.

Aspinall, E. 2011. "Democratization and Ethnic Politics in Indonesia: Nine Theses." *Journal of East Asian Studies* 11 (2): 289–319.

Asyathri, Helmia, Keppi Sukesi, and Yayuk Yuliati. 2014. "Diplomasi hibrida: Perempuan dalam resolusi konflik Maluku." *Indonesian Journal of Women's Studies* 2 (1): 18–31.

Atkinson, Jane Monnig. 1987. "Religions in Dialogue: The Construction of an Indonesian Minority Religion." In *Indonesian Religions in Transition,* edited by Rita Smith Kipp and Susan Rodgers, 171–86. Tucson: University of Arizona Press.

A'yun, Rafiqa Qurrata. 2017. "AILA's Unsuccessful Petition: A Narrow Escape from Overcriminalisation." *Indonesia at Melbourne* (blog), December 19. http: //indonesiaatmelbourne.unimelb.edu.au/ailas-unsuccessful-petition-a -narrow-escape-from-overcriminalisation/.

Aziz, Zakaria Ahmad. 2016. "Model pembelajaran PAI bagi Waria di Pondok Pesantren Waria Al Fatah Celenan Jagalan Banguntapan Bantul Yogyakarta." MA thesis, Sunan Kalijaga State Islamic University, Yogyakarta.

Babcock, Tim. 1981. "Muslim Minahasans with Roots in Java: The People of Kampung Jawa Tondano." *Indonesia* 32:75–92.

Bagir, Zainal Abidin. 2013. "Defamation of Religion in Post-Reformasi Indonesia: Is Revision Possible?" *Australian Journal of Asian Law* 13 (2): 1–16.

———. 2015. "Indonesia." In *Keeping the Faith: A Study of Religious Freedom in ASEAN Countries,* edited by Jaclyn Neo, 138–94. Jakarta: Human Rights Resource Center.

———. 2018. "The Politics and Law of Religious Governance." In Hefner 2018b, 284–95.

Bakker, L. 2016. "Organized Violence and the State." *Bijdragen tot de Taal-, Land-en Volkenkunde* 172 (2–3): 249–77.

Bamualim, C. S. 2011. "Islamic Militancy and Resentment against Hadhramis in Post-Suharto Indonesia: A Case Study of Habib Rizieq Syihab and His Islamic Defenders Front." *Comparative Studies of South Asia, Africa and the Middle East* 31 (2): 267–81.

Bangsa Online. 2016. "Penolakan muktamar HTI meluas, Ansor Bojonegoro minta aparat batalkan." April 30. www.bangsaonline.com/berita/22294/penolakan -muktamar-hti-meluas-ansor-bojonegoro-minta-aparat-batalkan.

Barron, Patrick, Sana Jaffrey, and Ashutosh Varshney. 2014. *How Large Conflicts Subside: Evidence from Indonesia.* Indonesian Social Development Paper No. 18. Jakarta: World Bank.

Bartels, Dieter. 1977. *Guarding the Invisible Mountain: Intervillage Alliances, Religious Syncretism, and Ethnic Identity among Ambonese Christians and Muslims in the Moluccas.* Ithaca, NY: Cornell University Press.

———. 2017. *Di bawah naungan Gunung Nunusaku: Muslim-Kristen hidup berdampingan di Maluku Tengah.* Vol. 2. Jakarta: KPG.

Barth, Fredrik. 1993. *Balinese Worlds.* Princeton, NJ: Princeton University Press.

Barton, Greg. 2005. *Jemaah Islamiyah: Radical Islamism in Indonesia.* Singapore: Ridge Books.

BBC Indonesia. 2016. "Kehadiran di HTI, tegas Bima Arya, tak berarti mendukung." February 11. www.bbc.com/indonesia/berita_indonesia/2016/02/16 0211_indonesia_bima_arya_hti.

Beaman, Jean. 2016. "Citizenship as Cultural: Towards a Theory of Cultural Citizenship." *Sociology Compass* 10:845–57.

Berenschot, Ward, and Gerry van Klinken. 2018. "Informality and Citizenship: The Everyday State in Indonesia." *Citizenship Studies* 22 (2): 95–111.

———, eds. 2019a. *Citizenship in Indonesia: Perjuangan atas hak, identitas, dan partisipasi.* Jakarta: Yayasan Pustaka Obor Indonesia.

———. 2019b. Introduction to *Citizenship in Indonesia: Perjuangan atas hak, identitas, dan partisipasi.* In Berenschot and Klinken 2019, 1–44.

Berita Maluku Online. 2015. "Banda sebagai Warisan Dunia, Thalib: Pempus sementara usulkan ke UNESCO." March 14. www.beritamalukuonline.com /2015/03/banda-sebagai-warisan-dunia-thalib.html.

Bertrand, Jacques. 2002. "Legacies of the Authoritarian Past: Religious Violence in Indonesia's Moluccan Islands." *Pacific Affairs* 75 (1): 57–85.

———. 2004. *Nationalism and Ethnic Conflict in Indonesia.* Cambridge: Cambridge University Press.

Blackburn, S. 2007. *Kongres Perempuan Pertama: Tinjauan ulang.* Jakarta: Yayasan Obor Indonesia.

Bowen, John A. 2005. "Normative Pluralism in Indonesia: Regions, Religions and Ethnicities." In *Multiculturalism in Asia,* edited by Will Kymlicka and Baogong He, 152–69. Oxford: Oxford University Press.

———. 2010. *Can Islam Be French? Pluralism and Pragmatism in a Secularist State.* Princeton, NJ: Princeton University Press.

BPS [Badan Pusat Statistik] Kota Manado. 2016a. "Banyaknya desa, rumah tangga, penduduk dan penduduk per rumah tangga tahun 2014." Manado Kota Badan Pusat Statistik. https://manadokota.bps.go.id/linkTabelStatis/view/id/3.

———. 2016b. "Jumlah penduduk menurut kecamatan dan agama yang dianut Kota Manado, 2010." Manado Kota Badan Pusat Statistik. https://manadokota .bps.go.id/linkTabelStatis/view/id/34.

Bräuchler, Birgit. 2003. "Cyberidentities at War: Religion, Identity, and the Internet in the Moluccan Conflict." *Indonesia* 75:123–51.

———. 2009a. "Cultural Solutions to Religious Conflicts? The Revival of Tradition in the Moluccas, Eastern Indonesia." *Asian Journal of Social Science* 37 (6): 872–91.

———. 2009b. "Mobilizing Culture and Tradition for Peace: Reconciliation in the Moluccas." In *Reconciling Indonesia: Grassroots Agency for Peace*, edited by Birgit Bräuchler, 97–118. London: Routledge.

———. 2015. *The Cultural Dimension of Peace: Decentralization and Reconciliation in Indonesia.* London: Palgrave Macmillan.

———. 2017. "Changing Patterns of Mobility, Citizenship and Conflict in Indonesia." *Social Identities* 23 (4): 1–16.

Bray, Sri Paweling. 2016. *Islam Jowo bertutur sabdaraja: Pertarungan kebudayaan, Khasebul (Katholik) dan kerja misi, kronologi munculnya sabdaraja.* Yogyakarta: Komunitas Jowo, Pejuang Mataram Islam.

Brenner, Suzanne. 2011. "Private Moralities in the Public Sphere: Democratization, Islam, and Gender in Indonesia." *American Anthropologist* 113 (3): 478–90.

Brownlee, Jason, Tarek Masoud, and Andrew Reynolds. 2015. *The Arab Spring: Pathways of Repression and Reform.* Oxford: Oxford University Press.

Bruinessen, Martin van. 2002. "Genealogies of Islamic Radicalism in Post-Suharto Indonesia." *South East Asia Research* 10 (2): 117–54.

———, ed. 2013a. *Contemporary Developments in Indonesian Islam: Explaining the "Conservative Turn."* Singapore: ISEAS.

———. 2013b. "Introduction: Contemporary Developments in Indonesian Islam and the 'Conservative Turn' of the Early Twenty-First Century." In Bruinessen 2013a, 1–20.

Bruner, Edward. 2004. *Culture on Tour: Ethnographies of Travel.* Chicago: University of Chicago Press.

Buehler, Michael. 2016. *The Politics of Shari'a Law: Islamist Activists and the State in Democratizing Indonesia.* Cambridge: Cambridge University Press.

Bulbeck, C. 1998. *Re-orienting Western Feminism: Women's Diversity in a Postcolonial World.* Cambridge: Cambridge University Press.

Burhani, Ahmad Najib. 2013a. "Liberal and Conservative Discourses in the Muhammadiyah: The Struggle for the Face of Reformist Islam in Indonesia." In Bruinessen 2013a, 105–44.

———. 2013b. "When Muslims Are Not Muslims: The Ahmadiyya Community and the Discourse of Heresy in Indonesia." PhD diss., University of California, Santa Barbara.

Burhanudin, Jajat, and Oman Fathurahman. 2004. *Tentang perempuan Islam: Wacana dan gerakan.* Jakarta: Gramedia Pustaka Utama, PPIM UIN Jakarta.

Burnet, Ian. 2013. *Spice Island.* Kenthurst, New South Wales: Rosenberg.

Bush, Robin. 2015. "Religious Politics and Minority Rights during the Yudhoyono Administration." In *The Yudhoyono Presidency: Indonesia's Decade of Stability and Stagnation,* edited by Edward Aspinall, Marcus Mietzner, and Dirk Tomsa, 239–57. Singapore: ISEAS.

Bush, Robin, and Budhy Munawar-Rachman. 2014. "NU and Muhammadiyah: Majority Views on Religious Minorities in Indonesia." In *Religious Diversity in Muslim-Majority States in Southeast Asia: Areas of Toleration and Conflict,* edited by Bernhard Platzdasch and Johan Saravanamuttu, 16–50. Singapore: ISEAS.

Butt, Simon. 2016. "Between Control and Appeasement: Religion in Five Constitutional Court Decisions." In *Religion, Law and Intolerance in Indonesia,* edited by Tim Lindsey and Helen Pausacker, 42–67. New York: Routledge.

Butt, Simon, and Tim Lindsey. 2012. *The Constitution of Indonesia: A Contextual Analysis.* Oxford: Hart.

Case, William. 2011. "What Ails Democracy in East Asia?" *Australian Journal of International Affairs* 65 (3): 360–70.

Cederroth, Sven. 1996. "From Ancestor Worship to Monotheism: Politics of Religion in Lombok." *Temenos* 32:7–36.

Centre for Humanitarian Dialogue. 2011. *The Centre for Humanitarian Dialogue in 2011.* Geneva: Centre for Humanitarian Dialogue.

Chalil, Muhammad. 1936. *Kesopanan perempuan Islam.* Yogyakarta: Penyiaran Islam.

———. 1954. *Nilai wanita.* Bandung-Jakarta: Al-Ma'arif.

Challand, Benoit. 2017. "Citizenship and Violence in the Arab Worlds: A Historical Sketch." In *The Transformation of Citizenship,* vol. 3, *Struggle, Resistance, and Violence,* edited by Juergen Makert and Bryan S. Turner, 93–112. New York: Routledge.

Chaplin, Chris. 2018. "Salafi Islamic Piety as Civic Activism: Wahdah Islamiyah and Differentiated Citizenship in Indonesia." *Citizenship Studies* 22 (2): 208–23.

————. 2019. "Kebajikan Islam salafi sebagai aktivisme masyarakat: Wahdah Islamiyah dan kewarganegaraan terdiferensiasi di Indonesia." In Berenschot and Klinken 2019, 227–56.

Chauvel, Richard. 1990. *Nationalists, Soldiers and Separatists: The Ambonese Islands from Colonialism to Revolt, 1880–1950*. Leiden: KITLV Press.

Cooley, Frank L. 1961. "Altar and Throne in Central Moluccan Societies: A Study of the Relationship between the Institutions of Religion and the Institutions of Local Society Undergoing Rapid Social Change." PhD diss., Yale University.

Crouch, Melissa. 2014. *Law and Religion in Indonesia: Conflict and the Courts in West Java*. London: Routledge.

Daniels, Timothy P. 2017. "Interplay of Sharia Projects: Between *Ketuanan Melayu*, Islam, and Liberal Rights in Malaysia." In *Sharia Dynamics: Islamic Law and Sociopolitical Processes*, edited by Timothy P. Daniels, 141–68. New York: Palgrave Macmillan.

Davidson, J. S. 2008. *From Rebellion to Riots: Collective Violence on Indonesian Borneo*. Madison: University of Wisconsin Press.

Deeb, L., and M. Harb. 2013. *Leisurely Islam: Negotiating Geography and Morality in Shi'ite South Beirut*. Princeton, NJ: Princeton University Press.

de Jonge, Christiaan, Arnold Parengkuan, and Karel Steenbrink. 2008. "How Christianity Obtained a Central Position in Minahasa Culture and Society." In *A History of Christianity in Indonesia*, edited by Jan S. Aritonang and Karel A. Steenbrink, 419–54. Leiden: Brill.

Detik. 2016. "Tak ada izin dan dapat ancaman, muktamar HTI di ITC dibubarkan." Detik, May 1. news.detik.com/berita-jawa-timur/d-3201012/tak-ada-izin-dan-dapat-ancaman-muktamar-hti-di-itc-dibubarkan.

Doorn-Harder, Nelly van. 2006. *Women Shaping Islam: Indonesian Muslim Women Reading the Qur'an*. Urbana-Champaign: University of Illinois Press.

Duncan, Christopher R. 2005a. "The Other Maluku: Chronologies of Conflict in North Maluku." *Indonesia* 80:53–80.

————. 2005b. "Unwelcome Guests: Relations between Internally Displaced Persons and Their Hosts in North Sulawesi, Indonesia." *Journal of Refugee Studies* 18 (1): 25–46.

————. 2009a. "Monument and Martyrdom: Memorializing the Dead in Postconflict Maluku." *Brijdragen tot de Taal-, Land- en Volkenkunde* 165 (4): 429–58.

————. 2009b. "Reconciliation and Revitalization: The Resurgence of Tradition in Postconflict Tobelo, Maluku, Eastern Indonesia." *Journal of Asian Studies* 68 (4): 1077–1104.

———. 2013. *Violence and Vengeance: Religious Conflict and Its Aftermath in Eastern Indonesia.* Ithaca, NY: Cornell University Press.

Dzuhayatin, Siti Ruhaini. 2001. "Gender and Pluralism in Indonesia." In *The Politics of Multiculturalism: Pluralism and Citizenship in Malaysia, Singapore, and Indonesia,* edited by Robert W. Hefner, 253–67. Honolulu: University of Hawai'i Press.

———. 2015. *Rezim gender Muhammadiyah; Kontestasi gender, idenitas dan eksistensi.* Yogyakarta: UIN Sunan Kalijaga, Suka Press.

Elson, Robert E. 2013. "Two Failed Attempts to Islamize the Indonesian Constitution." *Sojourn: Journal of Social Issues in Southeast Asia* 28 (3): 379–437.

Emon, Anver M. 2012. *Religious Pluralism and Islamic Law: Dhimmis and Others in the Empire of Law.* Oxford: Oxford University Press.

Engle Merry, Sally. 1988. "Legal Pluralism." *Law and Society Review* 22 (5): 869–96.

Erb, Maribeth. 2003. " 'Uniting the Bodies and Cleansing the Village': Conflicts over Local Heritage in a Globalizing World." *Indonesia and the Malay World* 31 (1): 129–39.

Errington, S. 1990. "Recasting Sex, Gender, and Power." In *Power and Difference: Gender in Island Southeast Asia,* edited by J. M. Atkinson and S. Errington, 1–58. Stanford, CA: Stanford University Press.

Evans, Peter. 1996. "Government Action, Social Capital and Development: Reviewing the Evidence on Synergy." *World Development* 24 (6): 1119–32.

Fachrudin, Azis. 2018. *Polemik tafsir Pancasila.* Yogyakarta: CRCS.

Fathoni. 2016. "Resmi PBNU sikapi perilaku seksual menyimpang LGBT." NU Online, February 25, 2016. www.nu.or.id/post/read/66045/resmi-pbnu-sikapi -prilaku-seksual-menyimpang-lgbt.

Fealy, Greg. 2016a. "Bigger Than Ahok: Explaining the 2 December Mass Rally." *Indonesia at Melbourne* (blog), December 7, 2016. http://indonesiaatmelbourne .unimelb.edu.au/bigger-than-ahok-explaining-jakartas-2-december-mass -rally/.

———. 2016b. "The Politics of Religious Intolerance in Indonesia: Mainstreamism Trumps Extremism?" In *Religion, Law and Intolerance in Indonesia,* edited by Tim Lindsey and Helen Pausacker, 115–31. New York: Routledge.

Feener, R. Michael. 2007. *Muslim Legal Thought in Modern Indonesia.* Cambridge: Cambridge University Press.

Feillard, Andrée. 1999. *NU vis a vis negara: Pencarian isi, bentuk dan makna.* Yogyakarta: LKiS.

Feillard, Andrée, and Rémy Madinier. 2006. *La fin de l'innocence? L'Islam indonésien face à la tentation radicale de 1967 à nos jours.* Paris: Les Indes Savantes.

Feith, Herbert. [1962] 2006. *The Decline of Constitutional Democracy in Indonesia.* Singapore: Equinox.

Fenwick, Stewart Ferguson. 2015. "Is Rawlsian Liberalism Compatible with Islam? A Case Study of Post-Soeharto Indonesia." PhD diss., Melbourne Law School, University of Melbourne.

Fofid, Rudi. 2014. "Beribu Headline Tanpa Deadline." In Manuputty et al. 2014, 15–37.

Fraser, Nancy. 2000. "Rethinking Recognition." *New Left Review* 3 (3): 107–20.

———. 2001. "Recognition without Ethics?" *Theory, Culture and Society* 18 (2–3): 21–42.

Friedmann, Yohanan. 2003. *Tolerance and Coercion in Islam: Interfaith Relations in the Muslim Tradition.* Cambridge: Cambridge University Press.

Gandapurnama, Baban. 2017. "Penjelasan Habib Rizieq soal tesis miliknya terkait Pancasila." Detik, February 13, 2017. https://news.detik.com/berita/d-3421726 /penjelasan-habib-rizieq-soal-tesis-miliknya-terkait-pancasila.

Gaylord, Wendy. 2007. "Reformasi, Civic Education, and Indonesian Secondary School Teachers." In *How Diverse Societies Form Democratic Citizens,* edited by Doyle Stevick and Bradley A. U. Levinson, 45–67. Lanham, MD: Rowman and Littlefield.

Gillespie, Piers. 2007. "Current Issues in Indonesian Islam: Analysing the 2005 Council of Indonesian Ulama Fatwa No. 7 Opposing Pluralism, Liberalism, and Secularism." *Journal of Islamic Studies* 18 (2): 202–40.

Glenn, E. N. 2011. "Constructing Citizenship: Exclusion, Subordination, and Resistance." *American Sociological Review* 76 (1): 1–24.

GMIM (Gereja Masehi Injili Minahasa). 2017. "Peta pelayanan GMIM." https://www.gmim.or.id/peta-pelayanan/.

Goebel, Zane. 2010. *Language, Migration, and Identity: Neighborhood Talk in Indonesia.* Cambridge: Cambridge University Press.

Goody, J. 1976. *Production and Reproduction: A Comparative Study of the Domestic Domain.* Cambridge: Cambridge University Press.

Gregg, G. 1998. "Culture, Personality, and the Multiplicity of Identity: Evidence from North African Life Narratives." *Ethos* 26 (2): 120–52.

Hadiz, Vedi R. 2016. *Islamic Populism in Indonesia and the Middle East.* Cambridge: Cambridge University Press.

———. 2017. "Indonesia's Year of Democratic Setbacks: Towards a New Phase of Deepening Illiberalism?" *Bulletin of Indonesian Economic Studies* 53 (3): 261–78.

Hadiz, Vedi, and Inaya Rakhmani. 2017. "Marketing Morality in Indonesia's Democracy." *Asian Currents,* December 21. http://asaa.asn.au/marketing-morality -indonesias-democracy/.

Hamayotsu, Kikue, and Ronnie Nataatmadja. 2016. "Indonesia in 2015." *Asian Survey* 56 (1): 129–37.

Hansen, T. B. 1999. *The Saffron Wave: Democracy and Hindu Nationalism in Modern India.* Princeton, NJ: Princeton University Press.

Harjati, Arum. 2013. "Memutar balik kodrat perempuan menghancurkan ketahanan keluarga." Hizbut Tahrir, April 17. https://hizbut-tahrir.or.id/?s=a.%09 Memutar+balik+Kodrat+Perempuan+Menghancurkan+Ketahanan+Keluarga.

Harsono, Andreas. 2012. "No Model for Muslim Democracy." *New York Times*, May 21. www.nytimes.com/2012/05/22/opinion/no-model-for-muslim-de mocracy.html.

Hasan, Noorhaidi. 2006. *Laskar Jihad: Islam, Militancy, and the Quest for Identity in Post-New Order Indonesia.* Ithaca, NY: Southeast Asia Program, Cornell University.

Hashemi, Nader, and Danny Postel, eds. 2017. *Sectarianization: Mapping the New Politics of the Middle East.* Oxford: Oxford University Press.

Hasyim, Syafiq. 2014. "Council of Indonesian Ulama (Majelis Ulama Indonesia, MUI) and Its Role in the Shariatisation of Indonesia." PhD diss., Free University, Berlin.

Hauser-Schäublin, Brigitta, ed. 2013. *Adat and Indigeneity in Indonesia.* Göttingen: Universitätsverlag Göttingen.

Hefner, Robert W. 1987. "Islamizing Java? Religion and Politics in Rural East Java." *Journal of Asian Studies* 46 (3): 533–54.

———, ed. 1998. *Democratic Civility: The History and Cross-Cultural Possibility of a Modern Political Ideal.* New Brunswick, NJ: Transaction Press.

———. 2000. *Civil Islam: Muslims and Democratization in Indonesia.* Princeton, NJ: Princeton University Press.

———. 2001. "Introduction: Multiculturalism and Citizenship in Malaysia, Singapore, and Indonesia." In *The Politics of Multiculturalism: Pluralism and Citizenship in Malaysia, Singapore, and Indonesia,* edited by Robert Hefner, 1–58. Honolulu: University of Hawai'i Press.

———. 2005a. "Introduction: Modernity and the Remaking of Muslim Politics." In *Remaking Muslim Politics: Pluralism, Contestation, Democratization,* edited by Robert W. Hefner, 1–36. Princeton, NJ: Princeton University Press.

———. 2005b. "Muslim Democrats and Islamist Violence in Post-Soeharto Indonesia." In *Remaking Muslim Politics: Pluralism, Contestation, Democratization,* edited by Robert W. Hefner, 273–301. Princeton, NJ: Princeton University Press.

———. 2009. "Islamic Schools, Social Movements, and Democracy in Indonesia." In *Making Modern Muslims: The Politics of Islamic Education in South-*

east Asia, edited by Robert W. Hefner, 55–105. Honolulu: University of Hawai'i Press.

———. 2011a. *Shari'a Politics: Shari'a Law and Politics in the Modern World.* Bloomington: Indiana University Press.

———. 2011b. "Where Have All the *Abangan* Gone? Religionization and the Decline of Non-standard Islam in Contemporary Indonesia." In Picard and Madinier 2011, 71–91.

———. 2013. "Islamization and the Changing Ethical Imagination in Java." *Indonesia* 96:187–202.

———. 2016. "Shari'a Law and the Quest for a Modern Muslim Ethics." In *Shari'a Law and Modern Muslim Ethics*, edited by Robert W. Hefner, 1–34. Bloomington: Indiana University Press.

———. 2018a. "Introduction: Indonesia at the Crossroads—Imbroglios of Religion, State, and Society in an Asian Muslim Nation." In Hefner 2018b, 3–30.

———, ed. 2018b. *Routledge Handbook of Contemporary Indonesia.* New York: Routledge.

———. 2019. "Whatever Happened to Civil Islam? Islam and Democratization in Indonesia, 20 Years On." *Asian Studies Review* 43 (3): 375–96. https://doi.org/10.1080/10357823.2019.1625865.

Hendriks, I. W. J. 2014. "Khotbah damai dari mimbar Masjid Al-Fattah." In Manuputty et al. 2014, 129–40.

Henley, David, and Jamie S. Davidson. 2008. "In the Name of Adat: Regional Perspectives on Reform, Tradition, and Democracy in Indonesia." *Modern Asian Studies* 42 (4): 815–52.

Hoesterey, J. B. 2018. "Public Diplomacy and the Dissemination of 'Moderate Islam.'" In Hefner 2018b, 406–16.

Holland, Dorothy, Donald M. Nonini, Catherine Lutz, L. Bartlett, M. Frederick–McGlathery, T. C. Guldbrandsen, and E. G. Murillo, eds. 2007. *Local Democracy under Siege: Activism, Public Interests, and Private Politics.* New York: NYU Press.

Honneth, Axel. 1995. *The Struggle for Recognition: The Moral Grammar of Social Conflicts.* Cambridge, MA: MIT Press.

———. 2001. "Recognition." *Proceedings of the Aristotelian Society* 75 (1): 111–26.

———. 2012. *The I in the We: Studies in the Theory of Recognition.* Somerset, NJ: John Wiley.

Hooker, M. B. 2003. *Indonesian Islam: Social Change through Contemporary Fatawa.* Honolulu: University of Hawai'i Press.

Hoon, Chang-Yau. 2014. "God and Discipline: Religious Education and Character Building in a Christian School in Jakarta." *South East Asia Research* 22 (4): 505–24.

Hosen, Nadirsyah. 2016. "The Constitutional Court and 'Islamic' Judges in Indonesia." *Australian Journal of Asian Law* 16 (2): 1–11.

Hoskins, Janet. 2002. "Predatory Voyeurs: Tourism and 'Tribal Violence' in Remote Indonesia." *American Ethnologist* 29 (4): 797–828.

Howell, Julia Day. 2008. "Modulations of Active Piety: Professors and Televangelists as Promoters of Indonesian 'Sufism.'" In *Expressing Islam: Religious Life and Politics in Indonesia*, edited by Greg Fealy and Sally White, 40–62. Singapore: ISEAS.

HTI (Hizbut Tahrir Indonesia). 2007a. "Gubernur Sultra ikut nonton bareng film Liputan KKI 2007." *Al-Wa'ie*, no. 86, October.

———. 2007b. "Ilusi demokrasi, ifakta dan cita-cita." *Al-Wa'ie*, no. 82, June.

———. 2007c. "Muslimah berjuang meneggakan syariah." *Al-Wa'ie*, no. 82.

———. 2007d. "Pernyataan Hizbut Tahrir Indonesia tentang casus Ahmadiyah." December 24. http://hizbut-tahrir.or.id/2007/12/26/pernyataan-hizbut-tahrir-indonesia-tentang-kasus-ahmadiyah/.

———. 2008a. "HTI tegaskan berantas pornografi." [HTI confirms eradicating pornography] October 29. http://hizbut-tahrir.or.id/2008/10/29/hti-tegaskan-berantas-pornografi/.

———. 2008b. "Liputan media HTI di daerah demo terkait RUU pornografi." [HTI media coverage in the demonstration area related to the pornography bill] October 28. http://hizbut-tahrir.or.id/2008/10/28/liputan-media-hti-di-daerah-demo-terkait-ruu-pornografi/.

———. 2008c. "RUU pornografi: Pertarungan Islam versus sekularisme." [pornography bill: the fight of islam vs secularism] *Al-Wa'ie*, 99:VIII.

———. 2009a. "KH Hasyim Asy'ari dan NU: Pejuang syariah." December 6. http://hizbut-tahrir.or.id/2009/12/06/kh-hasyim-asy%E2%80%99ari-dan-nu-pejuang-syariah/.

———. 2009b. "Kunjungan Silaturrahmi HTI Pasuruan ke diknas kabupaten dan Kota Pasuruan HTI." March 11. http://hizbut-tahrir.or.id/2009/03/11/kunjungan-silaturrahmi-hti-pasrusun-ke-diknas-kabupaten-dan-kota-pasuruan/.

———. 2010a. "Bolehkah menjadi pengacara." January 1. http://hizbut-tahrir.or.id/2010/01/01/bolehkah-menjadi-pengacara/.

———. 2010b. "Catatan jubir: Impuls kecil respon besar." August 8. http://hizbut-tahrir.or.id/2010/06/08/catatan-jubir-impuls-kecil-respon-besar/.

———. 2010c. "Dari Kongres Umat Islam Indonesia (KUII)-V: Indonesia butuh pemimpin bertakwa dan sistem yang berdasarkan Syariah." *Al-Islam*, no. 506.

———. 2010d. "Hizbut Tahrir diundang dan siap sukseskan Kongres Umat Islam Indonesia ke V." April 22. http://hizbut-tahrir.or.id/2010/04/22/hizbut-tahrir -diundang-dan-siap-sukseskan-kongres-umat-islam-ke-v/.

———. 2010e. "Kasman Singodimejo: Singa Podium, penuntut Islam sebagai dasar negara." October 10. http://hizbut-tahrir.or.id/2010/10/10/kasman-singo dimejo-singa-podium-penuntut-islam-sebagai-dasar-negara/.

———. 2010f. "KH Ahmad Dahlan: Mengembalikan umat pada Syariah." February 9. http://hizbut-tahrir.or.id/2010/02/09/kh-ahmad-dahlan-mengemba likan-umat-pada-syariah/.

———. 2010g. "MUI Riau: Semestinya kepemimpinan umat menyatu dengan kepemimpinan negara untuk terapkan Syariah." May 9. http://hizbut-tahrir.or .id/2010/05/09/mui-riau-semestinya-kepemimpinan-umat-menyatu-dengan -kepemimpinan-negara-untuk-terapkan-syariah/.

———. 2012. "Kegigihan para pejuang syariah dan khilafah di Bumi Nusantara." May 1. http://hizbut-tahrir.or.id/2012/05/01/kegigihan-para-pejuang-syariah -dan-khilafah-di-bumi-nusantara/.

———. 2015. "Nasehat Menggugah Hadratus Syaikh KH: Hasyim Asy'ari untuk menjaga persatuan." June 25. http://hizbut-tahrir.or.id/2015/06/25/nasehat -menggugah-hadratus-syaikh-kh-hasyim-asyari-untuk-menjaga-persatuan/.

Huda, Mas Alamil, and Hazliansyah. 2017. "Yenny Wahid: Kemenangan Anies-Sandi Bukan Kemenangan Kelompok Radikal." *Republika*, April 29. http:// republika.co.id/berita/nasional/politik/17/04/29/op5twf280-yenny-wahid -kemenangan-aniessandi-bukan-kemenangan-kelompok-radikal.

Hudzaifah, Edy. 2015. "Spanduk 'Tolak Sabda Raja' bertebaran di Kota Yogyakarta." *Kiblat*, July 4. www.kiblat.net/2015/07/04/spanduk-tolak-sabda-raja-berteba ran-di-kota-yogyakarta.

Human Rights Watch. 2013. *In Religion's Name: Abuses against Religious Minorities in Indonesia.* New York: HRW.

Hurd, Elizabeth Shakman. 2014. "Alevis under Law: The Politics of Religious Freedom in Turkey." *Journal of Law and Religion* 29 (3): 416–35.

Husein, Muhammad. 2011. *Fiqh seksualitas: Risalah Islam untuk pemenuhan hak-hak seksualitas.* Jakarta: PKBI.

ICG (International Crisis Group). 2000a. "Indonesia: Overcoming Murder and Chaos in Maluku." Report, December 19. https://www.crisisgroup.org/asia /south-east-asia/indonesia/indonesia-overcoming-murder-and-chaos -maluku.

———. 2000b. "Indonesia's Maluku Crisis: The Issues." Briefing, July 19. https:// www.crisisgroup.org/asia/south-east-asia/indonesia/indonesias-maluku -crisis-issues.

————. 2003. "Jemaah Islamiyah in South East Asia: Damaged but Still Danger-
ous." Report, August 26. https://www.crisisgroup.org/asia/south-east-asia/in
donesia/jemaah-islamiyah-south-east-asia-damaged-still-dangerous.

————. 2005. "Recycling Militants in Indonesia: Darul Islam and the Australian Embassy Bombing." Report, February 22. International Crisis Group,
Jakarta. https://www.crisisgroup.org/asia/south-east-asia/indonesia/recycling
-militants-indonesia-darul-islam-and-australian-embassy-bombing.

————. 2007. "Indonesia: Jemaah Islamiyah's Current Status." Report, May 3.
https://www.crisisgroup.org/asia/south-east-asia/indonesia/indonesia-je
maah-islamiyah-s-current-status.

————. 2008. "Indonesia: Implications of the Ahmadiyah Decree." Briefing, July 7.
https://www.crisisgroup.org/asia/south-east-asia/indonesia/indonesia-im
plications-ahmadiyah-decree.

————. 2010. "Indonesia: 'Christianisation' and Intolerance." Asia Briefing No.
114, November 24. https://d2071andvip0wj.cloudfront.net/b114-indonesia
-christianisation-and-intolerance.pdf.

————. 2011. "Indonesia: Trouble Again in Ambon." Briefing, October 4. https://
www.crisisgroup.org/asia/south-east-asia/indonesia/indonesia-trouble-again
-ambon.

————. 2012a. "Defying the State." Briefing, August 30. https://www.crisisgroup
.org/asia/south-east-asia/indonesia/indonesia-defying-state.

————. 2012b. "Indonesia: Cautious Calm in Ambon." Briefing, February 13.
https://www.crisisgroup.org/asia/south-east-asia/indonesia/indonesia-cau
tious-calm-ambon.

Ichwan, M. N. 2005. "Ulama, State and Politics: Majelis Ulama Indonesia after Su-
harto." *Islamic Law and Society* 12 (1): 45–72.

————. 2013. "Towards a Puritanical Moderate Islam: The Majelis Ulama Indonesia and the Politics of Religious Orthodoxy." In Bruinessen 2013a, 60–104.

————. 2017. "MUI, Gerakan Islamis, dan Umat mengambang." *Maarif* 11 (2):
87–104.

Indonesia Timur. 2017. "Buka Pesta Rakyat Banda, gubenur minta dibenahi lagi."
Indonesia Timur, October 11. https://indonesiatimur.co/2017/10/11/buka
-pesta-rakyat-banda-gubernur-minta-dibenahi-lagi/.

Indonesian Constitutional Court. 2007. Decision No.12/PUU-V/2007.

————. 2008. Decision No. 19/PUU-VI/2008.

IPAC (Institute for Policy Analysis of Conflict). 2016. "Rebuilding after Communal Violence: Lessons from Tolikara, Papua." June 13. www.understanding
conflict.org/en/conflict/read/52/Rebuilding-after-Communal-Violence-Les
sons-from-Tolikara-Papua.

————. 2018a. "After Ahok: The Islamist Agenda in Indonesia." April 6. www
.understandingconflict.org/en/conflict/read/69/After-Ahok-The-Islamist
-Agenda-in-Indonesia.

————. 2018b. "The West Kalimantan Election and the Impact of the Anti-Ahok
Campaign." February 21. http://understandingconflict.org/en/conflict/read
/68/The-West-Kalimantan-Election-and-the-Impact-of-the-Anti-Ahok-Cam
paign.

————. 2019. "Anti-Ahok to Anti-Jokowi: Islamist Influence on Indonesia's 2019
Election Campaign." Report No. 55, March 15. http://understandingconflict
.org/en/conflict/read/80/Anti-Ahok-To-Anti-Jokowi-Islamist-Influence-on
-Indonesias-2019-Election-Campaign.

Isin, E. F. 2008. "Theorising Acts of Citizenship." In *Acts of Citizenship*, edited by
E. F. Isin and G. Nielsen, 15–44. London: Zed Books.

Isin, E. F., and P. Nyers. 2014. "Introduction: Globalizing Citizenship Studies."
In *Routledge Handbook of Global Citizenship Studies*, edited by E. F. Isin and
P. Nyers, 1–11. New York: Routledge.

It, S. 2005. "The Women's Movement in Indonesia: With Special Reference to the
'Aisyiyah Organization." PhD diss., Temple University.

Jacobsen, Michael. 2004. "Factionalism and Secession in North Sulawesi Province,
Indonesia." *Asian Journal of Political Science* 12 (1): 65–94.

Jaelani, Ahmad. 2016. "Pandangan Islam terhadap LGBT." Hizbut Tahrir, February 3. https://hizbut-tahrir.or.id/2016/02/13/pandangan-islam-terhadap-lgbt.

Jaffrey, Sana, and Ihsan Ali-Fauzi. 2016. "Street Power and Electoral Politics in
Indonesia." *New Mandala*, April 5. www.newmandala.org/street-power-and
-electoral-politics-in-indonesia/.

Jamhari. 2000. "Popular Voices of Islam: Discourse on Muslim Orientations in
South Central Java." PhD diss., Australian National University, Canberra.

Jaringan Islam Liberal. 2005. "Bachtiar Effendy dan Syamsu Rizal Panggabean:
KUII IV hanya ajang silaturahmi." Islam Lib, September 11. http://islamlib
.com/id/artikel/kuii-iv-hanya-ajang-silaturahmi/ [no longer available on-
line].

Jaringan News. 2015. "Tuasikal Abua: Mari kabarkan pada dunia tengah aman."
Jaringan News, September 20. www.jaringannews.com/sosok/Sosok/72775
/Tuasikal-Abua-Mari-Kabarkanpada-Dunia-Maluku-Tengah-Aman/.

Jones, Sidney. 2013. "Indonesian Government Approaches to Radical Islam since
1998." In *Democracy and Islam in Indonesia*, edited by Mirjam Künkler and Alfred Stepan, 109–25. New York: Columbia University Press.

Joppke, Christian. 2017. *Is Multiculturalism Dead? Crisis and Persistence in the Constitutional State*. Cambridge: Polity Press.

Kadir, Hatib Abdul. 2019. "Ambon di bawah orde baru: Transformasi kapitalisme pada masyarakat pinggiran." *Dialektika* 12 (2). https://jurnal.iainambon.ac .id/index.php/DT/article/view/1115.

Kamal, Aulia. 2016. "Negara dalam pusaran konflik rumah ibadah: Problem persepsi dalam pembentukan dan eskalasi konflik rumah ibadah Kristen di Aceh Singkil." MA thesis, Universitas Gadjah Mada, Yogyakarta.

Karsenti, Bruno. 2017. *La question juive des modernes: Philosophie de l'émancipation.* Paris: PUF.

Keane, Webb. 2016. *Ethical Life: Its Natural and Social Histories.* Princeton, NJ: Princeton University Press.

Kenji, Tsuchiya, and James Siegel. 1990. "Invincible Kitsch or as Tourists in the Age of Des Alwi." *Indonesia* 50:61–76.

Kersten, Carool. 2015. *Islam in Indonesia: The Contest for Society, Ideas, and Values.* London: Hurst.

Kingsbury, Damien. 2017. "Jakarta Elections Mark Indonesia's Increasingly Conservative Turn." *Crikey,* April 20. https://www.crikey.com.au/2017/04/20/ja karta-elections-mark-indonesias-increasingly-conservative-turn.

Kleinman, Arthur. 1991. *Rethinking Psychiatry: From Cultural Category to Personal Experience.* New York: Free Press.

Klinken, Gerry van. 2001. "The Maluku Wars: Bringing Society Back In." *Indonesia* 71:1–26.

———. 2007. *Communal Violence and Democratization in Indonesia: Small Town Wars.* New York: Routledge.

———. 2014. "Ale rasa beta rasa—Menyusun sejarah bersama di Ambon." In Manuputty et al. 2014, 1–11.

Klinken, Gerry van, and Ward Berenschot. 2018. "Everyday Citizenship in Democratizing Indonesia." In Hefner 2018b, 151–62.

Kloos, David, and Ward Berenschot. 2016. "Citizenship and Islam in Malaysia and Indonesia." In *Citizenship and Democratization in Southeast Asia,* edited by Ward Berenschot, Henk S. Nordholt, and Laurens Bakker, 178–207. Leiden: Brill.

Knaap, Gerrit. 1995. "The Demography of Ambon in the Seventeenth Century: Evidence from Colonial Proto-censuses." *Journal of Southeast Asian Studies* 26 (2): 227–41.

———. 2003. "Headhunting, Carnage and Armed Peace in Amboina, 1500–1700." *Journal of the Economic and Social History of the Orient* 46 (2): 165–92.

Kolimon, Merry. 2017. "Heboh ini surat pendeta Merry Kolimon dari NTT untuk menyikapi vonis terhadap AHOK." *Pos Kupang,* May 10. http://kupang.tribun

news.com/2017/05/10/heboh-ini-surat-pendeta-mery-kolimon-dari-ntt
-untuk-menyikapi-vonis-terhadap-ahok.

Komara, Rina. 2009. "Pro dan kontra poligamai, untuk apa?" Hizbut Tahrir, October 27. https://hizbut-tahrir.or.id/2009/10/27/poligami-dalam-pandangan
-syariat.

Komnas Perempuan. 2001. *Report of the First Three Years (1998–2001)*. Jakarta: Komnas Perempuan.

Kompas. 2014. "Saya Jokowi, bagian dari Islam yang Rahmatan Lil Alamin." May 24. https://nasional.kompas.com/read/2014/05/24/1429414/. Saya. Jokowi. Bagian .dari. Islam.yang. Rahmatan. Lil. Alamin.

———. 2017. "HTI resmi dibubarkan." July 19. http://nasional.kompas.com
/read/2017/07/19/10180761/hti-resmi-dibubarkan-pemerintah.

Kosel, Sven. 2010. "Christianity, Minahasa Ethnicity, and Politics in North Sulawesi: 'Jerusalem's Veranda' or Stronghold of Pancasila?" In *Christianity in Indonesia: Perspectives of Power*, edited by Susanne Schroter, 291–322. New Brunswick, NJ: Transaction.

KOWANI. 1958. "Women and Citizenship in Indonesia." Unpublished paper presented at the First Asia Africa Women's Conference, Colombo, Sri Lanka.

Kresna, Mawa. 2017. "Pengikut HTI dalam Bayang-Bayang Pengawasan." *Tirto,* July 21. https://tirto.id/pengikut-hti-dalam-bayang-bayang-pengawasan
-cs81.

Kroeskamp, Hendrik. 1974. *Early Schoolmasters in a Developing Country: A History of Experiments in School Education in 19th Century Indonesia*. Assen: Van Gorcum.

Kurniawan, Wawan. 2012. "Gerakan tandingan feminisme: Tinjauan terhadap respon MHTI Kota Bandung" *wey's* (blog), August 9. https://aweygaul.word press.com/2012/08/09/gerakan-tandingan-feminisme-tinjauan-terhadap
-respon-muslimah-hizbut-tahrir-indonesia-mhti-kota-bandung.

Kuru, Ahmed T. 2009. *Secularism and State Policies toward Religion: The United States, France, and Turkey*. Cambridge: Cambridge University Press.

Laclau, E. 2005. *On Populist Reason*. London: Verso.

Laidlaw, J. 2014. *The Subject of Virtue: An Anthropology of Ethics and Freedom*. Cambridge: Cambridge University Press.

Lape, Peter. 2010. "Pendahuluan: Kontak orang Banda (Bandanese) dengan Eropa dan kolonialisme di pulau Banda Maluku Indonesia." In *Destinasi Banda Neira brand pariwisata Indonesia Timur: Sejarah masa lalu, kekayaan maluku masa kini, dan dinamika Bandanese*, edited by B. Bungin, 2–15. Jakarta: Kaki Langit Kencana Perdana Media Group.

Lattu, Izak. 2014. "Orality and Interreligious Relationships: The Role of Collective Memory in Christian-Muslims Engagements in Maluku Indonesia." PhD diss., Graduate Theological Union, Berkeley.

LBH Jakarta. 2017. "#JakartaKritis: Demokrasi yang jernih dan hak atas Kota." *Bantuan Hukum*, April 11. https://www.bantuanhukum.or.id/web/jakarta kritis-demokrasi-yang-jernih-dan-hak-atas-kota/.

Lev, Daniel S. 1966. *The Transition to Guided Democracy: Indonesian Politics, 1957–1959*. Ithaca, NY: Modern Indonesia Project, Southeast Asia Program, Dept. of Asian Studies, Cornell University.

Li, Tania M. 2014. *Land's End: Capitalist Relations on an Indigenous Frontier*. Durham, NC: Duke University Press.

Liddle, R. William, and Saiful Mujani. 2007. "Leadership, Party, and Religion: Explaining Voting Behavior in Indonesia." *Comparative Political Studies* 40 (7): 832–57.

———. 2013. "Indonesian Democracy: From Transition to Consolidation." In *Democracy and Islam in Indonesia*, edited by Mirjam Kunkler and Alfred Stepan, 24–50. New York: Columbia University Press.

Lindsey, Tim. 2012. *Islam, Law and the State in Southeast Asia*. Vol. 1. Indonesia. London: Tauris.

Lindsey, Tim, and Simon Butt. 2016. "State Power to Restrict Religious Freedom: An Overview of the Legal Framework." In *Religion, Law and Intolerance in Indonesia*, edited by Tim Lindsey and Helen Pausacker, 19–41. New York: Routledge.

Lindsey, Tim, and Helen Pausacker, eds. 2016. *Religion, Law and Intolerance in Indonesia*. New York: Routledge.

Liow, Joseph C. 2009. *Piety and Politics: Islamism in Contemporary Malaysia*. New York: Oxford University Press.

Loth, Vincent C. 1995. "Pioneers and Perkeniers: The Banda Islands in the 17th Century." *Cakalele* 6:13–35.

Maarif, Samsul. 2017. *Pasang surut rekognisi agama leluhur dalam politik agama di Indonesia*. Yogyakarta: Program Studi Agama dan Lintas Budaya/CRCS, Universitas Gadjah Mada.

MacIntyre, Alasdair. 1984. *After Virtue: A Study in Moral Theory*. 3rd ed. Notre Dame: University of Notre Dame Press.

Mahendra, Yusril Ihza. 2017. "Di Era Jokowi, Pancasila lebih banyak dibenturkan dengan umat Islam." Kantor Berita Politik RMOL, June 7. http://politik.rmol .co/read/2017/06/07/294601/Di-Era-Jokowi,-Pancasila-Lebih-Banyak-Diben turkan-Dengan-Umat-Islam-.

Mamduh, Nafal. 2018. "Sikap ITS tangani 3 dosen bisa bungkam kebebasan ber-pendapat." *Tirto,* May 23, 2018. https://tirto.id/sikap-its-tangani-3-dosen-bisa -bungkam-kebebasan-berpendapat-cKXW.

Manuputty, Jacky. 2012. "Provokator damai." *Aceh Kita,* March 21. www.acehkita .com/opini-provokator-damai.

Manuputty, Jacky, Zairin Salampessy, Ihsan Ali-Fauzi, and Irsyad Rafsadi, eds. 2014. *Carita orang basudara.* Ambon: Lembaga Antar Iman Maluku and PUSAD Paramadina.

Marsden, M. 2005. *Living Islam: Muslim Religious Experience in Pakistan's North-West Frontier.* Cambridge: Cambridge University Press.

Media Project. 2011. "Religious Cooperation Pacifies Ambon." September 26. http://themediaproject.org/article/give-peace-ambon [no longer accessible].

Meijer, Roel, and Nils Butenschøn, eds. 2017. *The Crisis of Citizenship in the Arab World.* Leiden: Brill.

Menchik, Jeremy. 2016. *Islam and Democracy in Indonesia: Tolerance without Liber-alism.* New York: Cambridge University Press.

Metro TV News. 2016. "Muktamar HTI di cirebon batal digelar." January 5. http: //jabar.metrotvnews.com/read/2016/05/01/521869/muktamar-hti-di-cirebon -batal-digelar.

———. 2017. "Menguji kempuhan UU ormas." October 25. http://video.metro twnews.com/metro-pagi-prime-time/MkMMlamk-menguji-keampuhan— uu-ormas.

Mietzner, Marcus. 2009. *Military Politics, Islam, and the State in Indonesia: From Turbulent Transition to Democratic Consolidation.* Singapore: ISEAS.

———. 2014. "Successful and Failed Democratic Transitions from Military Rule in Majority Muslim Societies: The Cases of Indonesia and Egypt." *Contemporary Politics* 20 (4): 435–52.

———. 2017. "Indonesia in 2016." *Asian Survey* 57 (1): 165–72.

Mietzner, Marcus, and Burhanuddin Muhtadi. 2018. "Explaining the 2016 Islamist Mobilisation in Indonesia: Religious Intolerance, Militant Groups and the Politics of Accommodation." *Asian Studies Review* 42 (3): 479–97.

Mietzner, Marcus, Burhanuddin Muhtadi, and Rizka Halida. 2018. "Entrepreneurs of Grievance: Drivers and Effects of Indonesia's Islamist Mobilization." *Bijdra-gen tot de Taal-, Land-, en Volkenkunde* 174 (2/3): 158–87.

Modood, Tariq. 2007. *Multiculturalism: A Civic Idea.* Cambridge: Polity Press.

Moosa, Ebrahim. 2001. "The Poetics and Politics of Law after Empire: Reading Women's Rights in the Contestation of Law." *UCLA Journal of Islamic and Near Eastern Law* 1:1–46.

Mouffe, Chantal. 2000. "Deliberative Democracy or Agonistic Pluralism." Working paper, Political Science Series No. 72, Institute for Advanced Studies, Vienna.

———. 2005. "The 'End of Politics' and the Challenge of Right-Wing Populism." In *Populism and the Mirror of Democracy*, edited by Francisco Panizza, 50–71. London: Verso.

———. 2013. *Agonistics: Thinking the World Politically.* London: Verso.

Moustafa, Tamir. 2013. "Liberal Rights versus Islamic Law? The Construction of a Binary in Malaysiani Politics." *Law and Society Review* 47 (4): 771–802.

———. 2018. *Constituting Religion: Islam, Liberal Rights, and the Malaysian State.* Cambridge: Cambridge University Press.

Movanita, Ambaranie Nadia Kemala. 2017. "HTI resmi dibubarkan pemerintah." *Kompas*, July 19. http://nasional.kompas.com/read/2017/07/19/10180761/hti-resmi-dibubarkan-pemerintah.

Mubarok, Z. Muhmmad. 2008. *Genealogi Islam radikal di Indonesia: Gerakan, pemikiran dan prospek demokrasi.* Jakarta: Pustaka LP3ES.

Mudzhar, Mohamad Atho. 1993. *Fatwas of the Council of Indonesia Ulama: A Study of Islamic Legal Thought in Indonesia, 1975–1988.* Jakarta: Indonesian Netherlands Cooperation in Islamic Studies.

Muhammadiyah. 2015. "Negara Pancasila sebagai darul ahdi wa syahadah." Unpublished paper, Muktamar Muhammdayah Ke-47, Makassar.

Muhyidin, Teguh. 2013. "Konstruksi gender dalam Fiqih Ibadah wanita—Menjadi Imam Sholat bagi laki-laki: Studi analisis pemikiran majlis tarjih Muhammadiyyah." MA thesis, Sunan Kalijaga State Islamic University, Yogyakarta.

Mujib, Ibnu, and Yance Z. Rumahuru. 2010. *Paradigma transformatif masyarakat dialogue: Membangun fondasi dialog agama-agama berbasis teologi humanis.* Yogyakarta: Pustaka Pelajar.

Mulia, M. Siti. 2005. *Muslimah reformis: Perempuan pembaru keagamaan.* Bandung: Mizan.

———. 2011. *Membangun surga di bumi.* Jakarta: Elex Media Komputindo.

Mulkhan, Abdul Munir. 2006. "Sendang Ayu: Pergulatan Muhammadiyah di kaki bukit barisan." *Suara Muhammadiyah*, January 2.

Muslimah Hizbut Tahrir Indonesia (MHTI). n.d. *Selayang Pandang Muslimah Hizbut Tahrir Indonesia chapter campus* (Brochure).

Muslim Media News. 2014. "Pandangan KH. Hasyim Muzadi terhadap Gerakan Khilafah." March 24. www.muslimedianews.com/2014/03/pandangan-kh-hasyim-muzadi-terhadap.html.

———. 2015. "Nasehat sang kyai untuk Felix Siauw terkait nasionalisme." February 3. www.muslimedianews.com/2015/02/nasehat-sang-kyai-untuk-felix-siauw.html#ixzz4Ced8OJvK.

Mutaqin, Z. A. 2014. "Penghayat, Orthodoxy, and the Legal Politics of the State: The Survival of Agama Djawa Sunda (Madraisism) in Indonesia." *Indonesia and the Malay World* 42 (122): 1–23.

Nakamura, Mitsuo. 2012. *The Crescent Arises over the Banyan Tree: A Study of the Muhammadiyah Movement in a Central Javanese Town, c. 1910s–2010.* 2nd enl. ed. Singapore: ISEAS Press.

Nashir, Haedar. 2007. *Manifestasi gerakan Tarbiyah: Bagaimana sikap Muhammadiyah.* Yogyakarta: Suara Muhammadiyah.

NU Online. 2015a. "Konsep Islam nusantara mampu cegah Islam transnasional." August 31. www.nu.or.id/post/read/61923/konsep-islam-nusantara-mampu -cegah-islam-transnasional.

———. 2015b. "Teks Deklarasi Hubungan Islam-Pancasila pada Munas NU 1983." December 16. www.nu.or.id/post/read/64325/teks-deklarasi-hubungan-islam -pancasila-pada-munas-nu-1983.

———. 2016. "Diminta teken surat pernyataan, HTI pilih bubarkan diri." May 2. www.nu.or.id/post/read/67816/diminta-teken-surat-pernyataan-hti-pilih -bubarkan-diri.

Nurdin, Ahmad Ali. 2005. "Islam and State: A Study of the Liberal Islamic Network in Indonesia, 1999–2004." *New Zealand Journal of Asian Studies* 7 (2): 20–39.

Olle, John. 2009. "The Majelis Ulama Indonesia versus 'Heresy': The Resurgence of Authoritarian Islam." In *State of Authority: The State in Society in Indonesia,* edited by Gerry van Klinken and Joshua Barker, 95–116. Ithaca, NY: Cornell Southeast Asia Program Publications.

Ong, A. 1996. "Cultural Citizenship as Subject Making." *Current Anthropology* 37 (5): 737–62.

Osman, Mohamed Nawab Mohamed. 2018. *Hizbut Tahrir Indonesia and Political Islam: Identity, Ideology and Religio-Political Mobilization.* New York: Routledge.

Panggabean, Samsu Rizal. 2014. "Penghindaran positif, segregasi, dan kerjasama komunal di Maluku." In Manuputty et al. 2014, 389–94.

———. 2017. "Dua kota dua cerita: Mengapa kekerasan terjadi di Ambon tapi tidak di Manado?" In *Ketika agama bawa damai, bukan perang: Belajar dari "Imam dan Pastor,"* edited by Ihsan Ali-Fauzi, 117–56. Jakarta: PUSAD Paramadina.

Parwito. 2012. "Diskusi di LKiS dibubarkan, polisi periksa Irshad Manji." *Merdeka,* May 10. https://www.merdeka.com/peristiwa/diskusi-di-lkis-dibubarkan-po lisi-periksa-irshad-manji.html.

Pasundan Ekspres. 2016. "Muslimat NU: LGBT itu haram." *Pasundan Ekspres,* February. http://pasundanekspres.com/muslimat-nu-lgbt-itu-haram/22.

Patty, Rahmat Rahman. 2013. "Tolak perkebunan tebu, Koalisi Save Aru Galang dukungan." *Kompas,* December 10. http://regional.kompas.com/read/2013 /12/10/1411587/Tolak. Perkebunan. Tebu. Koalisi. Save. Aru. Galang. Dukungan.

Pausacker, Helen. 2013. "Morality and the Nation: Pornography and Indonesia's Islamic Defenders Front." PhD diss, University of Melbourne Law School.

Pengurus Besar NU (Nahdlatul Ulama). 2015. Anngaran Dasar [Organizational Statutes]. Jakarta: Nahdatul Ulama National Headquarters.

Picard, Michel. 2011. "From *Agama Hindu Bali* to *Agama Hindu* and Back: Toward a Relocalization of Balinese Religion?" In Picard and Madinier 2011, 117–41.

Pimpinan Pusat 'Aisyiyah. 2004. *Sejarah pertumbuhan dan perkembangan 'Aisyiyah.* Yogyakarta: Pimpinan Pusat 'Aisyiyah.

———. 2015. *Tuntunan menuju keluarga sakinah.* Yogyakarta: Pimpinan Pusat 'Aisyiyah.

———. n.d. "Sejarah 'Aisyiyah." Accessed March 20, 2016. www.aisyiyah.or.id /id/page/sejarah.html.

Pimpinan Pusat Muhammadiyah. 2005. *Anggaran dasar* [Organizational statutes]. Yogyakarta: Muhammadiyah National Headquarters.

Pimpinan Pusat Muslimat Nahdatul Ulama. n.d. Accessed February 16, 2016. www.muslimat-nu.or.id.

Pinontoan, Denni. 2017. "Pilkada Jakarta dan ormas adat dalam politik lokal Minahasa." CRCS UGM, May 12. https://crcs.ugm.ac.id/news/10923/pilkada -jakarta-dan-ormas-adat-dalam-politik-lokal-minahasa.html.

Pomalingo, Samsi. 2004. "Dialog antarumat beragama: Studi kasus BKSAUA Di Manado, Sulawesi Utara." MA thesis, Universitas Gadjah Mada, Yogyakarta.

Pranowo, Bambang. 1991. "Creating Islamic Tradition in Rural Java." PhD diss., Monash University, Melbourne.

Putra, G. B. A. Muhammad. 2017. *Perempuan-perempuan pemburu surga: Menyibak rahasia kejayaan 'Aisyiyah.* Yogyakarta: Suara Muhammadiyah.

Putsanra, Dipna Videlia. 2018. "Argumen lemah rektor UIN yogya soal larangan cadar." *Tirto,* March 7. https://tirto.id/argumen-lemah-rektor-uin-yogya-soal -larangan-cadar-cFMy.

Qibtiyah, Alimatul. 2007. "Islamic Feminism and Global Feminism: Problems, Methods, and Solution in Indonesian Context." In *Moving with the Times: The Dynamic of Contemporary Islam in a Changing Indonesia,* edited by N. Hasan and M. N. Ichwan, 228–56. Yogyakarta: CISForm, Sunan Kalijaga State Islamic University.

————. 2012. "Feminist Identity and the Conceptualisation of Gender Issues in Islam: Muslim Gender Studies Elites in Yogyakarta, Indonesia." PhD diss., Western Sydney University, Sydney.

————. 2015a. "Hak perempuan dalam Muhammadiyah." *SKH Kedaulatan Rakyat,* April 6.

————. 2015b. "Homosexuality in Islam." *Musawa: Jurnal Studi Gender dan Islam* 16 (2): 197–209.

————. 2015c. "Quo-Vadis kepemimpinan perempuan?" *SKH Kedaulatan Rakyat,* February 25.

————. 2016. "Perempuan dan media dalam Aksi 'Bela Islam.'" *Maarif* 11 (2): 168–87.

Qodir, Zuly. 2009. *Gerakan sosial Islam: Manifesto kaum beriman.* Yogyakarta: Pustaka Pelajar.

————. 2017. "Muhammadiyah dan Aksi Damai Bela Islam: Rejuvenasi politik umat Islam?" *Maarif* 11 (2): 135–54.

Rahman, Fazlur. 1982. *Islam and Modernity: Transformation of an Intellectual Tradition.* Chicago: University of Chicago Press.

Rakhmani, Inaya. 2016. *Mainstreaming Islam in Indonesia: Television, Identity and the Middle Class.* New York: Palgrave Macmillan.

Ramadan, Tariq. 2009. *Radical Reform: Islamic Ethics and Liberation.* Oxford: Oxford University Press.

Ramstedt, Martin. 2004. *Hinduism in Modern Indonesia.* London: Routledge.

Reeson, Margaret. 2015. *Live Peace: Joy Balazo and Young Ambassadors for Peace.* Moreland, Victoria: Acorn Press.

Ricklefs, M. C. 2006. *Mystic Synthesis in Java: A History of Islamization from the Fourteenth to the Early Nineteenth Centuries.* Norwalk, CT: East Bridge.

————. 2007. *Polarising Javanese Society: Islamic and Other Visions (c. 1830–1930).* Singapore: NUS Press.

————. 2012. *Islamisation and Its Opponents in Java: C. 1930 to the Present.* Singapore: NUS Press.

Ridwan, Nur Khaliq. 2008. *Regenerasi NII: Membedah Jaringan Islam Jihadi di Indonesia.* Jakarta: Penerbit Erlangga.

Rinaldo, R. 2013. *Mobilizing Piety: Islam and Feminism in Indonesia.* New York: Oxford University Press.

Robinson, Kathryn. 2009. *Gender, Islam and Democracy in Indonesia.* London: Routledge.

Rochmah, A. Iffah. 2016. "Pernyataan Muslimah Hizbut Tahrir Indonesia: Konggress Ibu Nusantara 4 (KIN) 2016, Negara soko guru ketahanan keluarga."

Hizbut Tahrir, December 17. https://hizbut-tahrir.or.id/2016/12/17/pernya
taan-muslimah-hizbut-tahrir-indonesia-kongres-ibu-nusantara-4-kin-2016
-negara-soko-guru-ketahanan-keluarga.

Ropi, Ismatu. 2012. "The Politics of Regulating Religion: State, Civil Society and the Quest for Religious Freedom in Modern Indonesia." PhD diss., Australian National University, Canberra.

Rosaldo, Renato. 1989. "Imperialist Nostalgia." *Representations* 26:107–22.

Ruhulessin, John Chr. 2005. *Etika publik: Menggali dari tradisi Pela di Maluku.* Salatiga: Satya Wacana University Press.

Saeed, Abdullah. 2005. "Introduction: The Qur'an, Interpretation and the Indonesian Context." In *Approaches to the Qur'an in Contemporary Indonesia*, edited by Abdullah Saeed, 107–34. London: Oxford University Press.

Salampessy, Zairin. 2014. "Ketika memilih setia pada prinsip." In Manuputty et al. 2014, 39–58.

Salim, Arskal. 2008. *Challenging the Secular State: The Islamization of Law in Modern Indonesia.* Honolulu: University of Hawai'i Press.

Salim, Hairus H. S., Najib Kailani, and Nikmal Azekiyah. 2011. *Politik ruang publik sekolah: Negosiasi dan resistensi di SMUN di Yogyakarta.* Yogyakarta: CRCS.

Salimah. 2004. "AILA, untuk pengokohan keluarga Muslim Indonesia." https://www.salimah.or.id/2014/berita-salimah/aila-untuk-pengokohan-keluarga-muslim-indonesia.

Salvatore, Armando. 2016. *The Sociology of Islam: Knowledge, Power and Civility.* Hoboken, NJ: John Wiley and Sons.

Sandel, Michael. 1984. "The Procedural Republic and the Unencumbered Self." *Political Theory* 12 (1): 81–96.

Savirani, Amalinda, and Edward Aspinall. 2017. "Adversarial Linkages: The Urban Poor and Electoral Politics in Jakarta." *Journal of Current Southeast Asian Affairs* 36 (3): 3–34.

Schielke, S. 2010a. "Being Good in Ramadan: Ambivalence, Fragmentation, and the Moral Self in the Lives of Young Egyptians." In *Islam, Politics, Anthropology*, edited by Filippo Osella and Benjamin Soares, 23–38. Hoboken, NJ: John Wiley.

———. 2010b. "Second Thoughts about the Anthropology of Islam, or How to Make Sense of Grand Schemes in Everyday Life." Working Paper No. 2, Zentrum Moderner Orient, Berlin.

———. 2015. *Egypt in the Future Tense: Hope, Frustration, and Ambivalence before and after 2011.* Bloomington: Indiana University Press.

Schulte Nordholt, Henk. 2007. "Bali: An Open Fortress." In *Renegotiating Boundaries: Local Politics in pos-Suharto Indonesia*, edited by Henk Schulte Nordholt and Gerry van Klinken, 387–416. Leiden: KITLV Press.

Seksi Integrasi Pengolahan dan Diseminasi Statistik. 2015a. *Kota Ambon dalam angka 2015*. Ambon: Badan Pusat Statistik Kota Ambon.

———. 2015b. *Statistik migrasi Indonesia: Hasil survei penduduk antar sensus 2015*. Jakarta: Badan Pusat Statistik.

Setiawan, Farid. 2006. "Ahmad Dahlan menangis (tanggapan terhadap tulisan Abdul Munir Mulkhan)." *Suara Muhammadiyah*, February 20.

Shihab, Rizieq. 2015. "Pancasila tergantung siapa yang mengurus 'memimpin.'" YouTube, uploaded November 15. https://www.youtube.com/watch?v=9thYJ FxPCu4.

———. 2017. "Speech in Masjid PUSDAI Bandung." YouTube, uploaded February 13. https://www.youtube.com/watch?v=niAOx_20Vb8&t=496s.

Sholih, Mufti. 2018. "Sanksi membayangi dosen PTN yang membela HTI." *Tirto*, May 8. http://tirto.id/sanksi-membayangi-dosen-ptn-yang-membela -hti-cJ5e.

Sidel, John T. 2006. *Riots, Pogroms, Jihad: Religious Violence in Indonesia*. Ithaca, NY: Cornell University Press.

———. 2008. "The Manifold Meanings of Displacement: Explaining Interreligious Violence, 1999–2001." In *Conflict, Violence, and Displacement in Indonesia*, edited by Eva-Lotta E. Hedman, 29–59. Ithaca, NY: Cornell Southeast Asia Program.

Simanjutak, Laurencius. 2012. "Batal di UGM, Irsyad Manji diskusi di LKiS Yogya." Merdeka.com, May 9, 2012. https://www.merdeka.com/peristiwa /batal-di-ugm-irshad-manji-diskusi-di-lkis-yogya.html.

Simon, Gregory M. 2014. *Caged In on the Outside: Moral Subjectivity, Selfhood, and Islam in Minangkabau, Indonesia*. Honolulu: University of Hawai'i Press.

Sirry, Mun'im A., ed. 2004. *Fiqih lintas agama: Membangun masyarakat inklusif-pluralis*. Jakarta: Yayasan Wakaf Paramadina.

Smith-Hefner, Nancy J. 2007. "Javanese Women and the Veil in Post-Soeharto Indonesia." *Journal of Asian Studies* 66 (2): 389–420.

———. 2019. *Islamizing Intimacies: Youth, Sexuality, and Gender in Contemporary Indonesia*. Honolulu: University of Hawai'i Press.

Soares, B. F. 2005. *Islam and the Prayer Economy: History and Authority in a Malian Town*. Ann Arbor: University of Michigan Press.

Soegijono, Simon Pieter. 2011. *Papalele: Potret aktivitas pedagang kecil di Ambon*. Salatiga: Program Pascasarjana Universitas Kristen Satya Wacana.

Soselisa, Hermien L. 2000. "Sagu Salempeng Tapata Dua: Conflict and Resource Management in Central Maluku." *Cakalele: Maluku Research Journal* 11:67–82.

Soumokil, Tontji. 2011. *Reintegrasi sosial pasca konflik Maluku.* Salatiga: Fakultas Ilmu Sosial dan Komunikasi Universitas Kristen Satya Wacana.

Spyer, Patricia. 2002. "Fire without Smoke and Other Phantoms of Ambon's Violence: Media Effects, Agency, and the Work of Imagination." *Indonesia* 74: 21–36.

Stange, Paul. 1986. "'Legitimate' Mysticism in Indonesia." *Review of Indonesian and Malaysian Affairs* 20 (2): 76–117.

Steenbrink, Karel A. 2003. *Catholics in Indonesia, 1808–1942: A Documented History.* Leiden: KITLV Press.

Stepan, Alfred. 2011. "The Multiple Secularisms of Modern Democratic and Non-democratic Regimes." In *Rethinking Secularism,* edited by Craig Calhoun, Mark Juergensmeyer, and Jonathan VanAntwerpen, 114–44. Oxford: Oxford University Press.

———. 2014. "Muslims and Toleration: Unexamined Contributions to the Multiple Secularisms of Modern Democracies." In *Boundaries of Toleration,* edited by Alfred Stepan and Charles Taylor, 267–96. New York: Columbia University Press.

Stokke, Kristian. 2017. "Politics of Citizenship: Towards an Analytic Framework." In *Politics of Citizenship in Indonesia,* edited by Eric Hiariej and Kristian Stokke, 23–53. Jakarta: Yayasan Pustaka Obor Indonesia.

Suara 'Aisyiyah. 2016. "Pernyataan Sikap Pimpinan Pusat 'Aisyiyah tentang LGBT." Statement no. 069/PPA/A/III/2016. Its four points posted in "Pimpinan Pusat 'Aisyiyah Ambil Sikap Terkait Kontroversi LGBT," *Suara Muhammadiyah,* March 25, http://www.suaramuhammadiyah.id/2016/03/25/pimpinan-pusat -aisyiyah-ambil-sikap-terkait-kontroversi-lgbt/.

Suara Islam. 2010a. "Mengharap terobosan dari KUII Ke-5." May 8. www.suara -islam.com/news/muhasabah/komentar-mak/765-mengharap-terobosan -dari-kuii-ke-5-.

———. 2010b. "MUI gelar KUII V, Ormas kontroversial tak diundang." April 8. www.suara-islam.com/news/berita/nasional/673-mui-gelar-kuii-v-ormas -kontroversial-tak-diundang.

Sulistiyanto, Priyambudi. 2018. "Indonesia in 2017: Jokowi's Supremacy and His Next Political Battles." In *Southeast Asian Affairs 2018,* 153–66. Singapore: ISEAS Press.

Suryadinata, Leo, ed. 2008. *Ethnic Chinese in Contemporary Indonesia.* Singapore: ISEAS.

Suseno, Frans Magnis. 2017. "Kembalikan kesepakatan bangsa." *Kompas,* May 19.

Sutanto, Trisno. 2018. "The Decolonization of Adat Communities: Notes from PGI's 2018 Seminar on Religions." *CRCS Newsletter,* May. https://crcs.ugm .ac.id/perspective/12682/the-decolonization-of-adat-communities.html [no longer available online].

Swazey, Kelli. 2013. "A Place for Harmonious Difference: Christianity and the Mediation of Minahasan Identity in the North Sulawesi Public." PhD diss., University of Hawai'i, Honolulu.

Syabab Indonesia. 2015. "Inilah pandangan KH Hasyim asy'ari tentang nation dan nasionalisme." June 25. www.syababindonesia.com/2015/02/inilah-pandan gan-kh-hasyim-asyari.html [no longer available online].

Syafieq and Abdullah Alawi. 2016. "Intoleransi di daerah karena kegaduhan anti-Ahok di Jakarta?" NU Online, November 1. www.nu.or.id/post/read/72595 /intoleransi-di-daerah-karena-kegaduhan-anti-ahok-di-jakarta-.

Syam, Shaliandri D. 2005. "Gagasan kespro: Tak seindah janjinya." *Al-Wa'ie,* no. 64, December.

Tahun, Marthen. 2014. "Fractured Ecumenism and Attempts at Fence-Mending: Relations between Pentecostals and Non-Pentecostals in Indonesia." In *Aspirations for Modernity and Prosperity: Symbols and Sources behind Pentecostal/ Charismatic Growth in Indonesia,* edited by Christine E. Gudorf, Zainal Abidin Bagir, and Marthen Tahun, 139–70. Adelaide: ATF Theology.

Taji-Farouki, Suha. 1996. *Fundamental Quest: Hizb Al-Tahrir and the Search for the Islamic Caliphate.* London: Grey Seal Books.

Talle, Kari. 2013. "Vigilante Citizenship: Sovereign Practices and the Politics of Insult in Indonesia." *Bijdragen tot de Taal-, Land-en Volkenkunde* 169 (2–3): 183–212.

Tamanaha, Brian Z. 2008. "Understanding Legal Pluralism: Past to Present, Local to Global." *Sydney Law Review* 30:375–411.

Tambayong, Yapi. 2007. *Kamus bahasa dan budaya Manado.* Jakarta: PT Gramedia Pustaka Utama.

Taylor, Charles. 1994. *Multiculturalism and the "Politics of Recognition."* Princeton, NJ: Princeton University Press.

Tempo. 2015. "NU dan Muhammadiyah protes sabda Raja Yogya." May 7. https:// m.tempo.co/read/news/2015/05/07/058664246/nu-dan-muhammadiyah -protes-sabda-raja-yogya.

———. 2016. "Kampus ISI yogya & warga bantul tolak gerakan HTI." June 17. https://m.tempo.co/read/news/2016/06/17/078780855/kampus-isi-yogya -warga-bantul-tolak-gerakan-hti.

Thalib, Usman, and La Raman. 2015. *Banda dalam sejarah perbudakan di Nusantara: Swastanisasi dan praktik kerja paksa di Perkebunan Pala Kepulauan Banda tahun 1770–1860.* Yogyakarta: Penerbit Ombak.

Thufail, Fadjar. 2012. "When Peace Prevails on Kasih Hill: The Protestant Church and the Politics of Adat in Minahasa." *Asian Ethnicity* 13 (4): 359–71.

Timor Express. 2015. "Brigade Meo turunkan Papan HTI di Oesapa." October 1. www.timorexpress.com/20151001094341/brigade-meo-turunkan-papan-hti -di-oesapa#ixzz48UIw5VL7.

Toisuta, Hasbollah. 2014. "Khotbah damai dari mimbar Masjid Al-Fattah." in Manuputty et al. 2014, 151–62.

Tomsa, Dirk. 2017. "Indonesia in 2016: Jokowi Consolidates Power." *Southeast Asian Affairs* 2017:149–62.

Turner, Bryan. 2011. *Religion and Modern Society: Citizenship, Secularization and the State.* Cambridge: Cambridge University Press.

Tyson, Adam. 2011. "Being Special, Becoming Indigenous: Dilemmas of Special Adat Rights in Indonesia." *Asian Journal of Social Science* 39 (5): 652–73.

Ufen, Andreas. 2008. "From Aliran to Dealignment: Political Parties in Post-Suharto Indonesia." *South East Asia Research* 16 (1): 5–41.

US Bureau of Democracy, Human Rights and Labor. 2015. "International Religious Freedom Report: Indonesia." www.state.gov/j/drl/rls/irf/religiousfreedom /index.htm?year=2015&dlid=256107.

Varshney, A., M. Z. Tadjoeddin, and S. R. Panggabean. 2004. "Patterns of Collective Violence in Indonesia, 1990–2003." Working paper, United Nations Support Facility for Indonesian Recovery, Jakarta. http://citeseerx.ist.psu.edu/viewdoc /download?doi=10.1.1.560.7694&rep=rep1&type=pdf.

Vreede-de Stuers, C. 1960. *The Indonesian Woman: Struggles and Achievements.* Gravenhage: Mouton.

Warburton, Eve, and Liam Gammon. 2017. "Class Dismissed? Economic Fairness and Identity Politics in Indonesia." *New Mandala,* May 5. www.newmandala .org/economic-injustice-identity-politics-indonesia/.

Weintraub, Andrew. 2010. *Dangdut Stories: A Social and Musical History of Indonesia's Most Popular Music.* New York: Oxford University Press.

———. 2018. "Nation, Islam, and Gender in *Dangdut,* Indonesia's Most Popular Music." In *Routledge Handbook of Contemporary Indonesia,* ed. Robert W. Hefner, 366–77. New York: Routledge.

Wilson, Chris. 2008. *Ethno-Religious Violence in Indonesia: From Soil to God.* New York: Routledge.

Wilson, Ian Douglas. 2006. "Continuity and Change: The Changing Contours of Organized Violence in Post-New Order Indonesia." *Critical Asian Studies* 38 (2): 265–97.

———. 2008. "'As Long as It's Halal': Islamic *Preman* in Jakarta," In *Expressing Islam: Religious Life and Politics in Indonesia,* edited by Greg Fealy and Sally White, 192–210. Singapore: ISEAS.

———. 2015. "Resisting Democracy: Front Pembela Islam and Indonesia's 2014 Elections." *ISEAS Perspective* 10:32–40.

———. 2017. "Jakarta: Inequality and the Poverty of Elite Pluralism." *New Mandala*, April 19. www.newmandala.org/jakarta-inequality-poverty-elite-pluralism/=.

Winn, Philip. 2002. "'Everyone Searches, Everyone Finds': Moral Discourse and Resource Use in an Indonesian Muslim Community." *Oceania* 72 (4): 275–92.

———. 2010. "Slavery and Cultural Creativity in the Banda Islands." *Journal of Southeast Asian Studies* 41 (3): 365–89.

Winters, Jeffrey A. 2013. "Oligarchy and Democracy in Indonesia." *Indonesia* 96: 11–33.

Woodward, Mark R., and Amanah Nurish. 2017. "Quo vadis FPI dalam aksi Bela Islam." *Maarif* 11 (2): 105–22.

Wrangham, Rachel. 1999. Management or Domination? Planning Tourism in the Banda Islands, Eastern Indonesia." *International Journal of Contemporary Hospitality Management* 11 (2/3): 111–15.

Wrangham, R., S. Cox, N. Frost, R. Hitch, S. Kuriake, S. Maskat, S. Ohoirat, S. Robbins, and S. Wilson, eds. 1996. *Spice Islands 1995: Tradition, Tourism and Development in the Banda Islands, Eastern Indonesia.* Canterbury: University of Kent.

Yildirim, Y. 2009. "The Medina Charter: A Historical Case of Conflict Resolution." *Islam and Christian–Muslim Relations* 20 (4): 439–50.

Yourman, Julius. 1939. "Propaganda Techniques within Nazi Germany." *Journal of Educational Sociology* 13 (3): 148–63.

Yuliawati. 2017. "PBNU dan 13 organisasi Islam dukung perppu ormas Anti-Pancasila." *Kata Data*, July 12. https://katadata.co.id/berita/2017/07/12/pbnu-dan-13-organisasi-islam-dukung-perppu-ormas-anti-pancasila.

Zeghal, Malika. 2016. "Constitutionalizing a Democratic Muslim State without Shari'a: The Religious Establishment in the Tunisian 2014 Constitution." In *Shari'a Law and Modern Muslim Ethics*, edited by Robert W. Hefner, 107–34. Bloomington: Indiana University Press.

Zuhadi, Syamsul. 1989. "The Indonesian Council of Ulama." *Indonesia and the Malay World* 18 (50): 31–41.

Zurn, Christopher. 2000. "Anthropology and Normativity: A Critique of Axel Honneth's 'Formal Conception of Ethical Life.'" *Philosophy and Social Criticism* 26 (1): 115–24.

CONTRIBUTORS

Mohammad Iqbal Ahnaf received his PhD in government from the Victoria University of Wellington in New Zealand and teaches at the Center for Religious and Cross-Cultural Studies, Graduate School, at Gadjah Mada University. He has authored numerous articles and books on Islam, citizenship, and cultural politics in modern Indonesia.

Zainal Abidin Bagir teaches at the Center for Religious and Cross-Cultural Studies, Graduate School, at Gadjah Mada University and is the current director of the Indonesian Consortium for Religious Studies, a consortium of Gadjah Mada University, Sunan Kalijaga State Islamic University and Duta Wacana Chrisian University, all in Yogyakarta. He has authored and edited numerous books and articles on religion, law, and plurality in Indonesia.

Robert W. Hefner is professor of anthropology and global affairs and a senior research associate at the Institute on Culture, Religion, and World Affairs at the Pardee School of Global Affairs at Boston University. He has authored or edited twenty books on Islam, Indonesia, and modernity and is currently completing a book on the politics and ethics of recognition and citizenship.

Erica M. Larson is a visiting assistant professor at Hanover College in Indiana and received her PhD from the Department of Anthropology at Boston University, specializing in the anthropology of education, ethics, and religious pluralism. Her research takes an anthropological approach to understanding how schools contribute to socializing views of the nation and a public ethic for engaging religious diversity.

Alimatul Qibtiyah earned her PhD at the University of Iowa and is associate professor of Islam and gender studies at the Sunan Kalijaga State Islamic University in Yogyakarta, Indonesia. She is also a member of the National Executive of 'Aisyiyah, a four-million-strong women's organization affiliated with Muhammadiyah, the largest Islamic reformist organization in the world and is now a commissioner at the Indonesian National Commission on Violence Against Women.

Kelli Swazey obtained her PhD in anthropology at the University of Hawaii-Manoa and has been a researcher and visiting professor at the Center for Religious and Cross-Cultural Studies and the Department of Anthropology, Gadjah Mada University. She has authored numerous articles and directed two documentary films on religion, ethnicity, and politics in Indonesia, with a special focus on eastern Indonesia.

Marthen Tahun is a staff researcher at the Center for Religious and Cross-Cultural Studies at Gadjah Mada University, Yogyakarta. He is the author and editor of numerous articles and books on Christianity and religious affairs in Indonesia. He is currently completing his PhD in history at the Protestant Theological University in the Netherlands.

CPSIA information can be obtained
at www.ICGtesting.com
Printed in the USA
LVHW010518120723
752154LV00004B/150